The Routledge Introductory Persian Course, Second Edition

The Routledge Introductory Persian Course: Farsi Shirin Ast, Second Edition is an innovative course designed for students who are new to the language.

Focusing on grammatical and communicative competence, the course contains 15 lessons combining dialogues and texts with grammar explanations, exercises and audio materials to guide and support the student through the key skills of reading, writing, speaking and listening.

Key features include:

- Lively, content-based materials – the language is taught and practiced through a variety of dialogues and texts on the culture, history, and traditions of Iran
- Complete vocabulary lists – each vocabulary entry contains the English meaning, the part of the speech in Persian, as well as a sample sentence in Persian
- Colloquial situational dialogues – students are introduced to spoken Persian from the outset
- Carefully controlled exercises – new grammatical points are practiced in a variety of controlled exercises that bridge between students' existing information and the new information
- Audio material – students can develop natural pronunciation by imitating the audio recordings of the vocabulary, dialogues, and texts available freely online
- Glossaries – comprehensive Persian to English and English to Persian glossaries

The course provides everything that students and instructors need for an engaging and effective learning environment.

Revised and updated, this new edition includes more vocabulary and grammar activities, and clearer learning outcomes.

Pouneh Shabani Jadidi is Senior Lecturer of Persian Language and Linguistics at the Institute of Islamic Studies, McGill University, Montreal, and is the current President of the American Association of Teachers of Persian (2018–2020).

Dominic Parviz Brookshaw is Senior Research Fellow in Persian at Wadham College, Oxford, and Associate Professor of Persian Literature at The Oriental Institute, University of Oxford.

The Routledge Introductory Persian Course
Farsi Shirin Ast

Second Edition

Pouneh Shabani-Jadidi and
Dominic Parviz Brookshaw

فارسی شیرین است

پونه شعبانی جدیدی

و

دومینیک پرویز بروکشا

LONDON AND NEW YORK

Second edition published 2020
by Routledge
2 Park Square, Milton Park, Abingdon, OX14 4RN

Simultaneously published in the USA and Canada by Routledge
52 Vanderbilt Ave, New York, NY 10017

Routledge is an imprint of the Taylor & Francis Group, an informa business

© 2020 Pouneh Shabani Jadidi & Dominic Parviz Brookshaw

All images © Dominic Parviz Brookshaw

The right of Pouneh Shabani Jadidi & Dominic Parviz Brookshaw to be identified as authors of this work has been asserted by them in accordance with sections 77 and 78 of the Copyright, Designs and Patents Act 1988.

All rights reserved. No part of this book may be reprinted or reproduced or utilised in any form or by any electronic, mechanical, or other means, now known or hereafter invented, including photocopying and recording, or in any information storage or retrieval system, without permission in writing from the publishers.

First edition published by Routledge 2010

British Library Cataloguing-in-Publication Data
A catalogue record for this book is available from the British Library

Library of Congress Cataloging-in-Publication Data
A catalog record for this book has been requested

ISBN 13: 978-1-138-49678-1 (hbk)
ISBN 13: 978-1-138-49679-8 (pbk)
ISBN 13: 978-1-351-02066-4 (ebk)

Typeset in Sabon
by Apex CoVantage, LLC
Printed and bound by CPI Group (UK) Ltd, Croydon CR0 4YY

Contents

Introduction   ix

Lesson 1: The Persian alphabet   1   **درس اول: الفبای فارسی**
- Persian alphabet   2   الفبای فارسی
- Orthography   5   املاء
- Spelling hints   6   راهنمای املائی
- Persian alphabet with examples   9   الفبای فارسی با مثال
- What's going on in town? Getting to know someone   13   در شهر چه خبره؟ آشنایی

Lesson 2: Introduce yourself. Where are you from?   15   **درس دوم : خودتان را معرفی کنید. کجایی هستید؟**
- New vocabulary   16   واژگان
- Dialogue: Accent   20   گفتگو : لهجه
- To be/to have   21   بودن / داشتن
- Uses of *ezafe*   23   اضافه
- What's going on in town? Introducing yourself   25   در شهر چه خبره؟ معرفی

Lesson 3: Is Iran or Canada larger?   27   **درس سوم: ایران بزرگتر است یا کانادا؟**
- New vocabulary   28   واژگان
- Dialogue: The new professor   30   گفتگو : استاد جدید
- Negation   31   نفی
- Adjectives (comparative – superlative)   32   صفت (برتر - عالی)
- Reading: Canada and Iran   34   خواندن: کانادا و ایران
- What's going on in town? Asking for directions   35   در شهر چه خبره؟ آدرس پرسیدن

Lesson 4: How many provinces does Iran have?   37   **درس چهارم: ایران چند استان دارد؟**
- New vocabulary   38   واژگان
- Dialogue: Gilan Province   41   گفتگو : استان گیلان
- Subjective pronouns   42   ضمیرشخصی فاعلی
- Objective pronouns   42   ضمیرشخصی مفعولی
- Possessive pronouns   43   ضمیرملکی
- Reading: Gilan   44   خواندن: گیلان
- Word order in Persian   45   ترتیب کلمات
- What's going on in town? At the bank   47   در شهر چه خبره؟ در بانک

Lesson 5: What do you know about Noruz?   49   **درس پنجم: در مورد نوروز چه می دانید؟**
- New vocabulary   50   واژگان

Dialogue: Noruz 54	گفتگو: نوروز
Sentences 55	جمله
Narrative sentences 55	جملات اخباری
Questions – Yes/No and Wh-questions 55	جملات پرسشی
Indirect questions 57	جملات پرسشی غیر مستقیم
Exclamatory sentences 57	جملات تعجبی
Reading: New Year 58	خواندن: سال نو
Numbers 59	اعداد
Time expressions 61	زمان
What's going on in town? At the cinema 63	در شهر چه خبره؟ در سینما
Lesson 6: What day is the weekend in Iran? 65	**درس ششم: آخر هفته در ایران چه روزی است؟**
New vocabulary 66	واژگان
Dialogue: Friday 68	گفتگو: جمعه
Verbs 69	فعل
Past tense 69	گذشته (ماضی)
Present tense 70	حال (مضارع)
The present stem 70	بن مضارع
Future verbs 71	آینده (مستقبل)
Reading: The days of the week 73	خواندن: روزهای هفته
What's going on in town? At the grocer's 74	در شهر چه خبره؟ دربقالی
Lesson 7: What is your favourite sport? 77	**درس هفتم: ورزش مورد علاقه شما چیست؟**
New vocabulary 78	واژگان
Dialogue: Football 81	گفتگو: فوتبال
Present subjunctive 82	مضارع التزامی
Past subjunctive 84	ماضی التزامی
Imperative verbs 84	فعل امری
Reading: Sports 85	خواندن: ورزش
Months and seasons 86	فصلها و ماه های سال
What's going on in town? Sightseeing 87	در شهر چه خبره؟ گردش در شهر
Lesson 8: Do you haggle? 89	**درس هشتم: آیا شما چانه می زنید؟**
New vocabulary 90	واژگان
Dialogue: The mountain 93	گفتگو: کوه
Past progressive tense 94	ماضی استمراری
Present perfect tense 95	ماضی نقلی
Past perfect tense 96	ماضی بعید
Reading: Haggling 97	خواندن: چانه زدن
Verb review 98	افعال را مرور کنیم!
What's going on in town? In the summer 99	در شهر چه خبره؟ در تابستان
Lesson 9: What do you believe in? 101	**درس نهم: شما به چه اعتقاد دارید؟**
New vocabulary 102	واژگان
Dialogue: University credits 105	گفتگو: واحدهای دانشگاهی
Nouns 106	اسم

Orthographic rule 107
Numericals 107
Determiners 108
Demonstrative adjectives 108
Demonstrative pronouns 109
Definite and indefinite markers 109
Reading: Religion 111
What's going on in town? At the
restaurant 112

Lesson 10: Are women and men equal? 115
New vocabulary 116
Dialogue: Moving house 119
Prepositions (Time; Place; Means and manner;
Instrument; Accompaniment) 120
Reflexive and emphatic pronouns 122
Reading: A traditional way of thinking 123
What's going on in town? In class 124

Lesson 11: Where is Persepolis? 127
New vocabulary 128
Dialogue: Shopping 130
Relative clauses 131
Reading: Tourist sights 132
What's going on in town?
At the post office 133

**Lesson 12: Is pop music better or
traditional music?** 135
New vocabulary 136
Dialogue: Favourite singer 138
Adverbial clauses 139
Conditional sentences 140
Possible conditionals (present or future
condition) 140
Possible conditionals (past condition) 140
Impossible conditionals 140
Impersonal constructions 141
Reading: Education 142
What's going on in town? At the doctor's
surgery 143

**Lesson 13: What kind of a university
is your university?** 147
New vocabulary 148
Dialogue: The police station 150

قانون املائی
صفت شمارشی
صفت و ضمیر نامشخص
صفت اشاره
ضمیر اشاره
نشانه های معرفه و نکره
خواندن: دین
در شهر چه خبره؟ در رستوران

درس دهم: آیا زن و مرد برابرند؟
واژگان
گفتگو: اسباب کشی
حرف اضافه
(زمان، مکان، حالت، وسیله، همراهی)
ضمایر انعکاسی وتأکیدی
خواندن: تفکر سنتی
در شهر چه خبره؟ در کلاس

درس یازدهم: تخت جمشید کجاست؟
واژگان
گفتگو: خرید
عبارت وصفی
خواندن: مراکز جهانگردی
در شهر چه خبره؟ در پستخانه

**درس دوازدهم: موسیقی پاپ بهتر است یا
سنتی؟**
واژگان
گفتگو: خواننده مورد علاقه
عبارت قیدی
جملات شرطی
شرط ممکن
(شرط حال یا آینده)
شرط ممکن (شرط گذشته)
شرط غیرممکن
عبارت غیر شخصی
خواندن: آموزش و پرورش
در شهر چه خبره؟ در مطب دکتر

**درس سیزدهم: دانشگاه شما چه نوع
دانشگاهی است؟**
واژگان
گفتگو: اداره پلیس

Passive constructions 150
Reading: Different kinds of university 152
What's going on in town? At the
bookstore 153

Lesson 14: Are you single or married? 155
New vocabulary 156
Dialogue: The birthday present 158
Reading: Traditional marriage practices 159
Compounding 160
Derivatives 161
Conjunctions 162
What's going on in town? Travelling 163

Lesson 15: Why do you stand on ceremony? 165
New vocabulary 166
Dialogue: Beeping your car horn 168
Causative verbs 169
Reading: Book Fair 170
A review of verb tenses 170
Past 170
Present 171
Future 172
Subjunctive 172
What's going on in town? Standing on
ceremony 174

Persian–English glossary 177
English–Persian glossary 227
Index 273

مجهول
خواندن: انواع دانشگاه
در شهر چه خبره؟ درکتابفروشی

درس چهاردهم: مجرد هستید یا متأهل؟
واژگان
گفتگو: هدیه تولد
خواندن: ازدواج به سبک سنتی
مرکب سازی
مشتقات
کلمات ربط
در شهر چه خبره؟ سفر

درس پانزدهم: چرا آنقدر تعارف می کنید؟
واژگان
گفتگو: بوق
افعال سببی
خواندن: نمایشگاه کتاب
مروری بر زمانها
گذشته (ماضی)
حال (مضارع)
آینده (مستقبل)
التزامی
در شهر چه خبره؟ تعارف

Introduction

The Routledge Introductory Persian Course: Farsi Shirin Ast is a coursebook intended for the instruction of modern Persian language at university level. It is not "teach yourself" book, but it has been designed to be as user-friendly as possible. The subtitle of this coursebook, *Farsi Shirin Ast*, means "Persian is sweet". We believe learning a language should be an enjoyable experience, and we have designed this coursebook in such a way that it will appeal to both student and instructor alike. The formal, written Persian presented in this coursebook is that of contemporary Iran, although the considerable overlap in written Iranian Persian (*Farsi*) and written Afghan Persian (*Dari*) is so great that Persian learners intending to use their language within a formal Afghan context will also find this coursebook of benefit. This new edition is a revised second edition drawn up by the authors in 2019. Several exercises have been added to help students internalize the material better.

◼ The authors

The Routledge Introductory Persian Course: Farsi Shirin Ast is co-authored by Dr Pouneh Shabani Jadidi, and Professor Dominic Parviz Brookshaw.

Pouneh Shabani-Jadidi is Senior Lecturer of Persian Language and Linguistics at McGill University. She holds a PhD in Linguistics from the University of Ottawa (2012) as well as a PhD in Applied Linguistics from Tehran Azad University (2004).

She has taught Persian language and linguistics as well as Persian literature and translation at McGill University, the University of Oxford, the University of Chicago, and Tehran Azad University since 1997.

She has published on morphology, psycholinguistics, translation, teaching Persian as a second language, and second language acquisition. She is the author of *Processing Compound Verbs in Persian: A Psycholinguistic Approach to Complex Predicates* (Leiden and University of Chicago Press, 2014). She has also published three proficiency-based textbooks for Persian, namely *The Routledge Introductory Persian Course* and *The Routledge Intermediate Persian Course* (2010, 2012, with Dominic Brookshaw) as well as *What the Persian Media Says* (Routledge, 2015) and The Routledge Advanced Persian Course (2019). She is co-editor of *The Oxford Handbook of Persian Linguistics* (2018). She is also the translator of *The Thousand Families: Commentary on Leading Political Figures of Nineteenth Century Iran*, by Ali Shabani (Peter Lang, 2018, with Patricia Higgins). In addition, she has translated *Hafez in Love (Hafez-e Nashenide-Pand)*, by Iraj Pezeshkzad (Syracuse University Press, 2020, with Patricia Higgins). Her present project is editing *The Routledge Handbook of Persian as a Second Language* (forthcoming in 2020).

She serves as reviewer for *International Journal of Iranian Studies, International Journal of Applied Linguistics, Sage Open Journal, Frontiers in Psychology, International Journal of Psycholinguistic Research*, and *LINGUA*. Currently, she is president of the American Association of Teachers of Persian (2018–2020).

Dominic Parviz Brookshaw is Senior Research Fellow in Persian at Wadham, and Associate Professor of Persian Literature at The Oriental Institute University of Oxford. He holds a DPhil from Oxford in medieval Persian poetry, and a BA from Oxford in Arabic with Persian.

The current focus of Professor Brookshaw's research is the intersection between performance, patronage, and desire in texts produced by poets and other literati who were active in Shiraz in the fourteenth century CE. In his wider research, Brookshaw examines the emergence and genesis of Persian wine poetry in the eastern Iranian lands in the tenth and eleventh centuries, the relationship of this poetry to the earlier Arabic *khamriya*, the heteroerotic and homoerotic dynamics of Persian and Arabic lyric poetry, and the interplay between the bacchic and the panegyric in the Persian *ghazal*.

In terms of the modern period, Brookshaw looks at women poets and their royal patrons in the first half of the Qajar period (circa 1797–1848), and he is currently working on a monograph in which he investigates the role played by poetry in the formation of a royal cultural policy in early nineteenth-century Iran. Brookshaw's research on modern/ist twentieth-century Persian poetry is centred on Iranian poets and their dialogue with (and ultimate subversion of) the Persian poetic canon. His other research interests include poets of the Iranian diaspora, non-Muslim religious minorities in Iran, and Persian language learning. Before arriving at Wadham in September 2013, Brookshaw taught Persian literature and language at Stanford University (2011–2013), the University of Manchester (2007–2011), McGill University (2005–2007), and the University of Oxford (2002–2005). From 2004–2014 he served as Assistant Editor for Iranian Studies. He is a former member of the Board of the International Society for Iranian Studies, and of the Governing Council of the British Institute of Persian Studies.

Some of his publications include *Hafiz and His Contemporaries: Poetry, Performance and Patronage in Fourteenth-century Iran* (I.B. Tauris/Bloomsbury, 2019), *Ruse and Wit: The Humorous in Arabic, Persian, and Turkish Narrative* (Ilex Foundation/Harvard University Press, 2012), *Forugh Farrokhzad, Poet of Modern Iran: Iconic Woman and Feminine Pioneer of New Persian Poetry* (co-edited with Nasrin Rahimieh) (I.B. Tauris, 2010), *Media Persian: An Essential Vocabulary* (Edinburgh University Press, 2011), and *The Routledge Introductory Persian Course* and *The Routledge Intermediate Persian Course* (2010, 2012, with Pouneh Shabani-Jadidi).

The language instruction approach used in this coursebook

Unlike traditional approaches to language teaching, which are based on developing the *grammatical competence* of second/foreign language students, more recent approaches to teaching second/foreign languages have instead focused on *communicative competence*. The many example sentences in the vocabulary section are meant to provide a rich spectrum of input to the students, similar to a child receiving ample input before beginning to speak. In traditional methodologies which emphasize grammatical competence, the focus is on the sentence, which can often result in students being unable to actually use the language in context. Learning the target language in isolated sentences can lead to learners becoming unable to deal with more complex portions of written language, such as paragraphs and short texts. This is why in this book, from the very first lesson, students are exposed to dialogues, and in later lessons, to short texts. Coursebooks which focus primarily on the production or translation of single sentences in the traditional grammar translation method create a language learning process that is synthetic and artificial, rather than authentic and automatic. More up-to-date methodologies which focus on communicative competence, however, place less emphasis on the explicit or direct teaching of grammar and instead stress language use and implicit or indirect instruction of grammar. This does not mean that formal instruction of grammar should be eliminated altogether, since adult learners have the ability to perceive abstract information. In fact, the contextualized formal instruction of grammar is arguably the most effective approach in adult second language learning. Students learn more successfully when they approach a second/foreign language as a means for acquiring information, rather than as an end in itself. In addition, language instruction is more efficient when all four skills of language learning (i.e. listening, reading, writing and speaking) are simultaneously practised within a true-to-life context in the target language. Content-based materials, such as those presented in this coursebook, provide such a comprehensive context for language instruction. Through a varied range of materials, the student's attention is focused on learning the content (whether vocabulary or grammatical constructions) on a more subconscious level, which is the level at which language acquisition occurs more successfully. In such an interactive content-based classroom, the student-teacher roles shift as the student and the teacher become collaborators in the language acquisition process. A student-centered atmosphere in the classroom boosts the students' motivation and self-confidence, while minimizing their affective inhibitions and stress. In such an atmosphere, students take the lead and the teacher follows, facilitating the flow of the lesson.

■ The structure of the coursebook

The Routledge Introductory Persian Course: Farsi Shirin Ast contains 15 lessons. Each lesson (apart from Lesson 1 in which the Persian alphabet and writing system are introduced) is composed of several sections, each designed to integrate language learning skills and facilitate language acquisition:

- A title in the form of a question followed by a photographic image and accompanying caption which should be used as the basis for pre-reading tasks.
- A vocabulary section in which Persian words are presented along with their English equivalent(s). In the vocabulary table, the part of speech of each new item is presented (in Persian), and a Persian sentence is provided where the new word is used in context (with accompanying English translation in Chapters 2–5).
- A dialogue, followed by comprehension questions in Persian.
- An explanation in English of the grammatical point(s) introduced in the dialogue, which includes Persian example sentences, usually accompanied by an English translation (see below). We have intentionally made these grammar explanations in English as brief as possible, since our preference is for the acquisition of Persian grammar *implicitly*, rather than *explicitly*.
- A short text in which the implicit focus is on the new grammatical point(s) introduced in the lesson, followed by comprehension questions in Persian.

- Additional exercises for students to practise the grammar and vocabulary introduced in the lesson. These take a variety of forms: multiple-choice, fill in the blanks, translation, word reordering, sentence completion, etc.
- A colloquial situational dialogue, followed by a table showing the relationship between the formal (or literary) and colloquial words and expressions used, as well as some additional related vocabulary so that students can recreate similar situational dialogues by substituting the words used in the original dialogue with other related words. The colloquial Persian presented in these sections (collectively entitled, *Dar shahr cheh khabar-eh?* "What's going on in town?"), is the informal spoken dialect of Tehran, which is the most widely understood colloquial form of Persian.
- A formal situational dialogue in form of a cloze test in order for students to practice the vocabulary and structure they learned in the lesson.

The coursebook ends with two comprehensive vocabulary sections, one Persian to English, the other English to Persian which includes the words introduced in the individual vocabulary sections at the beginning of each lesson with their English equivalent(s). There is also an index of grammatical terms at the very end of the book which students and instructors can use to easily locate where a particular grammar point is discussed in the coursebook.

How to use this coursebook

The title of each lesson is in the form of an engaging question in Persian which relates to the subject of the dialogue or the short text (or both) and which the instructor should use as a pre-reading exercise to prepare students for the topics covered in that lesson. In doing so, a connection will be made between the students' old information, and the new information being presented to them, thereby resulting in the internalization of the new information. The title is followed by a photographic image with an accompanying caption in Persian which the instructor can either use at the beginning as an aid to further discussion (along with the title), or else at the end of the lesson once the dialogue and short text have been covered. Each photo caption ends with an invitation to the students to do a brief websearch (in Persian script) to find out more about the subject of the photograph. The information the students find via the websearch can be discussed in brief before moving on to the next lesson. By making the title of each lesson a question in Persian, and providing each image with a Persian caption, we encourage students from the very beginning of the course to engage with Persian directly, rather than indirectly (through, say translation or transliterated Persian). Wherever possible (and with increasing frequency as the lessons progress), instructions are given in Persian, rather than English, for the same purpose.

The vocabulary section includes example sentences as well as parts of speech so that students can learn from the very beginning of their encounter with Persian how to use each word in context, as well as to identify its grammatical usage. These example sentences are introduced from the first lessons so that the students are exposed to a large amount of passive vocabulary and grammar required to gradually better comprehend the target language. In the first few chapters (2–5), English translations are provided for these example sentences to ease students into engaging with the passive vocabulary and grammar. After the first few lessons, the students can

xiii   **Introduction**

be asked to make similar sentences in Persian to the example sentences provided in the book, and – with the aid of a dictionary – translate the example sentences into English either in class, or else as a homework exercise. Putting their new vocabulary to use in this manner enables learners to make their passive vocabulary active. It should be mentioned, however, that the vocabulary presented in the coursebook is by no means exhaustive, and students be encouraged to use printed dictionaries and those available on the internet to broaden their vocabulary base. Instructors may also wish to introduce a certain amount of additional vocabulary where they feel it to be beneficial. The audio recordings of the vocabulary lists should be also used in tandem with the coursebook in order to help students to develop natural pronunciation in Persian. We have made a conscious, pedagogical decision not to use transliteration in our coursebook because, in our experience, it interferes with and ultimately delays the learner's connection with the Persian script and writing system. Likewise, short vowels are not marked so that from the beginning, students become accustomed to reading authentic Persian texts where short vowels are normally not shown.

The dialogues are based on real life settings and are intended to be used to familiarize students with the formal/literary register of Persian. Students can listen to the audio recordings of the dialogues as read by native speakers, and use them to gauge their own pronunciation. The dialogues are followed by comprehension questions in Persian which can be answered orally or in writing. Students are also invited to compose a modified version of the dialogue in their own words, which they can then act out in class in pairs. Controlled exercises of this type, on the one hand make students engage in a creative manner with the structures necessary to imitate natural style when producing Persian. On the other hand, these exercises also help students to internalize the vocabulary and structures introduced in the dialogue by requiring them to substitute the information presented in the dialogue with their own information.

As far as possible, we have endeavoured to explain the grammatical points in plain English. These brief grammar explanations are followed immediately by relevant examples so as to build the grammatical competence of the students as well as their communicative competence. In other words, there is as smooth a transition as possible from the explicit explanation of grammatical points to their implicit presentation in context. In addition, from the first lessons, students learn not only to form simple sentences and to analyse their constituent parts, but also to construct and analyse compound and complex sentences. The verb is said to be the head of the sentence. This is why in this coursebook, simple verbs have been introduced prior to other parts of speech (such as nouns and adjectives) in each grammar section. Moreover, since the first few lessons contain simple vocabulary, the main focus for the learners at the beginning will be the acquisition of verbs, which contain the core meaning of the sentence. It should be noted that not all the example Persian sentences given in the grammar sections are accompanied by English translations. This requires learners to engage more directly with the Persian constructions and to focus on grammatical patterns, rather than being distracted by decoding the semantic meaning. Students should, of course, be encouraged to look up any new vocabulary they encounter in the exercises in the glossary at the back of the book, or else in a dictionary.

The short texts introduce learners to larger blocks of language, and show them how phrases and sentences are connected in a paragraph. The texts contain information about modern and pre-modern Iranian society, literature, history and art; we firmly believe that the language should not be separated from its cultural context in second-language instruction. The audio recording of each short text should be used as a pre-reading exercise for listening comprehension. The audio should be played twice while students keep their books closed; the first time followed by several general comprehension questions delivered orally, and the second time followed by more detailed comprehension questions. Following this, the students can be asked to open their books and first read and then paraphrase the text in small groups. In this way, heritage students and absolute beginners can be paired or else divided into mixed groups to work together to better understand and summarize the text.

The colloquial dialogues are situational, in Tehrani dialect, and are aimed at familiarizing students with conversation in everyday situations. The formal/literary versus colloquial tables after each dialogue highlight the difference between the two registers of the language, and can be used on the one hand to help *ab initio* learners to convert their formal Persian into colloquial, and, conversely, help heritage learners to familiarize themselves with the relationship between the spoken form of Persian – which they are more comfortable with – and the formal, literary register. By including this colloquial section in each lesson, we hope to encourage instruction in colloquial Persian in the classroom, which should enable those students without Persian-speaking heritage, and those who do not have the opportunity to visit Iran, to learn to converse in a natural spoken register. We have chosen to draw a clear separation between the formal/literary and colloquial in our coursebook since we feel that by doing so a more level playing field is created for both heritage learners and *ab initio* students. Heritage learners commonly have limited knowledge of formal, written Persian, and so by focusing on this register of Persian, the learning environment becomes more homogenous.

■ Tentative syllabus

A tentative syllabus is suggested below, although it should be stressed that each class will have its own natural pace:

If introductory Persian is taught as a year-long course, with two semesters each of approximately 13 weeks, with around 40 hours of Persian instruction per semester, each lesson can be covered in two weeks (or six sessions) in the following manner:

Class 1: Pre-lesson discussion of the title, photograph, and caption and first half of vocabulary
Class 2: Second half of vocabulary
Class 3: Formal dialogue and first half of the grammar
Class 4: Reading and second half of the grammar
Class 5: Colloquial dialogue and cloze test dialogue
Class 6: Chapter quiz

If this pattern is followed, the first seven chapters can be covered in the first semester and the second eight chapters in the second semester.

Depending on the size of the class and the students' individual learning strategies, the instructor can adopt different teaching techniques which s/he feels will best facilitate the acquisition of the material. The more the students are involved in the class, the greater the chance they will acquire and retain the material covered. Bridging between the students' existing knowledge and the new information also facilitates learning. In addition, the students' autonomy can be built up by assigning different target-language-related tasks to them, such as generating sample sentences with the newly introduced vocabulary or writing dialogues and texts similar to those presented in the book or giving short presentations on the topics covered in each lesson. Language proficiency follows when the four key language skills – listening, reading, writing and speaking – are enhanced side-by-side in this kind of integrated approach.

We hope that you will enjoy using this coursebook, and look forward to receiving your feedback via email or the website.

Pouneh Shabani Jadidi and Dominic Parviz Brookshaw
Montreal and Oxford, March 2019

Parts of speech in Persian

noun (e.g. love, flower, kindness)	اسم
verb (e.g. goes, has arrived, will eat)	فعل
adjective (e.g. good, eager, faithful)	صفت
adverb (e.g. well, carefully, enthusiastically)	قید
preposition (e.g. on, without, by)	حرف اضافه
pronoun (e.g. it, her, themselves)	ضمیر
conjunction (e.g. and, otherwise, however)	حرف ربط
compound noun (e.g. ice cream, blackboard)	اسم مرکب
phrase (e.g. in the park, standing there, by means of)	عبارت
sentence (e.g. I study Persian.)	جمله

Lesson One

درس اول

الفبای فارسی

دیوار مسجد جامع نطنز
الفبای فارسی همان الفبای عربی است به اضافهٔ چهار حرف: پ، چ، ژ، گ. این صداها در عربی کلاسیک وجود ندارند و به همین دلیل به الفبای فارسی اضافه شده اند.
برای کسب اطلاعات بیشتر در مورد الفبای فارسی در اینترنت جستجو کنید.

Lesson 1 ■ The Persian Alphabet

الفبای فارسی

The Persian Alphabet

درس اول: الفبای فارسی
در شهر چه خبره؟ آشنایی

Chapter aims
Grammar:
1. The alphabet
2. Phonological and orthographic rules

Situation:
1. Meeting someone
2. Talking about jobs

■ Persian alphabet الفبای فارسی

pronunciation	final (stand alone)	final (attached)	medial	initial
/a:/[1] far	/alef/ ا	ـا	ـا	آ
/b/ bed	/be/ ب	ـب	ـبـ	بـ
/p/ pet	/pe/ پ	ـپ	ـپـ	پـ

[1] The letters which appear between / / are those of the phonetic alphabet. The /a:/ represents the long vowel as in the English word 'far', whereas /a/ indicates the short vowel as in 'rap'. Please note that the initial *alef* can represent /a/, /e/, or /o/, depending on the short vowel it carries.

pronunciation	final (stand alone)		final (attached)	medial	initial
/t/ ten	/te/	ت	ـت	ـتـ	تـ
/s/ set	/se/	ث	ـث	ـثـ	ثـ
/ǰ/ jet	/ǰi:m/	ج	ـج	ـجـ	جـ
/č/ chat	/če/	چ	ـچ	ـچـ	چـ
/h/ hat	/he/	ح	ـح	ـحـ	حـ
/x/[2] loch	/xe/	خ	ـخ	ـخـ	خـ
/d/ doll	/da:l/	د	ـد	ـد	د
/z/ zoo	/za:l/	ذ	ـذ	ـذ	ذ
/r/[3] red	/re/	ر	ـر	ـر	ر
/z/ zoo	/ze/	ز	ـز	ـز	ز
/ž/ beige	/že/	ژ	ـژ	ـژ	ژ
/s/ set	/si:n/	س	ـس	ـسـ	سـ
/š/ shoe	/ši:n/	ش	ـش	ـشـ	شـ
/s/ set	/sa:d/	ص	ـص	ـصـ	صـ
/z/ zoo	/za:d/	ض	ـض	ـضـ	ضـ
/t/ ten	/ta:/	ط	ـط	ـطـ	طـ

[2] This sound is not very common in English; it is close to the final sound of the word "loch".

[3] Persian /r/ is slightly different from the English /r/. Try rolling your tongue and you will get close to this sound!

Lesson 1 ■ *The Persian Alphabet*   **4**

pronunciation	final (stand alone)		final (attached)	medial	initial
/z/ zoo	/za:/	ظ	ظ	ظ	ظ
/ʔ/ bottle /boʔel/ (in Cockney accent)	/ʔeyn/	ع	ع	ـع	ع
/ɣ/ glottal /g/	/ɣeyn/	غ	غ	ـغ	غ
/f/ fat	/fe/	ف	ف	ـف	ف
/ɣ/ glottal /g/	/ɣa:f/	ق	ـق	ـق	ق
/k/ key	/ka:f/	ک	ـک	ک	ک
/g/ go	/ga:f/	گ	ـگ	گ	گ
/l/ love	/la:m/	ل	ـل	ـل	ل
/m/ me	/mi:m/	م	ـم	ـم	مـ
/n/ net	/nu:n/	ن	ـن	ـن	نـ
/v/[4] valley	/va:v/	و	ـو	ـو	و
/h/ hat	/he/	ه	ـه	ـهـ	هـ
/y/[5] yes	/ye/	ى	ـى	ـيـ	يـ

[4] This letter can also represent the short vowel /o/ and the long vowel /u:/, as in:

تو /to/

او /u:/

[5] This letter can also represent the long vowel /i:/, as in:

شیر /ši:r/

فارسی /fa:rsi:/

■ Orthography

There are 32 letters in Persian, which are written from right to left. These letters contain consonants and long vowels.

Vowels

Short vowels are not normally written in Persian. Unlike English, which has a rather complex system of vowels, Persian has only three long vowels:

آ ـ ا	/a:/	آب /a:b/ - کباب /kaba:b/ - دارا /da:ra:/
ای ـ یـ ـ ی[6]	/i:/	ایران /i:ra:n/ - دیو /di:v/ - کی /ki:/
او ـ ـو ـ و[7]	/u:/	او /u:/ - سوت /su:t/ - قو /ɣu:/

Persian vowels with examples

Persian vowels	initial		medial		final	
/a/	از	/az/	من	/man/	نه	/na/
/e/	اصفهان	/esfaha:n/	پدر	/pedar/	نوه	/nave/
/o/	امید	/omi:d/	مسلمان	/mosalma:n/	نو	/no/
/a:/	آب	/a:b/	مادر	/ma:dar/	پا	/pa:/
/i:/	ایران	/i:ra:n/	دین	/di:n/	آبی	/a:bi:/
/u:/	او	/u:/	موم	/mu:m/	مو	/mu:/

The three short vowels in Persian (/a/-/e/-/o/) are not normally indicated in writing.[8]

At the beginning of a word, the short vowel is carried either by ا or else by ع , e.g.:

امیر /ami:r/

امید /omi:d/

علم /ʔelm/

---

[6] Initial " یـ " is preceded by " ا " to produce the long vowel /i:/, as in " ایران " /i:ra:n/.

[7] Initial " و " is preceded by " ا " to produce the long vowel /u:/, as in " او " /u:/.

[8] In a few words in Persian, medial و is pronounced short (/o/), rather than long (/u:/), e.g.: /xoš/ خوش

If a word ends in /o/, then it will end in و , e.g.:

تو /to/

نو /no/

If the word ends in /e/, the short vowel is carried by a ه, which is often hough not always) silent, e.g.:

که /ke/

ستاره /seta:re/

ده /deh/

Spelling hints

1. To write a word, the letters in the word need to be attached to one another, but some letters only attach on the right, and not on the left.

These are the letters that attach **only** on the **right**:

ا   با /ba:/ ما /ma:/ آباد /a:ba:d/

د   آمد /a:mad/ مدد /madad/ دل /del/

ذ   کاغذ /ka:γaz/ نافذ /na:fez/ لذیذ /lazi:z/

ر   پر /por/ اگر /agar/ ضرر /zarar/

ز   ریز /ri:z/ بز /boz/ مرز /marz/

ژ   ویژه /vi:že/ پژمرده /pažmorde/ ژاله /ža:le/

و   هلو /holu:/ مو /mu:/ حلوا /halva:/

All other letters in the alphabet attach both on the left and on the right:

ب ـ بـ ـبـ ـب   لب /lab/ کبوتر /kabu:tar/ بوسه /bu:se/

پ ـ پـ ـپـ ـپ   چپ /čap/ کپی /kopi:/ پر /par/

ت ـ تـ ـتـ ـت   قدمت /γedmat/ کتری /ketri:/ توت /tu:t/

ث ـ ثـ ـثـ ـث   ثلث /sols/ کثرت /kesrat/ ثبت /sabt/

ن ـ نـ ـنـ ـن   آهن /a:han/ بندر /bandar/ نم /nam/

ی ـ یـ ـیـ ـی   پیری /pi:ri:/ پنیر /pani:r/ یاد /ya:d/

Practice: Please insert an /alef/ between every two letters above, e.g.: باپ، تاث.

ج ـ جـ ـجـ ـج   کج /kaĵ/ گنجشک /gonĵešk/ جهد /ĵahd/

چ ـ چـ ـچـ ـچ   پیچ /pi:č/ کچل /kačal/ چمن /čaman/

ح ـ حـ ـحـ ـح   صحیح /sahi:h/ محجوب /mahĵu:b/ حفظ /hefz/

خ ـ خـ ـخـ ـخ   ملخ /malax/ مختار /moxta:r/ خام /xa:m/

درس اول ◼ الفبای فارسی   7

Practice: Please insert a /dal/ between every two letters above, e.g.: جدچ

سمنو /samanu:/ مسلمان /mosalma:n/ نرگس /narges/	س ـ سـ ـس
شب /šab/ پشم /pašm/ پوشش /pu:šeš/	ش ـ شـ ـش
صاف /sa:f/ مصادف /mosa:def/ قصص qesas/	ص ـ صـ ـص
ضبط /zabt/ مضمون /mazmu:n/ قبض /ɣabz/	ض ـ ضـ ـض

Practice: Please insert a /zal/ between every two letters above, e.g.: سذش

طرف /taraf/ خطر /xatar/ فقط /faɣat/	ط ـ طـ ـط
ظفر /zafar/ مظهر /mazhar/ محفوظ /mahfu:z/	ظ ـ ظـ ـظ

Practice: Please insert a /re/ between the two letters above.

عجب /ʔajab/ معمول /maʔmu:l/ منع /manʔ/	عـ ـعـ ـع
غبغب /ɣabɣab/ چغندر /čoɣondar/ مبلغ /mablaɣ/	غـ ـغـ ـغ
فارسی /fa:rsi:/ کفن /kafan/ سقف /saqf/	فـ ـفـ ـف
قلب /ɣalb/ بشقاب /bošɣa:b/ طبقه /tabaɣe/	قـ ـقـ ـق

Practice: Please insert a /ze/ between every two letters above.

کار /ka:r/ نیمکت /ni:mkat/ لک لک /laklak/	کـ ـکـ ـک
گم /gom/ نگاه /nega:h/ سگ /sag/	گـ ـگـ ـگ
لوس /lu:s/ هلال /hela:l/ پل /pol/	لـ ـلـ ـل

Practice: Please insert a /zhe/ between every two letters above.

مکان /maka:n/ ممکن /momken/ نیم /ni:m/	مـ ـمـ ـم
هجرت /heǰrat/ نهنگ /nahang/ ده /deh/	هـ ـهـ ـه

Practice: Please insert a /vav/ between every two letters.

2.   As for pronunciation, there are some letters that are pronounced the same way:

ت ـ ط	/t/
ث ـ س ـ ص	/s/
ح ـ ه	/h/
ذ ـ ز ـ ض ـ ظ	/z/
غ ـ ق	/ɣ/

Lesson 1 ■ *The Persian Alphabet* **8**

3. As for orthography, there are some letters with dots below them. Write the corresponding sound for each letter below.

ب - ـب - ـبـ - بـ - ب

پ - ـپ - ـپـ - پـ - پ

ج - ـج - ـجـ - جـ - ج

چ - ـچ - ـچـ - چـ - چ

ی - ـی - ـیـ - یـ - ی

4. And there are some letters with dots above them. Write the corresponding sound for each letter below.

ت - ـت - ـتـ - تـ - ت

ث - ـث - ـثـ - ثـ - ث

خ - ـخ - ـخـ - خـ - خ

ز - ـز - ـزـ - زـ - ز

ژ - ـژ - ـژـ - ژـ - ژ

ش - ـش - ـشـ - شـ - ش

ض - ـض - ـضـ - ضـ - ض

ظ - ـظ - ـظـ - ظـ - ظ

غ - ـغ - ـغـ - غـ - غ

ف - ـف - ـفـ - فـ - ف

ق - ـق - ـقـ - قـ - ق

ن - ـن - ـنـ - نـ - ن

5. As noted above, short vowels are not normally represented by letters. See above for details on this.

6. The following symbols represent short vowels, which when written, are placed above or below the consonant that carries them.

/a/ ﹷ /a/ as in 'tap'   e.g. مَن /man/

/e/ ﹻ /e/ as in 'met'   e.g. مِس /mes/

/o/ ﹹ /o/ as in 'top'   e.g. شُل /šol/

7. If one letter is doubled in a word, only one letter is written and a ّ (*tašdi:d*) is placed above it, e.g.:

/bačče/ بچّه

/moʔallem/ معلّم

درس اول ■ الفبای فارسی

8. Another symbol used in Persian orthography is *hamze* (ء), which is a glottal stop like ع /ʔeyn/. The medial *hamze* is carried by a long vowel (أ - ؤ - ئ) as in:

/masʔale/	مسأله
/taʔsi:r/	تأثیر
/moʔmen/	مؤمن
/soʔa:l/	سؤال
/masa:ʔel/	مسائل
/vokala:ʔ/	وکلاء

9. There is another symbol used in Persian orthography, which is used mostly for adverbs. It is placed on alef (اً) and is called *tanvi:n*

/taɣriban/	تقریباً
/abadan/	ابداً

Practise the way letters are formed in Persian in different positions by copying the examples in the following table. Once you have copied out the words, try looking up their meanings in the dictionary.

■ Persian alphabet with examples الفبای فارسی با مثال

Final (stand alone)	final (attached)	medial	Initial
ا /da:ra:/ دارا	ا /da:na:/ دانا	ـا /ma:dar/ مادر	ا /ana:r/ انار
			ا /ensa:n/ انسان
			ا /ota:ɣ/ اتاق
			آ /a:b/ آب
ب /a:b/ آب	ـب /asb/ اسب	ـبـ /kabu:tar/ کبوتر	بـ /baha:r/ بهار
پ /tu:p/ توپ	ـپ /čap/ چپ	ـپـ /separ/ سپر	پـ /parva:ne/ پروانه
ت /tu:t/ توت	ـت /hast/ هست	ـتـ /seta:re/ ستاره	تـ /tar/ تر

Final (stand alone)	final (attached)	medial	Initial
ث /asa:s/ اثاث	ث /lous/⁹ لوث	ـثـ /mosallas/ مثلث	ثـ /sabt/ ثبت
ج /ta:J̌/ تاج	ج /ganJ̌/ گنج	ـجـ /masJ̌ed/ مسجد	جـ /J̌u: J̌e/ جوجه
چ /ɣa:rč/ قارچ	چ /gač/ گچ	ـچـ /bačče/ بچّه	چـ /čatr/ چتر
ح /louh/ لوح	ح /masi:h/ مسیح	ـحـ /sahra:/ صحرا	حـ /houle/ حوله
خ /ka:x/ کاخ	خ /mi:x/ میخ	ـخـ /taxfi:f/ تخفیف	خـ /xa:ne/ خانه
د /doru:d/ درود	ـد /komod/ کمد	ـد /meda:d/ مداد	د /da:ne/ دانه
ذ /ša:z/ شاذ	ذ /lazi:z/ لذیذ	ـذ /gozarna:me/ گذرنامه	ذ /zorrat/ ذرّت
ر /ma:r/ مار	ر /ši:r/ شیر	ـر /kare/ کره	ر /ru:ba:h/ روباه
ز /a:va:z/ آواز	ز /gaz/ گز	ـز /a:vi:za:n/ آویزان	ز /za:l/ زال
ژ /dež/ دژ	ژ /lož/ لژ	ـژ /vi:že/ ویژه	ژ /ža:le/ ژاله
س /aru:s/ عروس	س /mes/ مس	ـسـ /afsar/ افسر	سـ /si:r/ سیر
ش /mu:š/ موش	ش /keš/ کش	ـشـ /kašti/ کشتی	شـ /šahr/ شهر
ص /ɣors/ قرص	ص /xa:les/ خالص	ـصـ /fasl/ فصل	صـ /sadaf/ صدف
ض /hoUz/ حوض	ض /mari:z/ مریض	ـضـ /azole/ عضله	ضـ /zarb/ ضرب
ط /haya:t/ حیاط	ط /xatt/ خط	ـطـ /tu:ti:/ طوطی	طـ /tabl/ طبل
ظ /hefa:z/ حفاظ	ظ /ha:fez/ حافظ	ـظـ /ʔazi:m/ عظیم	ظـ /zarf/ ظرف

⁹ /ou/ This diphthong is found in English words such as go, show and mow.

Final (stand alone)	final (attached)	medial	Initial
ع شجاع /šoǰa:ʔ/	ـع شمع /šamʔ/	ـعـ جعبه / aʔbe/	عـ عینک /ʔeynak/
غ باغ /ba:ɣ/	ـغ تیغ /ti:ɣ/	ـغـ لغت /loɣat/	غـ غار /ɣa:r/
ف لاف /la:f/	ـف لیف /li:f/	ـفـ کلافه /kala:fe/	فـ فکر /fekr/
ق اجاق /oǰa:ɣ/	ـق قاشق /ɣa:šoɣ/	ـقـ قلقلی /ɣelɣeli:/	قـ قند /ɣand/
ک خاک /xa:k/	ـک نمک /namak/	ـکـ شکر /šekar/	کـ کاخ /ka:x/
گ برگ /barg/	ـگ سگ /sag/	ـگـ انگور /angu:r/	گـ گوساله /gu:sa:le/
ل خال /xa:l/	ـل گل /gol/	ـلـ البرز /alborz/	لـ لاله /la:le/
م خام /xa:m/	ـم نسیم /nasi:m/	ـمـ عمیق /ami:ɣ/	مـ مزرعه /mazraʔe/
ن کمان /kama:n/	ـن من /man/	ـنـ پنیر /pani:r/	نـ نمک /namak/
و سرو /sarv/ جارو / a:ru:/	ـو دیو /di:v/ مو /mu:/	ـو شلوار /š alva:r/ موش /mu:š/	و وسط /vasat/
ه ماه /ma:h/	ـه شبیه /šabi:h/	ـهـ مهر /mehr/	هـ هاله /ha:le/
ی گوی /gu:y/ روسری /ru:sari:/	ـی نی /ney/ بینی /bi:ni:/	ـیـ آسایش /a:sa:yeš/ شیر /ši:r/	یـ یار /ya:r/

▪ Persian syllable

Persian syllables can be comprised of (C)V(C)(C). In Persian, there is no initial consonant cluster, i.e., several consonants one after the other. When words are borrowed from other languages with initial consonant clusters, a vowel is inserted either before or after the first consonant. For example, Persian speakers would pronounce /sport/ as /esport/, and /flai/ as /felai/.

Unlike initial consonant clusters, there are quite a few final consonants, such as /rf/, /st/, qsh/,/ ft/, etc.

Lesson 1 ■ *The Persian Alphabet* **12**

■ Exercises

1. Combine the following letters and sounds to make a Persian word, and then look them up in the dictionary.

ب + ـَ + ر + ا + د + ـَ + ر ← بَرادَر

س + ـِ + ت + ا + ر + ـِ + ه ←

د + ـِ + ر + ـَ + خ + ت ←

گ + ـُ + ل ←

م + ـُ + ش + ک + ـِ + ل ←

گ + ـَ + ل + ل + ـِ + ه ←

ن + ـَ + ق + ا + ش ←

ا + و + ل + ـَ + ل ←

ت + ـَ + و + ـَ + ل + ل + ـُ + د ←

2. Combine the following letters, sounds and symbols to make a Persian word, and then look them up in the dictionary.

ع + ـُ + م + د + ـَ + ت + ا + ـً ← عمدتاً

ف + ـِ + ع + ل + ا + ـً ←

ت + ـَ + ق + ـَ + ب + ب + ـُ + ل ←

م + ـُ + ث + ـَ + ل + ل + ـَ + ث ←

ر + ـَ + س + ا + ء + ـِ + ل ←

3. Read the words below and write out their English equivalents. Some of them are brand names, others are foreign loan words commonly used in Persian. Note that when foreign words are written in Persian, short vowel sounds are often represented using long vowels.

پاریس	کامپیوتر	وب سایت	ایمیل
تنیس	فیلم	بسکتبال	فرم
سون آپ	والیبال	فوتبال	توشیبا
سونی	سینما	تویوتا	پاناسونیک
فورد	کاینکس	لنز	اسپری
سوپ	پیتزا	همبرگر	سس
اینترنت	لپتون	استاندارد	پارک
نسکافه	کافی نت	ماسک	هایلایت
گل	ویدئو	مدرن	پژو

مانیتور	سواچ	سی دی	رولکس
تایپ کیک	شیک	میلک	رنو
کافی شاپ	کاپوچینو	جین	فانتا
پارکینگ	بانک	فتوکپی	کوکاکولا
تی شرت	اسکیت بورد	تونل	پوستر
موبایل	هات داگ	مترو	تراکتور

در شهر چه خبره؟

آشنایی

مریم: سلام. اسم من مریمه.
علی: سلام. من علی ام.
مریم: شغل تو چیه؟
علی: من دکترم. تو چی؟
مریم: من معلمم.

این گفتگو را با کلمات زیر تمرین کنید

دکتر - دندانپزشک - مهندس - مهندس الکترونیک - مهندس مکانیک - مهندس شیمی - استاد - وکیل - دانشجو - کارمند - محقق - خلبان - راننده - پلیس

کتابی Literary	عامیانه Colloquial
مریم است	مریمه
چه	چی
چیست	چیه

جاهای خالی را پر کنید و بعد با کلمات زیر آن را در گروهتان تمرین کنید

ایران شناسی - کامپیوتر - هنر - معماری - پزشکی - ادبیات - اسلام شناسی - مطالعات خاورمیانه - حقوق مدیریت - اقتصاد - علوم سیاسی - زبان شناسی - مردم شناسی - جامعه شناسی - تربیت بدنی - جغرافیا - تاریخ

- سلام. اسم من پونه است. .... شما چیست؟
- سلام. اسم من آرین .... حال شما خوب است؟
- بله. من خوب هستم. مرسی. شما چطور؟

Lesson 1 ■ *The Persian Alphabet*   **14**

– من هم خوب .... ممنون. شما چه می خوانید؟

– من مهندسی می خوانم. شما ....؟

– من دندانپزشکی ....

– خوشوقتم.

– من هم . ...

– خداحافظ.

....

Lesson Two

درس دوم
خودتان را معرفی کنید.
کجایی هستید؟

میدان نقش جهان و مسجد شاه در شهر اصفهان
این میدان و مسجد به دستور شاه عباس کبیر حدوداً چهارصد سال پیش ساخته شدند.
برای کسب اطلاعات بیشتر در مورد شاه عباس و پایتخت او اصفهان در اینترنت جستجو کنید.

Lesson 2 ■ *Introduce yourself: Where are you from?*

خودتان را معرفی کنید.
کجایی هستید؟

*Introduce yourself:
Where are you from?*

درس دوم : خودتان را معرفی کنید. کجایی هستید؟
گفتگو: لهجه
دستور: بودن، داشتن
اضافه
در شهر چه خبره؟ معرفی

Chapter aims
Grammar:
1. The two most common verbs, 'to be' and 'to have'
2. The *ezafe*

Situation:
1. Introducing oneself
2. Introducing someone to someone else

واژگان

لغت Word	معنی انگلیسی English meaning	نقش دستوری Part of speech	مثال Example
سلام	Hello	اسم	به پدرت سلام کن. Say hello to your father.
خداحافظ!	Goodbye!	عبارت	وقتی می رفت گفت : خداحافظ. When he was leaving, he said, "Good-bye!"
اسم، نام	first name	اسم	اسم شما چیست؟ What is your name?

درس دوم ■ خودتان را معرفی کنید. کجایی هستید؟

مثال Example	نقش دستوری Part of speech	معنی انگلیسی English meaning	لغت Word
ببخشید، فامیلی شما چیست؟ Excuse me. What is your last name?	اسم	last name	فامیلی، نام خانوادگی
آیا شما خانم پارسا را می شناسید؟ Do you know Mrs Parsa?	اسم	Mrs; Miss; Ms	خانم
استاد فارسی ما آقای عارف است. Our Persian professor is Mr Aref.	اسم	Mr	آقا
من سه دختر و یک پسر دارم. I have three daughters and one son.	اسم	girl; daughter	دختر
پسر کوچک شما چند ساله است؟ How old is your little son?	اسم	boy; son	پسر
اسم دختر بزرگ شما چیست؟ What is your oldest daughter's name?	عبارت	What is . . .?	چیست؟
از دیدن شما بسیار خوشوقتم. I am very pleased to meet you.	عبارت	Pleased to meet you!	خوشوقتم!
ببخشید شما کجایی هستید؟ Excuse me. Where are you from?	جمله	Where are you from?	کجایی هستید؟
خواهر من معلم است و من هم همینطور. My sister is a teacher, and I am too.	قید	also; too	همینطور
شما چطور به دانشگاه می آیید؟ How do you come to university?	کلمه پرسشی	how; in what way	چطور
دیشب کجا رفتید؟ Where did you go yesterday?	کلمه پرسشی	where	کجا
من وقت ندارم با شما به سینما بروم. I don't have time to go to the movies with you.	اسم	time	وقت
خواهرم هم در ایران زندگی می کند. My sister also lives in Iran.	قید	too; also	هم
وقتی فارسی حرف می زنید کمی لهجهٔ انگلیسی دارید. When you speak Persian, you have a little bit of an English accent.	اسم	accent	لهجه
شیراز یکی از شهرهای بزرگ ایران است. Shiraz is one of the largest cities in Iran.	اسم	Shiraz (a city in southern Iran)	شیراز

Lesson 2 ■ *Introduce yourself: Where are you from?* **18**

مثال Example	نقش دستوری Part of speech	معنی انگلیسی English meaning	لغت Word
اصفهان یکی از شهرهای تاریخی ایران است. Isfahan is one of Iran's historical cities.	اسم	Esfahan (a city in central Iran)	اصفهان
پدر شما ایرانی است؟ Is your father Iranian?	اسم	Father	پدر
مادر من خیلی مهربان است. My mother is very kind.	اسم	mother	مادر
شما چند خواهر دارید؟ How many sisters do you have?	اسم	sister	خواهر
برادر شما کجا زندگی می کند؟ Where does your brother live?	اسم	brother	برادر
او هنوز بچه است. S/he is still a child.	اسم	child; baby	بچه
آیا با زن و بچه ات آمدی؟ Have you come with your wife and children?	اسم	woman; wife	زن
شوهرم مهندس کامپیوتر است. My husband is a computer engineer.	اسم	husband	شوهر
دایی من سه پسر دارد. My (maternal) uncle has three sons.	اسم	uncle (maternal)	دایی
یکی از خاله هایم در شیراز زندگی می کند. One of my (maternal) aunts lives in Shiraz.	اسم	aunt (maternal)	خاله
عموی من پارسال فوت کرد. My (paternal) uncle passed away last year.	اسم	uncle (paternal)	عمو
من عمه ام را خیلی دوست دارم. I like my (paternal) aunt very much.	اسم	aunt (paternal)	عمه
چند دختر دایی داری؟ How many cousins do you have?	اسم مرکب	cousin (daughter of maternal uncle)	دختردایی
دخترخاله من در امارات درس می خواند. My cousin studies in the Emirates.	اسم مرکب	cousin (daughter of maternal aunt)	دخترخاله
دختر عموی شما کجا کار می کند؟ Where does your cousin work?	اسم مرکب	cousin (daughter of paternal uncle)	دخترعمو

مثال Example	نقش دستوری Part of speech	معنی انگلیسی English meaning	لغت Word
دخترعمه من تار می زند. My cousin plays the *tar*.	اسم مرکب	cousin (daughter of paternal aunt)	دخترعمه
پسردایی من در ایران است. My cousin is in Iran.	اسم مرکب	cousin (son of maternal uncle)	پسر دایی
پسرخاله من نقاشی می کند. My cousin paints.	اسم مرکب	cousin (son of maternal aunt)	پسرخاله
مریم با پسرعمویش ازدواج کرد. Maryam married her cousin.	اسم مرکب	cousin (son of paternal uncle)	پسرعمو
امروز تولد پسرعمه ام است. Today is my cousin's birthday.	اسم مرکب	cousin (son of paternal aunt)	پسرعمه
مادربزرگم با ما زندگی می کند. My grandmother lives with us.	اسم مرکب	grandmother	مادربزرگ
پدربزرگ من مرد بزرگی بود. My grandfather was a great man.	اسم مرکب	grandfather	پدربزرگ
نوه شما چند سال دارد؟ How old is your grandchild?	اسم	grandchild	نوه
من ایرانی هستم. I am Iranian.	ضمیر	I	من
تو کجایی هستی؟ Where are you from?	ضمیر	you (singular informal)	تو
او برادر من است. He is my brother.	ضمیر	he; she	او
ما ایرانی هستیم. We are Iranian.	ضمیر	we	ما
شما کجایی هستید؟ Where are you from?	ضمیر	you (plural; formal singular)	شما
آنها انگلیسی هستند. They are English.	ضمیر	they	آنها
موی من سیاه است. My hair is black.	صفت	black	سیاه
استاد ما خوب درس می دهد. Our professor teaches well.	اسم	professor	استاد

مثال Example	نقش دستوری Part of speech	معنی انگلیسی English meaning	لغت Word
من برای خواندن به عینک نیاز دارم. I need glasses to read.	اسم	glasses	عینک
او در دانشگاه زبان فارسی می خواند. S/he studies Persian at university.	اسم	university	دانشگاه
خانهٔ شما کجاست؟ Where is your house?	اسم	house	خانه
برادر کوچک من به مدرسه می رود. My little brother goes to school.	اسم	school	مدرسه (مدارس)
چشمهای شما بسیار زیباست. Your eyes are very beautiful.	صفت	beautiful	زیبا
ماشین من خیلی قدیمی است. My car is very old.	صفت	old (of things)	قدیمی
پالتو من جدید است. My winter coat is new.	صفت	new	جدید
از دیدن شما بسیار خوشحالم. I am very glad to see you.	صفت	happy	خوشحال

گفتگو

لهجه

نیما: سلام خانم. اسم من نیماست. اسم شما چیست؟

سیما: سلام. اسم من سیماست.

نیما: خوشوقتم.

سیما: من هم همینطور. شما کجایی هستید؟

نیما: من اهل شیرازم. شما چطور؟

سیما: من تهرانی هستم ولی پدر و مادرم اصفهانی هستند.

نیما: ولی شما لهجهٔ اصفهانی ندارید.

سیما: شما هم همینطور.

نیما: لهجهٔ اصفهانی؟

سیما: نه لهجهٔ شیرازی!

درس دوم ■ خودتان را معرفی کنید. کجایی هستید؟   21

درک مطلب

نیما اهل کجا است؟

آیا سیما اصفهانی است؟

پدرومادر سیما کجایی هستند؟

شما کجایی هستید؟

پدرومادر شما کجایی هستند؟

بحث کنید و بنویسید

یک گفتگو بنویسید مانند گفتگوی لهجه وازاسم خودتان واسم یکی‌از دوستانتان استفاده کنید. در گفتگویتان سعی
کنید دو شهر دیگر ایران را نام ببرید.

دستور

بودن/ داشتن   ■ to be/to have

The infinitive "to be" in English is equivalent to بودن in Persian. As "to be" changes its form completely when it is used with different pronouns, بودن also changes its form for different subjects. Furthermore, as "to be" has a contracted form in English, بودن can also be contracted:

بودن

من خوشحالم.	←	من خوشحال هستم.
تو خوشحالی.	←	تو خوشحال هستی.
او خوشحال است.	←	او خوشحال هستی.
ما خوشحالیم.	←	ما خوشحال هستیم.
شما خوشحالید.	←	شما خوشحال هستید.
آنها خوشحالند.[1]	←	آنها خوشحال هستند.

---

[1] When it is joined to words ending in the sound /e/, written as (ه - ـه) and /i:/, written as (ی), an *alef* is added, except for third person singular:

ایرانی ایم	ایرانی ام	خسته ایم	خسته ام
ایرانی اید	ایرانی ای	خسته اید	خسته ای
ایرانی اند	ایرانی است	خسته اند	خسته است

Lesson 2 ■ *Introduce yourself: Where are you from?* **22**

The infinitive "to have" in English is equivalent to داشتن in Persian. This verb can combine with nouns to form a compound verb, as in دوست داشتن (to like).

داشتن

من لهجهٔ شیرازی دارم.
تو لهجهٔ شیرازی داری.
او لهجهٔ شیرازی دارد.
ما لهجهٔ شیرازی داریم.
شما لهجهٔ شیرازی دارید.
آنها لهجهٔ شیرازی دارند.

جاهای خالی را پر کنید

او یک خواهر.............(داشتن).
من شما را.....................(دوست داشتن).
آنها ماشین...................(داشتن).
او مریم...................(بودن).
شما کجایی................(بودن)؟
ما تهرانی.................(بودن).
تو اهل شیراز..................(بودن)؟
من و خواهرم یک برادر کوچک .... (داشتن).
پدر و مادر من در ایران .... (بودن).
تو اهل تهران .... (بودن)؟
شما چند کلاس .... (داشتن)؟
من و دوستم زبان فارسی را دوست .... (داشتن).

Note that if the word ends in the sound /h/, written as (ه - ـه), an *alef* is not added since the word does not end in a vowel, e.g. :

شاهیم	شاهم
شاهید	شاهی
شاهند	شاه است

When it is joined to words ending in the long vowels /a:/ (ا) and /u:/(و), a ی is added, except for third person singular:

دانشجوییم	دانشجویم	زیباییم	زیبایم
دانشجویید	دانشجویی	زیبایید	زیبایی
دانشجویند	دانشجوست	زیبایند	زیباست

■ Uses of *ezafe*

اضافه

Ezafe literally means "adding". The of-phrase in English (e.g. the capital city of Iran) is similar to one form of *ezafe* in Persian. In nominal phrases, all the words except for the final word take *ezafe*, which is indicated by inserting the short vowel /e/, e.g. :

/pa:ytaxt-e keš var-e i:ra:n/
Lit. the capital city of the country of Iran

پایتختِ کشورِ ایران

Ezafe is usually not indicated in written Persian, but it must be said in spoken Persian. When the word itself ends in the long vowel /a:/ or /u:/, then the sound /ye/ is added instead of the sound /e/. The sound /ye/ can be represented either by adding the letter ی or, when it follows silent "h" (ه - ـه), by a *hamze* (ء) or by the letter ی, e.g. :

عموی تو	لهجهٔ انگلیسی	بابای من	خانهٔ من
	(لهجه ی انگلیسی)		(خانه ی من)

Another important usage of *ezafe* is to connect adjectives to nouns.

the good boy	پسر خوب
the beautiful capital city of Iran	پایتختِ قشنگِ ایران
my kind mother	مادرِ مهربان من

Ezafe is also inserted between certain titles, such as آقا (Mr), خانم (Mrs) and the surname, e.g.:

Mr Khalili	آقای خلیلی
Mrs Ehsan	خانم احسان

If these titles are used after the first name, there is no *ezafe*, e.g.:

حسن آقا
پری خانم

Ezafe is also inserted between the first name and surname, e.g.:

پروین ِ احسان
محمد ِ خلیلی

Ezafe is generally omitted when the first name ends in a long vowel, e.g.:

آهو خردمند
رضا اکبری

Lesson 2 ■ *Introduce yourself: Where are you from?* **24**

جاهای خالی را پر کنید

سارا یک برادر.................(داشتن).

او اهل همدان.................(بودن).

شما کجایی.................(بودن)؟

تو لهجهٔ انگلیسی.................(داشتن).

ما ماشین.................(داشتن).

مریم دختر خاله من.................(بودن).

عمه من اهل شیراز.................(بودن).

مادربزرگ او دو نوه.................(داشتن).

آنها یک خواهر.................(داشتن).

عبارات زیر را به فارسی ترجمه کنید

1. My uncle's Persian accent
2. Mr. Esfahani's cousin
3. His English aunt
4. The name of our university
5. Their old house
6. Your beautiful school
7. Her black hair
8. Our professor's new glasses
9. My new house
10. His old mother
11. My cousin's old books
12. Their old grandfather
13. Our Canadian passports
14. My brother's new school
15. Her beautiful, large room
16. The door of the class
17. My sister's new husband
18. The capital of Afghanistan
19. Our Persian language professor
20. Your old mobile phone

جاهای خالی را با کلمات زیر پر کنید

هستند ـ کجایی ـ چیست ـ خسته اید ـ چطور ـ زیباست ـ نام

آنها دانشجو.............

دختر عمه ی من.

من ایرانی هستم. شما. . . . . ؟

پدرشما.................است؟ تهرانی؟

در شهر چه خبره؟ 🎧

معرفی

مینا: علی این مریمه. مریم همکار منه.

علی: سلام مریم خانوم.

مریم: سلام

علی: شما چی درس میدین؟

مریم: زبان فرانسه درس می دم.

علی: شما چند تا زبان بلدین؟

مریم: من سه تا زبان بلدم. فارسی و انگلیسی و فرانسه.

علی: چه خوب. از آشناییتون خوشحال شدم.

مریم: منم همینطور. خدافظ.

این گفتگو را با کلمات زیر تمرین کنید

آلمانی - ترکی - ژاپنی - چینی - هلندی - هندی - عربی - روسی - لهستانی - تایلندی

	عامیانه colloquial		کتابی literary
	منه		من است
	مریمه		مریم است
	خانوم		خانم
	آشناییتون		آشناییتان
	می دین		می دهید
	بلدین		بلدید
	منم		من هم
	می دم		می دهم
	خدافظ		خداحافظ
	چند تا		چند

Lesson 2 ■ *Introduce yourself: Where are you from?*   **26**

جاهای خالی را پر کنید و بعد گفتگو را در گروهتان تمرین کنید

- الو. بفرمایید.

- سلام مریم جان. رضا .... خوبی؟

- سلام رضا جان. .... ممنون. خانمت خوب ....؟

- بله. خدا را شکر. خیلی بهتر .... دیروز دکتر گفت بچه مان دختر .... و من خیلی خوشحال شدم.

- خانمت .... نشد؟

- نه خیلی. او .... دوست دارد.

- چه عجیب! معمولاً خانمها دختر دوست .... و آقایان پسر!

- درست .... ولی در فامیل ما، دختر کم است. پس من خوشحالم که بچه مان .... است.

- مبارک باشد رضا جان!

- ممنون مریم جان!

Lesson Three / درس سوم
ایران بزرگتر است یا کانادا؟

چند پرچم در قبرستان شهدا در شهر کاشمر
این شهدا کسانی هستند که در جنگ ایران و عراق کشته شدند.
برای کسب اطلاعات بیشتر در مورد <u>جنگ ایران و عراق</u> یا <u>جنگ تحمیلی</u> در اینترنت جستجو کنید.

ایران بزرگتر است یا کانادا؟

Is Iran or Canada larger?

درس سوم: ایران بزرگتر است یا کانادا؟
گفتگو: استاد جدید
دستور: نفی
صفت
خواندن: کانادا و ایران
در شهر چه خبره؟ آدرس پرسیدن

Chapter aims
Grammar:
1. Negation of the two verbs 'to be' and 'to have'
2. Adjectives and their comparative and superlative forms

Situation:
1. Comparing two entities
2. Asking for directions

واژگان

لغت	معنی انگلیسی	نقش دستوری	مثال
صبح بخیر!	Good morning!	عبارت	وقتی از خواب بیدار می شوی به همه بگو: صبح بخیر! When you wake up, say "Good morning!" to everyone.
عصر بخیر!	Good afternoon!	عبارت	وقتی وارد کلاس شد گفت: عصر بخیر! When she entered the class, she said, "Good afternoon!"
شب بخیر!	Good night!	عبارت	قبل از خوابیدن بگو: شب بخیر! Before sleeping, say, "Good night!"

مثال	نقش دستوری	معنی انگلیسی	لغت
امروز صبح کلاس فارسی دارم. I've got Persian class this morning.	قید / اسم	morning	صبح
ظهر برای ناهار کجا می روی؟ Where are you going for lunch at noon?	قید / اسم	noon	ظهر
بعضی ها بعد از ظهر می خوابند. Some people sleep in the afternoon.	قید / اسم	afternoon	بعد از ظهر
دیروز تا عصر دانشگاه بودم. Yesterday, I was at university until late afternoon.	قید / اسم	late afternoon	عصر
غروب خیلی زیباست. The sunset is very beautiful.	اسم / قید	sunset	غروب
بچه ها از شب و تاریکی می ترسند. Children are afraid of the night and of darkness.	اسم / قید	night; evening	شب
آیا شما اینجا زندگی می کنید؟ Do you live here?	قید	here	اینجا
آیا آنجا خیلی دور است؟ Is it very far to there?	قید	there	آنجا
آن کتاب مال من است. That book is mine.	اشاره صفت / ضمیر	that	آن
من این کتاب را نخوانده ام. I haven't read this book.	اشاره صفت / ضمیر	this	این
هوا بسیار سرد است. The weather is very cold.	قید	very	بسیار
هوا خیلی گرم است. The weather is very hot.	صفت / قید	very; many	خیلی
غذای آن رستوران خیلی بد بود. The food at that restaurant was very bad.	صفت / قید	bad	بد
هوای اینجا بدتر از آنجاست. The weather here is worse than there.	صفت تفضیلی	worse	بدتر
بدترین روز زندگیم روزی بود که پدرم فوت کرد. The worst day of my life was the day my father passed away.	صفت عالی	worst	بدترین
شما خیلی خوب رانندگی می کنید. You drive very well.	صفت / قید	well; good	خوب

لغت	معنی انگلیسی	نقش دستوری	مثال
بهتر	better	صفت تفضیلی	هوای اینجا بهتر از آنجاست. The weather here is better than the weather there.
بهترین	best	صفت عالی	تو بهترین دوست من هستی. You are my best friend.
دانشجو (دانشجویان)	university student	اسم	او دانشجوی دانشگاه مک گیل است. He is a student at McGill University.
مهندسی	engineering	اسم	برادر من مهندسی عمران می خواند. My brother studies civil engineering.
ممنون	Thanks; grateful	عبارت صفت	از شما بسیار ممنون هستم. I am very grateful to you.
خوشا به حالتان!	Lucky you!	عبارت	وقتی به آنها گفتیم که در دانشگاه قبول شدیم آنها گفتند خوشا به حالتان. When we told them that we had been admitted to university they said, "Lucky you!"
معذرت خواستن (خواه) از	to apologize to	فعل	او از من معذرت خواست. He apologized to me.
خواندن (خوان)	to study; to read	فعل	او علوم سیاسی می خواند. She studies political science.

گفتگو

استاد جدید

بابک: صبح بخیر. من بابک هستم. اینجا مهندسی می خوانم. شما چه می خوانید؟

پروین: صبح شما هم بخیر. من پروین پارسا هستم و اینجا دانشجو نیستم.

بابک: خوشا به حالتان! اینجا دانشگاهِ بسیار بدی است و بدترین اساتید را دارد.

پروین: خیلی ممنون! من استادِ جدیدِ این دانشگاه هستم!

بابک: خیلی معذرت میخواهم. ولی اینجا بهترین استادهای جدید را دارد.

درک مطلب

بابک چه می خواند؟

فامیلی پروین چیست؟

آیا پروین دانشجوست؟
اینجا چه جور دانشگاهی است؟
شغل پروین چیست؟

بحث کنید و بنویسید

یک گفتگو بنویسید مانند گفتگوی استاد جدید ولی درمورد دو تا از کلاس هایتان در دانشگاه. سپس این دو کلاس را با هم مقایسه کنید و بگویید کدام بهتر است.

دستور

نفی ■ Negation

In Persian, the verb is negated with (نـ) which is added to the beginning of the verb, and in compound verbs, to the beginning of the verbal part of the compound. For example:

من دیروز به دانشگاه نرفتم.

I didn't go to the university yesterday.

ما در ایران زندگی نمی کنیم .

We don't live in Iran.

Note that when (نـ) comes before (می), it is pronounced /ne/; otherwise, it is pronounced /na/.

The negative form of the present tense of بودن is irregular:

من دانشجو هستم.	← من دانشجو نیستم .
تو دانشجو هستی.	← تو دانشجو نیستی.
او دانشجوست.[1]	← او دانشجو نیست.
ما دانشجو هستیم.	← ما دانشجو نیستیم.

---

[1] Note that third person singular is the only form of this verb that does not start with a /h/ sound. There is another version of this form, which is هست, and it is used for emphasis or to indicate the existence of something.

She *is* a student.   او دانشجو هست.
God exists   خدا هست.

Lesson 3 ■ *Is Iran or Canada larger?* **32**

شما دانشجو هستید.   ← شما دانشجو نیستید.

آنها دانشجو هستند.   ← آنها دانشجو نیستند.[2]

Note that in Persian, sentences containing certain negative expressions, such as هیچ وقت (never), هیچ کس (no one) and هیچ جا (no where), require a negative verb, e.g.

هیچ وقت او را ندیده ام.

I have never seen him.

هیچ کس مرا دوست ندارد.

No one loves me.

امسال هیچ جا نرفتیم.

We didn't go anywhere this year.

جاهای خالی را با فعل «بودن» پر کنید

در کلاس فارسی دانشجویان خوبی . . . .

اساتید دانشگاه ما بد . . . .

من اهل آفریقا . . . .

آیا شما استاد جدید . . . . ؟

ببخشید ولی اسم من مریم . . . . من بهاره هستم.

زبان مردم فرانسه چینی . . . .

هوا در قطب شمال هیچ وقت گرم . . . .

■ Adjectives   صفت

In Persian, adjectives normally follow the noun, but superlative adjectives (which end in ترین)
come before the noun without *ezafe*, while positive and comparative adjectives (which end in تر)
follow the noun with *ezafe*, e.g.:

---

[2] Note that in Persian, in these types of sentences, the noun is definite, unlike in English, where the indefinite noun is used. In addition, the singular form of noun is used for plural subjects unless the noun is qualified by an adjective, e.g:

I am a student.	من دانشجو هستم.
We are students.	ما دانشجو هستیم.
We are good students.	ما دانشجویان خوبی هستیم.

When qualified by an adjective, the noun appears in the indefinite

I am a good student.	من دانشجوی خوبی هستم.

the bad university	دانشگاهِ بد
the worse university	دانشگاهِ بدتر
the worst university	بدترین دانشگاه
the new professor	استادِ جدید
the newer professor	استادِ جدیدتر
the newest professor	جدیدترین استاد

In order to form a comparative adjective in Persian, one adds the suffix تر to the positive adjective, e.g.:

beautiful → more beautiful	زیبا ← زیباتر
big → bigger	بزرگ ← بزرگتر

In order to form a superlative adjective in Persian, one adds the suffix ترین to the positive adjective, e.g. :

beautiful → the most beautiful	زیبا ← زیباترین
big → the biggest	بزرگ ← بزرگترین

There are a handful of exceptions to this rule, e.g.:

خوب ← بهتر ← بهترین
بسیار ← بیشتر ← بیشترین

عبارات زیر را به فارسی ترجمه کنید

1. The best father
2. Newer professors
3. More students
4. My best cousin
5. Shorter hair
6. The loudest voice
7. The fastest car
8. Your older sister
9. The easiest test
10. Their youngest son
11. My oldest friend
12. Your newest professor
13. The oldest cinema
14. The worst restaurant
15. The hardest language

خواندن

کانادا و ایران

من ایرانی هستم ولی در کانادا زندگی می کنم. ایران کشوری قدیمی است ولی کانادا کشور جدیدی است. پدرومادرمن در ایران هستند ولی خواهر و برادر من در کانادا زندگی می کنند. من در دانشگاه مک گیل مهندسی می خوانم. دانشگاه مک گیل یکی از قدیمی ترین دانشگاه های کانادا است.

جاهای خالی را پر کنید

کانادا کشوری .... است.
پدرومادرِمن در .... زندگی نمی کنند.
من در دانشگاهِ مک گیل تاریخ ....
دانشگاهِ مک گیل یکی از قدیمی ترین دانشگاه های کانادا ....
ایران از کانادا بزرگتر ....
خواهر من دو سال از من .... است.
زندگی در پایتخت .... از زندگی در شهر های کوچک است.
موی من از موی تو .... است.
فارسی یکی از .... زبانهای دنیا است.

جاهای خالی را با کلمات مناسب پر کنید

نیما لهجه ی اصفهانی ....

الف) ندارم   ب) ندارد
ج) نداریم   د) ندارند

سیما اهل کجا .... ؟

الف) هستید   ب) هستیم
ج) است   د) هستند

آنها .... ؟

الف) ایرانی ایم   ب) ایرانی است
ج) ایرانی اند   د) ایرانی اید

تو کجا .... می کنی؟

الف) ممنون   ب) غروب
ج) زندگی   د) ظهر

آنها .... ممتاز این دانشگاه هستند.

الف) دانشجویان   ب) هوا

ج) مهندسی   د) کشور

این دانشگاه .... اساتید را دارد.

الف) بهتر   ب) خوب

ج) بدتر   د) بهترین

در شهر چه خبره؟ 🎧

آدرس پرسیدن

نازلی: ببخشین آقا میدون ونک کجاس؟

عابر: مستقیم برین بعد بپیچین سمت چپ.

نازلی: میدون ونک از اینجا خیلی دوره؟

عابر: نه خیلی. با ماشین یه ده دیقه ای طول می کشه.

نازلی: مرسی.

عابر: خواهش می کنم.

این گفتگو را با کلمات زیر تمرین کنید

سمت راست - چهارراه - چراغ راهنمایی - ورود ممنوع - خیابان یکطرفه - شمال - جنوب - شرق - غرب - نزدیک - دور

	عامیانه colloquial		کتابی literary
	ببخشین		ببخشید
	برین		بروید
	بپیچین		بپیچید
	میدون		میدان
	کجاس		کجاست
	دوره		دور است
	یه		یک
	دیقه		دقیقه
	طول می کشه		طول می کشد

جاهای خالی را پر کنید و بعد گفتگو را در گروهتان تمرین کنید

– سلام امید. این ترم چند .... داری؟

– سلام میترا. این ترم پنج کلاس .... تو چطور؟

– من سه کلاس دارم: کلاس ادبیات و .... تاریخ و کلاس فلسفه.

– کدام .... سخت ترین کلاس است؟

– البته کلاس فلسفه. استادمان جوانترین .... این دانشگاه است ولی خیلی .... درس می دهد.

– برای من تاریخ از فلسفه .... است چون خیلی تاریخ باید حفظ کنیم.

نگارش: دو کشور را انتخاب کنید و با استفاده از واژگان این درس آنها را با هم مقایسه کنید. بعد در گروهتان با هم بحث کنید.

درس چهارم
ایران چند استان دارد؟

آرامگاه و مجسمه شاعر بزرگ ایران، فردوسی

فردوسی یک هزار سال پیش زندگی می کرد و نویسندهٔ حماسهٔ ملی ایران یعنی شاهنامه است. آرامگاه فردوسی در شهر تاریخی طوس در نزدیکی مشهد مرکز استان خراسان رضوی، واقع است. برای کسب اطلاعات بیشتر در مورد فردوسی و مشهد در اینترنت جستجو کنید.

Lesson 4 ■ *How many provinces does Iran have?*   **38**

ایران چند استان دارد؟

How many provinces does Iran have?

درس چهارم: ایران چند استان دارد؟
گفتگو: استان گیلان
دستور: ضمیر
ترتیب کلمات
خواندن: گیلان
در شهر چه خبره؟ دربانک

Chapter aims
Grammar:
1. Different kinds of pronoun
2. Word order

Situation:
1. Describing a place
2. At the bank

واژگان

لغت	معنی انگلیسی	نقش دستوری	مثال
حال (احوال)	state of being	اسم	حال شما چطور است؟ How are you?
مرسی	Thanks	عبارت	وقتی در را برایم باز کرد، گفتم: مرسی. When she opened the door for me, I said, "Thanks!"
متشکرم	Thank you	عبارت	وقتی سخنرانی ام تمام شد، گفتم: متشکرم. When my speech was finished, I said, "Thank you!"
فیلم	film	اسم	آخرین فیلمی که دیدی چه بود؟ What was the last film you saw?

درس چهارم ■ ایران چند استان دارد؟   39

مثال	نقش دستوری	معنی انگلیسی	لغت
زیبا یعنی قشنگ. "Beautiful" means "pretty".	عبارت	means; that is to say	یعنی
معنی این کلمه چیست؟ What is the meaning of this word?	اسم	meaning	معنی
شما چند زبان بلدید؟ How many languages do you know?	اسم	language	زبان
مردم این کشور بسیار مهربان هستند. The people of this country are very kind.	اسم	people	مردم
شیراز در کدام استان قرار دارد؟ Which province is Shiraz in?	اسم	province	استان
کشور شما در کدام قاره است؟ Which continent is your country in?	اسم	country	کشور
زندگی در روستا بسیار ساده تر است. Life in villages is much simpler.	اسم	village	روستا
خانم شما خیلی زیبا هستند [1]. Your wife is very beautiful.	صفت	beautiful	زیبا
خانهٔ قشنگی دارید. You have a beautiful house.	صفت	pretty	قشنگ
هیچ کس در این دنیا زشت نیست. No one in this world is ugly.	صفت	ugly	زشت
شهر رشت در شمال ایران است. The city of Rasht is in the north of Iran.	اسم	north	شمال
من در جنوب شهر زندگی می کنم. I live in the southern part of the city.	اسم	south	جنوب
زاهدان در شرق ایران است. Zahedan is in the east of Iran.	اسم	east	شرق
ترکیه در غرب ایران است. Turkey is to the west of Iran.	اسم	west	غرب
مرکز شهر همیشه شلوغ است. The city centre is always crowded.	اسم	centre	مرکز

[1] In Persian, a plural verb can be used for a singular subject to indicate respect, as in:

خانم شما خیلی زیبا هستند.

Lesson 4 ■ *How many provinces does Iran have?* **40**

مثال	نقش دستوری	معنی انگلیسی	لغت
رنگ چشمان شما خیلی زیباست. The colour of your eyes is very beautiful.	اسم	colour	رنگ
لطفاً آن شلوار سبز را برایم بیاورید. Please bring me those green trousers.	اسم / صفت	green	سبز
رنگ آبی را دوست دارم. I like the colour blue.	اسم / صفت	blue	آبی
قرمز رنگ مورد علاقه من است. Red is my favourite colour.	اسم / صفت	red	قرمز
قناری زرد است. Canaries are yellow.	اسم / صفت	yellow	زرد
موهای مادرم خیلی سفید شده است. My mother's hair has gone very white.	اسم / صفت	white	سفید
دریا طوفانی است. The sea is rough.	اسم	sea	دریا
آب دریاچه شور است. The water in the lake is salty.	اسم	lake	دریاچه
اقیانوس بسیار بزرگ است. The ocean is very big.	اسم	ocean	اقیانوس
خیلی نمک ریختی. غذا شور است. You added too much salt. The food is salty.	صفت	salty	شور
این آب میوه بسیار شیرین است. This fruit juice is very sweet.	صفت	sweet	شیرین
این دوا خیلی تلخ است. This medicine is very bitter.	صفت	bitter	تلخ
غذاهای هندی معمولاً تند هستند. Indian food is usually spicy.	صفت	spicy	تند
او از من معذرت خواست و من او را بخشیدم. He apologized to me, and I forgave him.	فعل	to forgive; to excuse	بخشیدن (بخش)
آیا همسرم را می شناسید؟ Do you know my wife?	فعل	to know; to be acquainted with	شناختن (شناس)
من دیروز این فیلم را دیدم. I saw this film yesterday.	فعل	to see	دیدن (بین)

گفتگو

استان گیلان

فیلیپ : سلام سیمین.
سیمین: سلام. حالت خوب است؟
فیلیپ: بله. تو چطوری؟
سیمین: من هم خوبم. مرسی.
فیلیپ: این چیست؟
سیمین: یک فیلم ایرانی بنام «گیلان».
فیلیپ: گیلان یعنی چه؟
سیمین : گیلان نام یکی از استان های ایران است.
فیلیپ: فیلم خوبی است؟
سیمین: بله. فیلم بسیار خوبی است.
فیلیپ : آیا گیلان استان زیبایی است؟
سیمین: بله. گیلان یکی از زیباترین استان های ایران است.

درک مطلب

نام فیلم سیمین چیست؟
آیا گیلان فیلمِ خوبی است؟
معنی گیلان چیست؟
آیا گیلان استان زیبایی است؟
چند شهر در ایران را نام ببرید.
چند استان در ایران را نام ببرید.

بحث کنید و بنویسید

یک گفتگو بنویسید مانند گفتگوی استان گیلان ولی درمورد استان خودتان. نام مرکز استانتان را بگویید و آن شهر را با شهر دیگری مقایسه کنید.

ضمیر

Pronouns

In Persian there are subjective, objective and possessive pronouns:

Lesson 4 ■ *How many provinces does Iran have?* **42**

Subjective pronouns

ضمير شخصى فاعلى

Subjective pronouns come before the predicate. The subjective pronoun and the personal suffix of the verb should agree in Persian.

من خوب هستم.

تو خوب هستى.

او خوب است.

ما خوب هستيم.

شما خوب هستيد.

آنها خوب هستند.

It should be noted that subjective pronouns are commonly omitted in Persian.

They are Iranian.	ايرانى هستند.
She is young.	جوان است.
I am happy.	خوشحال هستم.
You are hungry.	گرسنه هستيد.
You are beautiful.	زيبا هستى.
I saw him.	او را ديدم.
We are going to the movies.	به سينما مى رويم.

They are normally only mentioned in order to emphasize or contrast the subject, e.g.:

I will do that!	من آن كار را مى كنم!
I will do that, not *you*!	من آن كار را مى كنم، نه تو!

Note that شما is used to indicate plural "you" as well as polite singular "you". There is an alternative pronoun for the third person plural, ايشان , which is most commonly used (with a plural verb) to refer to the third person singular in polite conversation.

Objective pronouns

ضمير شخصى مفعولى

Objective pronouns are normally used before the verb, and they are either followed by the direct object marker or preceded by a preposition indicating the indirect object marker. In colloquial Persian, the direct objective pronouns are normally added to the verb as objective pronoun suffixes.

علی مرا بخشید. = علی بخشیدم.[2]
علی ترا بخشید. = علی بخشیدت.
علی او را بخشید. = علی بخشیدش.
علی ما را بخشید. = علی بخشیدمان.
علی شما را بخشید. = علی بخشیدتان.
علی آنها را بخشید. = علی بخشیدشان.

علی به من گفت.
علی به تو گفت.
علی به او گفت.
علی به ما گفت.
علی به شما گفت.
علی به آنها گفت.

Note that in compound verbs, the direct objective suffix is added to the nominal part, e.g.:

علی <u>دوستش دارد</u>.

Ali loves her.

معلم <u>تشویقمان کرد</u>.

The teacher encouraged us.

Possessive pronouns ضمیر ملکی

Note that the possessive pronoun suffixes are similar to the objective pronoun suffixes. However, there is a difference between these two kinds of suffixes. While the objective pronoun suffix is added to the verb, the possessive pronoun suffix is added to the noun:

بیژن **خواهر** مرا دید. = بیژن **خواهرم** را دید.
بیژن **خواهر** ترا دید. = بیژن **خواهرت** را دید.
بیژن **خواهر** او را دید. = بیژن **خواهرش** را دید.
بیژن **خواهر** ما را دید. = بیژن **خواهرمان** را دید.

---

[2] Note that in transitive verbs with direct objects in the past tense, the first person singular of the verb takes the same form as the third person singular plus the objective pronoun, e.g.:

بخشیدم

I forgave

مرا بخشید = بخشیدم

He forgave me.

Or

زدم

I hit.

مرا زد = زدم.

He hit me.

بیژن **خواهر شما** را دید. = بیژن **خواهرتان** را دید.
بیژن **خواهر آنها** را دید. = بیژن **خواهرشان** را دید.

برادر من کوچک است. = برادرم کوچک است.
برادر تو کوچک است. = برادرت کوچک است.
برادر او کوچک است. = برادرش کوچک است.
برادر ما کوچک است. = برادرمان کوچک است.
برادر شما کوچک است. = برادرتان کوچک است.
برادر آنها کوچک است. = برادرشان کوچک است.

جاهای خالی را با ضمیر مناسب پر کنید
مثال:

او دانشجو است.

استاد تکلیف . . . . دید.
. . . . سیمین نیست.
. . . . خوشحال هستند.
استاد نام . . . . خواند.
ما ایرانیان کشور . . . . را دوست داریم.
من تکلیف . . . . را انجام دادم.
. . . . تشنه اید؟
آنها درس . . . . را نخواندند.
پدر . . . . بخشید.
استاد . . . . دیدم.
ما . . . . می شناسیم.
آنها . . . . دوست ندارند.
. . . . در کانادا زندگی می کنم.
. . . . خسته ایم.
. . . . در کلاس هستی.

خواندن

گیلان

گیلان استانی است در شمال ایران. استان گیلان بسیار سبز است. این استان شهرهای بسیاری دارد. شهرهای استان گیلان خیلی زیبا هستند. مرکز این استان رشت است. زبان محلی مردم گیلان گیلکی است. دریای خزر هم در شمال ایران است. آب این دریا شور است.

درست یا غلط؟

استان گیلان در جنوب ایران است.
آب دریای خزر شیرین است.
زبان مردم گیلان ترکی است.
مرکز استان گیلان رشت است.

چهار سؤال برای متن بالا بنویسید

مثال : استان گیلان در کجای ایران است؟

ترتیب کلمات   ■ Word order in Persian

In Persian, the word order is basically **Subject – Object – Verb**. If the object is direct and specific, then it is followed by را:

کتابی خواندم.

I read a book.

کتاب تو را خواندم.

I read your book.

کتاب جدیدی خواندم.

I read a new book.

کتاب جدید را خواندم.

I read the new book.

کتاب جدید تو را خواندم.

I read your new book.

As for the adverbials, although Persian is a scrambling language and the order of the words can change based on the word that is emphasized, the basic order is:

subject – <u>adverb of time</u> – object – <u>adverb of manner</u> – <u>adverb of place</u> – verb

Lesson 4 ■ *How many provinces does Iran have?* 46

In the following examples, all adverbials are underlined. Remember that in Persian, the order of the adverbial can be changed to indicate the focus. Generally speaking, the adverbial that appears first is the most important. Look at the four versions of the sentence below. They all convey the English meaning, "I wrote my homework with my new pencil in the library today", but by rearranging the order of the phrase, the focus of the sentence is slightly altered.

امروز تکلیفم را با مداد جدیدم در کتابخانه نوشتم.

با مداد جدیدم امروز تکلیفم را در کتابخانه نوشتم.

در کتابخانه با مداد جدیدم امروز تکلیفم را نوشتم.

در کتابخانه امروز تکلیفم را با مداد جدیدم نوشتم.

جملات زیر را به فارسی ترجمه کنید

1. They studied Persian at university last year.
2. My father saw Mr Rezapour in his office yesterday.
3. I see my professor in class every day.
4. I went to school by bus yesterday.
5. Last month we moved to a new house.
6. They eat lunch at the university every day.
7. I took my son to school by car on Thursday.
8. We bought these shoes from that shop today.
9. He opens the door of the class with a key everyday.
10. Did you come to the university by metro yesterday?
11. The cities of Iran are bigger than the cities in Canada.
12. We learn Persian by reading, writing, listening, and speaking in Persian.

جاهای خالی را پر کنید

سیما: سلام، اسم من سیماست.

علی: . . . .

ب) چیست	الف)کجایی هستید
د) خداحافظ	ج) خوشوقتم

استاد فارسی ما . . . . حسن زاده است.

ب) خانم	د) پسر
الف) زن	ج) دختر

شما . . . . انگلیسی دارید.

ب) شیرازی	الف) لهجه
د) زبان	ج) اصفهان

چند . . . . دارید؟

الف) من   ب) آنها

ج) خواهر   د) ایشان

شما . . . . هستید؟

الف) مردم   ب) کجایی

ج) الفبا   د) اهل

برادر مادر من . . . . من است.

الف) دایی   ب) عمو

ج) عمه   د) خاله

خواهر پدر من . . . . من است.

الف) عمو   ب) دایی

ج) عمه   د) خاله

من یک دختر و یک پسر دارم. یعنی من دو . . . . دارم.

الف) برادر   ب) خواهر

ج) بچه   د) عمه

کامران: من ایرانی هستم. شما چطور؟

سوسن: من هم . . . .

الف) همینطور   ب) چکار

ج) چطور   د) چیست

من دو نوه دارم . . . . دختر هستند.

الف) این   ب) تو

ج) ما   د) آنها

در شهر چه خبره؟ 🎧

در بانک

حسن: ببخشین باجه خدمات ارزی کجاس؟

کارمند بانک: همینجاس جناب.

حسن: می خواستم این هزار دلارو تبدیل کنم. نرخ دلار امروز چنده؟

کارمند بانک: یه لحظه اجازه بدین نگاه کنم.

حسن: دستتون درد نکنه.

کارمند بانک: نرخش نهصد و بیست تومانه. پس هزار دلار می شه نهصد و بیست هزار تومان.

حسن: بسیار خب. متشکرم. هزار دلار خدمت شما.

Lesson 4 ■ *How many provinces does Iran have?* **48**

این گفتگو را با کلمات زیر تمرین کنید

نقد- چک- چک پول- حساب جاری- حساب پس انداز- واریز- برداشت- سپرده کوتاه مدت - سپرده بلند مدت

عامیانه colloquial	کتابی literary
چنده	چند است
می شه	می شود
درد نکنه	درد نکند
تومانه	تومان است
یه	یک
دستتون	دستتان
دلارو	دلار را
اجازه بدین	اجازه بدهید
ببخشین	ببخشید
کجاس	کجاست
همینجاس	همینجا است
بسیار خب	بسیار خوب

جاهای خالی را پر کنید و بعد گفتگو را در گروهتان تمرین کنید

- سلام امیر. چه خبر؟
- سلام مینا. امروز استادمان ضمیر .... یادمان داد.
- چه جالب! چه چیزهایی یاد گرفتید؟
- چیزهای .... یاد گرفتیم. یک امتحان .... داشتیم.
- امتحانت .... بود؟
- آسان بود. یعنی .... نبود ولی من دیر .... کلاس رسیدم.
- پس استاد عصبانی شد؟
- نه او خیلی .... است و به من گفت این بار می بخشمت.
- پس من هم ترم .... با او کلاس می گیرم!

نگارش: یک استان و یا ایالت در کشورتان را انتخاب کنید و با استفاده از واژگان این درس در مورد آن یک متن بنویسید. سپس آنرا در گروهتان بخوانید.

Lesson Five

درس پنجم
در مورد نوروز چه می دانید؟

درختان پر از شکوفه در یکی از روستاهای خراسان در فاصلهٔ چند کیلومتری نیشابور
این عکس یک هفته پس از سیزده به در گرفته شده است.
برای کسب اطلاعات بیشتر در مورد <u>سیزده به در</u> در اینترنت جستجو کنید.

در مورد نوروز چه می دانید؟

What do you know about Noruz?

درس پنجم: در مورد نوروز چه می دانید؟
گفتگو: نوروز
دستور: ساخت جمله
جملات پرسشی
جملات تعجبی
اعداد
زمان
خواندن: سال نو
در شهر چه خبره؟ در سینما

Chapter aims
Grammar:
1. Different kinds of sentences, including statements, questions, and exclamations
2. Numbers

Situation:
1. The Persian New Year
2. Telling the time
3. At the cinema

واژگان

لغت	معنی انگلیسی	نقش دستوری	مثال
در مورد	about	حرف اضافه	در مورد تاریخ ایران چه می دانید؟ What do you know about the history of Iran?
پیش از = قبل از	before	حرف اضافه	پیش از انقلاب در ایران زندگی می کردم. I lived in Iran before the revolution.

مثال	نقش دستوری	معنی انگلیسی	لغت
بعد از کلاس به سینما می رویم. We will go to the cinema after class.	حرف اضافه	after	پس از = بعد از
تا تابستان در این شهر هستیم. We will be in this town until the summer.	حرف اضافه	until	تا
هواپیما از روی دریاچه گذشت. The airplane passed over the lake.	حرف اضافه	over	از روی
من یک پدرم. علاوه بر این یک معلم هم هستم. I am a father. In addition, I am also a teacher.	عبارت ربطی	in addition	علاوه بر این
در نوروز همهٔ مردم لباس های نو می پوشند. Everyone wears new clothes at Noruz.	صفت	New	نو
اولین روز بهار نوروز است. The first day of spring is Noruz.	صفت	First	اولین
آخرین روز هفته در ایران جمعه است. The last day of the week in Iran is Friday.	صفت	last	آخرین
یک خبر جالب برایت دارم. I have an interesting piece of news for you.	صفت	interesting	جالب
نوروز اولین روز فروردین ماه است. Noruz is the first day of Farvardin.	اسم	Noruz (Iranian new year, March 21)	نوروز
فروردین اولین ماه سال ایرانی است. Farvardin is the first month of the Iranian year.	اسم	Farvardin (first month of the Iranian year)	فروردین
هر سال سفره هفت سین را من می چینم. I set the Haft-sin every year.	اسم	'Haft-sin' (Noruz table setting)	سفره هفت سین
ایرانیان در چهارشنبه سوری از روی آتش می پرند. Iranians jump over fire on Charshanbeh-suri.	اسم	last Tuesday night of the year in the Iranian calendar	چهارشنبه سوری
سفره را بچین. Set the table.	اسم	table cloth	سفره
چند جشن ایرانی را نام ببرید. Name a few Iranian festivals.	اسم	celebration; festival	جشن
آتش برای بچه ها خطرناک است. Fire is dangerous for children.	اسم	fire	آتش
من بازی شطرنج را دوست دارم. I like chess.	اسم	game	بازی

Lesson 5 ■ *What do you know about Noruz?* 52

مثال	نقش دستوری	معنی انگلیسی	لغت
در چهارشنبه سوری آتش بازی می کنند. They light fireworks on Charshanbeh-suri.	اسم مرکب	fireworks	آتش بازی
برای عیدی یک سکه طلا گرفتم. I got a gold coin as a gift for Noruz.	اسم	coin	سکه
چلوکباب را باید با سماق خورد. You must eat Chelo-kebab with sumac.	اسم	sumac	سماق
روی سالاد سرکه و روغن زیتون ریختم. I put vinegar and olive oil on the salad.	اسم	vinegar	سرکه
لباس گرم بپوش چون هوا سرد است. Put on warm clothes because it is cold.	اسم	clothes	لباس
من در یک مهمانی با او آشنا شدم. I met him at a party.	اسم	party	مهمانی
کی از همسرتان جدا شدید؟ When did you separate from your spouse?	اسم	spouse	همسر
چند چیز را نام ببرید که با حرف الف شروع شوند. Name several things that start with the letter "alef".	اسم	thing	چیز
حقوق ماهیانه شما چقدر است؟ How much is your monthly salary?	اسم	salary; law (the subject); rights	حقوق
من به هنر علاقمندم. I am interested in art.	اسم	art	هنر
من از بچگی نقاشی می کردم. I have painted since my childhood.	اسم	painting	نقاشی
طبیعت ایران بسیار متنوع است. The countryside in Iran is very varied.	اسم	countryside; nature	طبیعت
آنها خارج از شهر زندگی می کنند. They live outside of town.	اسم	outside; abroad	خارج
داخل کیفم را گشتم ولی کلیدم را پیدا نکردم. I searched inside my purse, but I didn't find my key.	اسم	inside	داخل
آیا درست است که سیزده عدد بدیمنی است؟ Is it true that 13 is an unlucky number?	اسم	number	عدد (اعداد)
درخت با حرف دال شروع می شود. "Derakht" starts with the letter "dal".	اسم	letter	حرف (حروف)

مثال	نقش دستوری	معنی انگلیسی	لغت
این درس واژگان بسیار سختی دارد. This lesson has very difficult words.	اسم	word	واژه (واژگان)، کلمه (کلمات)، لغت (لغات)
«صبح بخیر» یک عبارت است. "Good morning" is a phrase.	اسم	phrase	عبارت (عبارات)
با هر یک از لغات درس یک جمله بسازید. Make a sentence with each word from the lesson.	اسم	sentence	جمله (جملات)
در یک پاراگراف شرح حالتان را بنویسید. Write about yourself in one paragraph.	اسم	paragraph	پاراگراف
یک مقاله در مورد سنت ها و رسوم مردم کشورتان بنویسید. Write an article about the customs and traditions of the people in your country.	اسم	article; essay	مقاله (مقالات)
ساعت پنج است. It is five o'clock.	اسم	hour; o'clock; watch	ساعت (ساعات)
چند دقیقه طول می کشد؟ How many minutes will it take?	اسم	minute	دقیقه (دقایق)
هر دقیقه شصت ثانیه است. There are 60 seconds in every minute.	اسم	second	ثانیه
قرار بود ساعت هفت و ربع همدیگر را ببینیم. We were supposed to meet at 7:15.	اسم	quarter	ربع
شما درباره ایران چه می دانید؟ What do you know about Iran?	کلمه پرسشی	what?	چه؟
چه کسی امروز به خانه شما می آید؟ Who is coming to your house today?	کلمه پرسشی	who?	چه کسی؟
کی کلاستان تمام می شود؟ When will your class end?	کلمه پرسشی	when?	کی؟
کدام مداد مال شماست؟ Which pencil is yours?	کلمه پرسشی	which?	کدام؟
چرا دیشب نیامدی؟ Why didn't you come last night?	کلمه پرسشی	why?	چرا؟
چند برادر داری؟ How many brothers do you have?	کلمه پرسشی	how many?	چند؟
چقدر پول با خودت آوردی؟ How much money did you bring with you?	کلمه پرسشی	how much?	چقدر؟

لغت	معنی انگلیسی	نقش دستوری	مثال
شروع شدن (شو)	to begin (intransitive)	فعل	کلاس ما ساعت ده و سی دقیقه شروع می شود. Our class starts at 10:30.
شروع کردن (کن)	to begin (transitive)	فعل	من خواندن فارسی را پارسال شروع کردم. I started to study Persian last year.

گفتگو

نوروز

سام: چه می خوانی؟
ستاره: یک کتاب درمورد نوروز.
سام: نوروز چیست؟
ستاره: نوروز سال نو ایرانی است.
سام: اولین ماه سال ایرانی چیست؟
ستاره: فروردین.
سام: مردم ایران سال نو را چطور جشن می گیرند؟
ستاره: آنها سفرهٔ هفت سین می چینند، لباس نو می پوشند و به مهمانی می روند.
سام: سفرهٔ هفت سین چیست؟
ستاره: سفرهٔ هفت سین هفت چیز است که با حرف «س» شروع می شود مثل سکه سماق و سرکه.
سام: چه جالب!

درک مطلب

ستاره چه می خواند؟
نوروز چیست؟
اولین ماه سال در ایران چه ماهی است؟
سال نو را در ایران چطور جشن می گیرند؟
سفرهٔ هفت سین چیست؟

بحث کنید و بنویسید

یک گفتگو بنویسید مانند گفتگوی نوروز ولی درمورد سال نو در کشورخودتان. فرق بین نوروز و سال نو در کشورتان را توضیح دهید.

دستور

جمله

Sentences

In Persian, there are narrative, interrogative and exclamatory sentences.

جملهٔ اخباری

Narrative sentences

Narrative sentences have the order: subject + object + verb. The definite direct object is distinguished from the subject by using the direct object marker را, e.g.:

سام کتاب را دوست دارد.

Sam likes the book.

In this sentence, سام is the subject, while کتاب is the object, which is marked by the direct object marker را, and "دوست دارد" is the verb. Note that if the noun is generic, i.e. if the noun has a general rather than specific meaning, it appears in the singular definite form, i.e. without the added indefinite اسم ی and without the object marker را, as in:

سام کتاب دوست دارد.

Sam likes books.

جملهٔ پرسشی

Questions

The word order of questions in Persian is the same as narrative sentences, i.e.: subject + object + verb. To ask a yes/no question, either the tone is changed or the question word آیا is added to the beginning of the narrative sentence without making any other changes. Adding آیا to the beginning of a question makes it formal.

Does Sam like the book?   آیا سام کتاب را دوست دارد؟

    When asking a wh-question, since Persian is an *in situ* language, the word order is the same as in the statement, and the question word simply sits in place of the omitted word or phrase, e.g.:

Sam likes Setareh.   سام ستاره را دوست دارد.
Who does Sam like?   سام چه کسی را دوست دارد؟

In Persian, there are three kinds of questions: yes/no questions, interrogative and indirect questions.

Lesson 5 ■ *What do you know about Noruz?*   56

Yes/No questions

ایران **کشور** جدیدی است؟

Is Iran a new country?

تو **دو** خواهر داری؟

Do you have two sisters?

Wh-questions

چه کسی (کی) دو خواهر دارد؟

Who has two sisters?

چند خواهر داری؟

How many sisters do you have?

چقدر پول داری؟

How much money do you have?

اسم تو **چیست؟**

What is your name?

چه کسی را دوست داری؟

Whom do you like?

چه چیزی را دوست داری؟

What do you like?

کدام دختر خواهر توست؟

Which girl is your sister?

این کتاب **کی** است؟

Whose book is this?

برادر **کی** را دیدی؟

Whose brother did you see?

کجا زندگی می کنی؟

Where do you live?

ساعت چند کلاس داری؟

What time do you have class?

کی کلاس داری؟

When do you have class?

هوا **چطور** است ؟

How's the weather?

چرا فارسی می خوانی؟

Why are you studying Persian?

Indirect questions

نمی دانم او اینجاست یا **نه**.

I don't know if he is here.

نمی دانم اسم او (اسمش) چیست.

I don't know what his name is.

Exclamatory sentences

جملهٔ تعجبی

Exclamatory sentences express feelings and emotions. In Persian they start with چه ("how" or "what") and end with an exclamation mark, as in:

چه جالب !

How interesting!

If چه is followed by a noun, the noun appears in the indefinite form, e.g.:

چه‌هوایی!

What (great) weather!

چه کتابی!

What a (fine) book!

جملات زیر را مرتب کنید

شلوار- پوشیدی - قشنگی - چه!

می رود - مدرسه - او - به - کی؟

نوروز - می دانید - معنی - آیا - را؟

حرف می زنید - چقدر - فارسی - خوب!

با - سینما - نمی آیید - چرا - ما - به؟

با کلمات پرسشی داخل پرانتز جملات زیر را سؤالی کنید

مثال: او روزهای سه شنبه کار نمی کند. (چه روزهایی) ← او چه روزهایی کار نمی کند؟

خانوادهٔ آنها جمعه ها به پار می روند. (کجا)

سام در دانشگاه تهران رشته حقوق می خواند. (کی)

من هنر می خوانم چون نقاشی کردن را دوست دارم. (چرا)

بچه ها ساعت ۸ به مدرسه می روند. (ساعت چند)

همسرش را به ما معرفی کرد. (چه کسی را)

خواندن 🎧

سال نو

ایرانیان پیش از سال نوسفرهٔ هفت سین می چینند و آن را تا روز سیزده به در نگه می دارند. سیزده به در سیزدهمین روز سال نو است که ایرانیان در آن روز به خارج از خانه و یا به طبیعت می روند. علاوه براین ایرانیان آخرین سه شنبهٔ هر سال را با آتش بازی و پریدن از روی آتش جشن می گیرند. نام این روز چهارشنبه سوری است. جشنهای ایرانیان بسیار قدیمی و متنوع هستند.

درست یا غلط؟

ایرانیان آخرین سه شنبهٔ هر سال را با رفتن به خارج از خانه یا به طبیعت جشن می گیرند.

ایرانیان پس از سال نو سفرهٔ هفت سین می چینند.

ایرانیان سفرهٔ هفت سین را تا دهمین روز سال نگه می دارند.

جشنهای ایرانیان بسیار جدید و یکنواخت هستند.

درک مطلب

سیزده به در در چه روزی است؟

ایرانیان سیزده به در در چه کار می کنند؟

چند رسم مختلف در سال نو ایرانی را نام ببرید.

چهار سؤال برای متن بالا بنویسید

◼ Numbers اعداد

Ordinal (used before a noun)	Ordinal (used after a noun)	Cardinal	Cardinal
اولین	اول	یک	۱
دومین	دوم	دو	۲
سومین	سوم	سه	۳
چهارمین	چهارم	چهار	۴
پنجمین	پنجم	پنج	۵
ششمین	ششم	شش	۶
هفتمین	هفتم	هفت	۷
هشتمین	هشتم	هشت	۸
نهمین	نهم	نه	۹
دهمین	دهم	ده	۱۰
یازدهمین	یازدهم	یازده	۱۱
دوازدهمین	دوازدهم	دوازده	۱۲
سیزدهمین	سیزدهم	سیزده	۱۳
چهاردهمین	چهاردهم	چهارده	۱۴
پانزدهمین	پانزدهم	پانزده	۱۵
شانزدهمین	شانزدهم	شانزده	۱۶
هفدهمین	هفدهم	هفده	۱۷
هجدهمین	هجدهم	هجده	۱۸
نوزدهمین	نوزدهم	نوزده	۱۹
بیستمین	بیستم	بیست	۲۰
بیست و یکمین	بیست و یکم	بیست و یک	۲۱
بیست و.	بیست و.	بیست و.	
سی امین	سی ام	سی	۳۰

Ordinal (used before a noun)	Ordinal (used after a noun)	Cardinal	Cardinal
سی و یکمین	سی و یکم	سی و یک	۳۱
سی و.	سی و.	سی و.	
چهلمین	چهلم	چهل	۴۰
چهل و یکمین	چهل و یکم	چهل و یک	۴۱
چهل و.	چهل و.	چهل و.	
پنجاهمین	پنجاهم	پنجاه	۵۰
پنجاه و یکمین	پنجاه و یکم	پنجاه و یک	۵۱
پنجاه و.	پنجاه و.	پنجاه و.	
شصتمین	شصتم	شصت	۶۰
شصت و یکمین	شصت و یکم	شصت و یک	۶۱
شصت و.	شصت و.	شصت و.	
هفتادمین	هفتادم	هفتاد	۷۰
هفتاد و یکمین	هفتاد و یکم	هفتاد و یک	۷۱
هفتاد و	هفتاد و	هفتاد و	
هشتادمین	هشتادم	هشتاد	۸۰
هشتاد و یکمین	هشتاد و یکم	هشتاد و یک	۸۱
هشتاد و	هشتاد و	هشتاد و	
نودمین	نودم	نود	۹۰
نود ویکمین	نود ویکم	نود ویک	۹۱
نود و	نود و	نود و	
صدمین	صدم	صد	۱۰۰
صد و بیست و پنجمین	صد و بیست و پنجم	صد و بیست و پنج	۱۲۵
دویستمین	دویستم	دویست	۲۰۰
سیصدمین	سیصدم	سیصد	۳۰۰
چهارصدمین	چهارصدم	چهارصد	۴۰۰
پانصدمین	پانصدم	پانصد	۵۰۰
ششصدمین	ششصدم	ششصد	۶۰۰
هفتصدمین	هفتصدم	هفتصد	۷۰۰

درس پنجم ■ در مورد نوروز چه می دانید؟   61

Ordinal (used before a noun)	Ordinal (used after a noun)	Cardinal	Cardinal
هشتصدمین	هشتصدم	هشتصد	۸۰۰
نهصدمین	نهصدم	نهصد	۹۰۰
نهصد و نود و نهمین	نهصد و نود و نهم	نهصد و نود و نه	۹۹۹
هزارمین	هزارم	هزار	۱۰۰۰
دو هزارمین	دو هزارم	دو هزار	۲۰۰۰
نه هزارمین	نه هزارم	نه هزار	۹۰۰۰
یک میلیونمین	یک میلیونم	یک میلیون	۱۰۰۰۰۰۰
یک میلیاردمین	یک میلیاردم	یک میلیارد	۱۰۰۰۰۰۰۰۰۰

جاهای خالی در جملات زیر را با اعداد مناسب پر کنید

جمعه .... روز هفته است.

.... روز مهرماه در ایران بچه ها به مدرسه میروند.

من دو خواهر بزرگتر از خودم دارم. من دختر .... پدر و مادرم هستم.

هر ماه ایرانی یا .... روز یا .... روز دارد.

من .... سال پیش بدنیا آمدم.

ایران امسال سال .... است.

الآن ساعت .... است.

ایران .... استان دارد.

آمریکا .... ایالت دارد.

در ایران .... نفر زندگی می کنند.

زمان   ■ Time expressions

Cardinal numbers are used to tell the time in Persian, e.g.:

ساعت .... است.

It is five o'clock.	ساعت پنج است.
What time do you have class?	چه ساعتی کلاس دارید؟
At four o'clock.	ساعت چهار.
It is half past six.	ساعت شش و نیم است.

Lesson 5 ■ *What do you know about Noruz?* **62**

It is six thirty.	ساعت شش و سی دقیقه است.
It is a quarter past twelve.	ساعت دوازده و ربع است.
It is twelve fifteen.	ساعت دوازده و پانزده دقیقه است.
It is a quarter to nine.	ساعت یک ربع به نه است.
It is eight forty-five.	ساعت هشت و چهل و پنج دقیقه است.
It is ten fifty.	ساعت ده و پنجاه دقیقه است.
It is ten minutes to eleven.	ساعت ده دقیقه به یازده است.

Note that when reporting the time, *ezafe* is not added after ساعت, but when the time expression is an adverbial (e.g. at four o'clock), *ezafe* is added after ساعت, e.g.:

at four o'clock	ساعتِ چهار

Frequently in adverbial time expressions, ساعت is omitted altogether, e.g.:

What time are we going to have dinner?	ساعت چند شام می خوریم ؟
Seven.	هفت.
I will see you at ten.	ده می بینمت.

جملات زیر را به فارسی ترجمه کنید

1. It is a quarter to eight.
2. It is a quarter past seven.
3. It is ten past four.
4. It is two o'clock.
5. It is one fifty-five.
6. I will see you at eleven.
7. Our class starts at nine.
8. We'll meet you at three fifteen.
9. He arrived at seven forty-five.
10. The bus arrives at eight forty-seven.

جاهای خالی را با کلمات مناسب پر کنید

این دانشگاه . . . . دانشگاه آمریکا است.

ب) بهترین	الف) بدتر
د) خوب	ج) جدیدتر

این درس . . . . بسیار سختی دارد.

الف) مردان   ب) زنان
ج) درختان   د) واژگان

مردم در نوروز لباس . . . . می پوشند.

الف) کهنه   ب) شیرین
ج) نو   د) قدیمی

آنها . . . . شهر زندگی می کنند.

الف) خارج   ب) جشن
ج) هنر   د) رنگ

او یک کتاب . . . . ایران می خواند.

الف) از روی   ب) علاوه براین
ج) در مورد   د) بعد از

در شهر چه خبره؟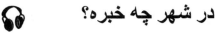

در سینما

رکسانا: دو تا بیلیت برای فیلم «باران».
بلیت فروش: چه سانسی؟ ساعت هفت خوبه؟
رکسانا: نه اگه دیرتر باشه بهتره. واسه سانس نه و نیم ندارین؟
بلیت فروش: چرا داریم. دو هزار تومان.
رکسانا: بفرمایین. اینم دو هزار تومان.
بلیت فروش: بهتره قبل از نه و ربع تو سالن باشین. درا رو نه و بیست دیقه می بندن.

این گفتگو را با کلمات زیر تمرین کنید

سینما- تئاتر- خیمه شب بازی- سیرک- کنسرت- نمایشگاه

کتابی literary	عامیانه colloquial
اگر	اگه
باشد	باشه

عامیانه colloquial	کتابی literary
بهتره	بهتر است
واسه	برای
دیقه	دقیقه
خوبه	خوب است
ندارین	ندارید
بفرمایین	بفرمایید
باشین	باشید
می بندن	می بندند
اینم	این هم
درا رو	درها را
بیلیت	بلیت
تو	داخل

جاهای خالی را پر کنید و بعد گفتگو را در گروهتان تمرین کنید

- سلام علی. امسال چه تاریخی و ساعت .... سال نو می شود؟
- سلام نسترن. امسال اول فروردین سه شنبه .... ۱۲ نیمه شب است.
- آیا بیدار می مانی؟
- حتماً! من و خانواده ام هرسال سر .... هفت سین می نشینیم و حافظ می خوانیم و .... داشتن سالی خوب آرزو می کنیم.
- چه خوب. .... به حالت! ما تنبل .... و .... شب بیدار نمی شویم! پیشاپیش سال .... مبارک!
- ممنون. سال نو تو هم ....!

نگارش: با استفاده از واژگان این درس یک متن در مورد جشن سال نو در کشورتان بنویسید و بعد آن را در گروهتان بخوانید.

درس ششم

آخر هفته در ایران چه روزی است؟

پنجشنبه بعد از ظهر و جمعه در ایران خیلی ها کار نمی کنند. یکی از تفریحات مورد علاقهٔ ایرانیان رفتن به باغ ها و پارک های عمومی است. این عکس در باغ فین در شهر تاریخی کاشان گرفته شده است. برای کسب اطلاعات بیشتر در مورد <u>کاشان</u> و <u>باغ فین</u> در اینترنت جستجو کنید.

آخر هفته در ایران چه روزی است؟

What day is the weekend in Iran?

درس ششم : آخر هفته در ایران چه روزی است؟
گفتگو : جمعه
دستور : فعل
گذشته (ماضی)
حال (مضارع)
آینده (مستقبل)
خواندن : روزهای هفته
در شهر چه خبره؟ در بقالی

Chapter aims
Grammar:
1. Different verb tenses, i.e. past, present, and future

Situation:
1. Talking about days of the week
2. At the store
3. *ta'arof*

واژگان

لغت	معنی انگلیسی	نقش دستوری	مثال
دیروز	Yesterday	قید / اسم	دیروز او را در کتابخانه دیدم.
امروز	Today	قید/ اسم	امروز هوا خیلی خوب است.
فردا	Tomorrow	قید / اسم	من فردا کلاس ندارم.
هرروز	every day	عبارت	ما هر روز به پارک می رویم.

درس ششم ■ آخر هفته در ایران چه روزی است؟ | 67

مثال	نقش دستوری	معنی انگلیسی	لغت
چند شنبه او را دیدی؟	عبارت	what day (of the week)	چند شنبه؟
شنبه اولین روز هفته است.	اسم/ قید	Saturday	شنبه
یکشنبه در ایران تعطیل نیست.	اسم/ قید	Sunday	یکشنبه
دوشنبه خیلی کار دارم.	اسم/ قید	Monday	دوشنبه
سه شنبه باید به مدرسهٔ پسرم بروم.	اسم/ قید	Tuesday	سه شنبه
تا چهارشنبه باید این کتاب را تمام کنم.	اسم/ قید	Wednesday	چهارشنبه
عصر پنج شنبه به دیدن او رفتم.	اسم/ قید	Thursday	پنج شنبه
جمعه چه کار می کنید؟	اسم/ قید	Friday	جمعه
سومین روز هفته دوشنبه است.	اسم	day	روز
هر هفته هفت روز دارد.	اسم	week	هفته
ماه آینده به سفر می رویم.	اسم	month	ماه
امسال سال خوبی بود.	اسم	year	سال
هر صد سال یک قرن است.	اسم	century	قرن (قرون)
در دههٔ اخیر کشور ما مشکلات زیادی داشته است.	اسم	decade	دهه
در آینده می خواهی چه کاره بشوی؟	اسم	future	آینده
بهتر است در زمان حال زندگی کنی نه در آینده و نه در گذشته.	اسم	present	حال
از گذشته چیزی یادم نیست.	اسم	past	گذشته
با آنها به سینما نرفتم چون خیلی درس داشتم.	کلمه ربط	since, because	چون
همه شما را دوست دارند زیرا شما مرد خوبی هستید.	کلمه ربط	because	زیرا
امروز هیچ جا نمی روم چون می خواهم درس بخوانم.	قید	nowhere	هیچ جا
فردا چند مهمان دارم.	اسم	guest	مهمان
امروز یک نامه دریافت کردم.	اسم	letter	نامه
نامه را در داخل پاکت گذاشتم.	اسم	envelope	پاکت
آیا روی پاکت تمبر چسباندی؟	اسم	stamp	تمبر
ببخشید پستخانه کجاست؟	اسم	post office	پستخانه

Lesson 6 ■ *What day is the weekend in Iran?* 68

مثال	نقش دستوری	معنی انگلیسی	لغت
تعداد دانشجویان کلاس چند نفر است؟	اسم	number, quantity	تعداد
هفت عددی فرد است.	صفت	odd number	فرد
هشت عددی زوج است.	صفت	even number	زوج
معلمان ما را به سه گروه تقسیم کرد.	اسم	group	گروه
معمولاً صبح زود بیدار می شوم.	قید	usually	معمولاً
آخر هفته او را می بینم.	عبارت	weekend	آخر هفته
در زبان فارسی استثناء زیاد وجود ندارد.	اسم	exception	استثناء
مردم ایران جمعه ها کار نمی کنند.	فعل	to work	کار کردن (کن)
آنها هنوز با مادرشان زندگی می کنند.	فعل	to live	زندگی کردن (کن)
من می خواهم شما را ببینم.	فعل	to want	خواستن (خواه)
شام چه می خوری؟	فعل	to eat	خوردن (خور)
مشقهایت را نوشتی؟	فعل	to write	نوشتن (نویس)
به من گفت که دیر برمی گردد.	فعل	to say; to tell	گفتن (گو)
چه لباس قشنگی پوشیده ای!	فعل	to wear	پوشیدن (پوش)
ساعت چند می خوابی؟	فعل	to sleep	خوابیدن (خواب)
آیا خبر جدید را شنیده ای؟	فعل	to hear	شنیدن (شنو)
من هر روز صبح ساعت هشت سر کار می روم.	فعل	to go to work	سرکار رفتن (رو)
ما در تابستان معمولاً به مسافرت می رویم.	فعل	to travel	مسافرت رفتن (رو)
این پول را بین خودت و خواهرت تقسیم کن.	فعل	to divide	تقسیم کردن (کن)

گفتگو

جمعه

فریبرز : دیروز کجا رفتی؟
سوسن : دیروز چند شنبه بود؟

فریبرز: دیروز جمعه بود.

سوسن: دیروز هیچ جایی نرفتم چون روزهای جمعه هم کار می کنم. تو چطور؟

فریبرز: روزهای جمعه معمولاً به رشت می روم. خواهرم آنجا زندگی می کند.

سوسن: آیا جمعهٔ آینده هم به رشت میروی؟

فریبرز: نه. جمعهٔ آینده استثنائاً به رشت نمی روم چون مهمان دارم.

درک مطلب

سوسن دیروز کجا رفت؟

دیروز چند شنبه بود؟

فریبرز دیروز کجا رفت؟

چرا فریبرز جمعهٔ آینده به رشت نمی رود؟

چرا فریبرز روزهای جمعه معمولاً به رشت می رود؟

شما روزهای جمعه کجا می روید؟

بحث کنید و بنویسید

یک گفتگو بنویسید مانند گفتگوی جمعه و توضیح دهید آخر هفته را معمولاً چطور، کجا و با چه کسانی می گذرانید.

دستور

فعل ▮ Verbs

Verbs in Persian are formed from the infinitive, which consists of the past stem and the infinitive marker ن e.g. رفتن، گفتن، دیدن.

گذشته (ماضی) *Past tense*

This tense is used to express actions that were completed in the past. To form the past stem, simply drop the infinitive marker ن from the infinitive.

The past stem, which ends in either د or ت is followed by fixed inflectional suffixes:

(/am/) for first person singular "I"
(/iː/) for second person singular "you"
nothing for third person singular "he/she/it"
(/iːm/) for first person plural "we"

(/i:d/) for second person plural or respected second person singular "you"

(/and/) for third person plural "they"

to buy   خریدن

خریدیم   خریدم

خریدید   خریدی

خریدند   خرید

من دیروز دو کتاب خریدم.

I bought two books yesterday.

او پارسال خانه اش را خرید.

He bought his house last year.

Present tense   حال (مضارع)

This tense is used to express an action in the present, which is either a habit or something done at the moment of speaking. The present tense in Persian can also be used to express actions in the future. Note that the verb endings are the same as the ones used for the past tense except for the third person singular, which is normally followed by د. In addition, in the present tense, the prefix می precedes the present stem.

The present stem   بن مضارع

Forming the present stem is not as easy as forming the past stem. To form the past stem, the infinitive marker ن is dropped (خریدن ← خرید), whereas to form the present stem, if the past stem ends in ید, the ید will be dropped (خرید ← خر). However, if the past stem ends in ند, the د will often be dropped (خواند ← خوان). And often if the past stem ends in خت, the خت will be usually replaced with ز (دوخت ← دوز). However, many simple verbs in Persian have irregular present stems which must be memorized, e.g.:

دیدن ← بین
شناختن ← شناس
آمدن ← آ
رفتن ← رو
نوشتن ← نویس

Note the present tense of the verb in the following examples.

تو زیاد کتاب می خوانی.

You read books a lot.

او هر روز یک کتاب می خواند.

She reads a book every day.

The present tense of داشتن and بودن are irregular and do not take می.

من تو را دوست دارم.

I love you.

من امروز مریض هستم.

I am ill today.

Note that if the present tense indicates an action that is in progress at the time of speaking, the present tense of " داشتن" can be used to emphasize that the action is taking place at the moment of speaking, and the conjugated form of داشتن is placed right after the subject, e.g.:

من دارم کتاب می خوانم.

I am reading a book.

شما دارید فارسی صحبت می کنید.

You are speaking Persian.

Future verbs   آینده (مستقبل)

As noted above, the present tense is often used in Persian to express a future action, e.g.:

We will go	می رویم
I will buy	می خرم
He will write	می نویسد

The future tense in Persian can also be made in the following way.

I will go	خواهم رفت
You will say	خواهی گفت
He will hear	خواهد شنید
We will see	خواهیم دید
You will come	خواهید آمد
They will read	خواهند خواند

Notice that the verb endings are the same as the ones used for the present tense. The first part of the verb is conjugated from the present stem خواه of the infinitive خواستن, while the main verb always appears as the past stem, e.g.: گفت، رفت، آمد. This form of the future verb is normally used in Persian to express a more emphatic meaning, e.g.:

I *will* go.	خواهم رفت.
You *will* see	خواهید دید

This emphatic form of the future is less common in spoken than in written Persian.

با هر یک از افعال زیر یک جمله برای زمان گذشته، یک جمله برای زمان حال و یک جمله برای زمان آینده بنویسید

to eat	خوردن
to spill	ریختن
to wear	پوشیدن
to sleep	خوابیدن
to cook	پختن
to like	دوست داشتن
to llive	زندگی کردن
to studye	درس خواندن

با درنظرگرفتن قیدهای زیر، جاهای خالی را در جملات زیر با زمان مناسب فعل پر کنید

yesterday	دیروز
tomorrow	فردا
every day	هرروز

من دیروز به دانشگاه . . . . (رفتن).

آنها هرروز ساعت ۸ . . . . (خوابیدن).

آنها روزهای جمعه کباب . . . . (خوردن).

من فردا لباس قرمز . . . . (پوشیدن).

او دیروز یک نامه . . . . (نوشتن).

من هفتهٔ آینده به اصفهان . . . . (رفتن).

درس ششم ▪ آخر هفته در ایران چه روزی است؟

خواندن

روزهای هفته

هر هفته ۷ روز دارد. در ایران اولین روز هفته شنبه است و آخرین روز هفته جمعه است. مردم ایران روزهای جمعه سرکار نمی روند. اکثر آنها یا به گردش می روند یا به مهمانی. شنبه، یکشنبه، دوشنبه، سه شنبه، چهارشنبه، پنج شنبه و جمعه روزهای هفته هستند. چون روزهای هفته با یک عدد آغاز می شوند، آنها را به دو گروه روزهای فرد (یکشنبه و سه شنبه و پنج شنبه) و روزهای زوج (شنبه و دوشنبه و چهارشنبه) تقسیم می کنیم.

درک مطلب

هر هفته چند روز دارد؟
در ایران اولین روز هفته چه روزی است؟
مردم ایران چه روزی سرکار نمی روند؟
روزهای هفته را به چند گروه تقسیم می کنیم؟

چهار سؤال برای متن بالا بنویسید

جملات زیر را به فارسی ترجمه کنید

1. Each day has 24 hours.
2. In Iran, people don't work on Fridays.
3. It is a quarter past 12.
4. We have Persian class at 10:35.
5. I bought a car yesterday.
6. Did you buy the Persian book today?
7. I drink my coffee with milk.
8. He comes to school by bus every day.
9. Next week we will go to Tehran.
10. I saw him on the street this morning.
11. I WILL go to Iran next summer.
12. I drink my coffee with milk at 8:00 every morning.
13. I was going to work when I saw my colleague.
14. Did you hear the good news?
15. I WILL write my biography one day.

در شهر چه خبره؟

در بقالی

خانم انصاری: سلام حاج آقا. از اون روغن زیتونی که هفته پیش بردم دارین؟
بقال: سلام خانم مهندس. اتفاقاً تموم شده ولی یکی از اون بهتر برامون از ترکیه رسیده. قیمتشم مناسبه.
خانم انصاری: چنده مگه؟
بقال: قابل شما رو نداره خانم مهندس. چاهار هزار و پونصد.
خانم انصاری: قربون دستتون. دو تا بدین.

این گفتگو را با کلمات زیر تمرین کنید

پنیر- شیر- کره- ماست- حبوبات- برنج- ترشی- آبلیمو- سرکه- تخم مرغ- نان

	عامیانه colloquial		کتابی literary
	اون		آن
	پونصد		پانصد
	تموم		تمام
	برامون		برایمان
	قربون		قربان
	دستتون		دستتان
	قیمتشم		قیمتش هم
	دارین		دارید
	بدین		بدهید
	مناسبه		مناسب است
	چنده		چند است
	مگه		مگر
	نداره		ندارد
	چاهار		چهار

جاهای خالی را پر کنید و بعد گفتگو را در گروهتان تمرین کنید

– سلام استاد. هفته‌ی........... من به کلاس نیامدم. چه درسی .... خواندیم و .... تکلیفی داشتیم؟

– سلام خانم تهرانی. هفته‌ی پیش در .... ایران پیش .... اسلام خواندیم و دانشجویان یک متن درباره‌ی این .... نوشتند.

– خیلی .... استاد. آیا من می توانم این .... را هفته‌ی آینده .... شما بیاورم؟

– حتماً. لطفاً از اینترنت استفاده .... و برای نوشتن متنتان .... کتابخانه بروید.

– چشم استاد. ممنون که به من اجازه .... تکلیفم را هفته‌ی .... بیاورم.

– خواهش .... خانم تهرانی.

نگارش: با استفاده از واژگان این درس، برنامه‌ی هفتگی تان را بنویسید و بعد آن را با برنامه‌ی هفتگی دوستتان مقایسه کنید.

Lesson Seven

درس هفتم
ورزش مورد علاقه شما چیست؟

یک مغازه لوازم ورزشی در تهران
دوتا از ورزشهایی که از همه بیشتر مورد علاقه ایرانیان می باشند فوتبال و کشتی هستند.
برای اطلاعات بیشتر در مورد تیم ملی فوتبال ایران در اینترنت جستجو کنید.

Lesson 7 ■ *What is your favourite sport?*

ورزش مورد علاقه شما چیست؟

What is your favourite sport?

درس هفتم: ورزش مورد علاقه شما چیست؟
گفتگو: فوتبال
دستور: مضارع التزامی
ماضی التزامی
فعل امری
فصلها و ماه های سال
نام ماه های میلادی به فارسی
خواندن: ورزش
در شهر چه خبره؟ گردش در شهر

Chapter aims
Grammar:
1. Present and past subjunctive
2. Imperatives

Situation:
1. Discussing the Persian months and seasons
2. Sightseeing

واژگان

مثال	نقش دستوری	معنی انگلیسی	لغت
پریروز او را در خیابان دیدم.	قید	the day before yesterday	پریروز
پس فردا به دیدن مادرم می روم.	قید	the day after tomorrow	پس فردا
قبلاً این فیلم را دیده ام.	قید	previously; already	قبلاً

درس هفتم ■ ورزش مورد علاقه شما چیست؟   79

مثال	نقش دستوری	معنی انگلیسی	لغت
شاید او هم با ما بیاید.	قید	maybe; perhaps	شاید
باید خوب درس بخوانی.	قید	must	باید
نباید دروغ بگویی.	قید	must not	نباید
لطفاً این اسکناس را خرد کنید.	قید	please	لطفاً
می‌توانیم با هم به دیدن او برویم.	قید	together	با هم
به غیر از مریم همه امتحان دادند.	حرف اضافه	except for	به غیر از، به جز
هنگام بهار طبیعت بسیار زیبا می‌شود.	حرف اضافه	at the time of	هنگام
ببخشید آجیل کیلویی چند است؟	اسم	nuts	آجیل
حتی از فکرش هم می‌ترسم.	اسم	thought	فکر (افکار)
از ایدهٔ او خوشم آمد.	اسم	idea	ایده
ماشین جدیدتان مبارک!	اسم	car	ماشین
من رانندگی بلد نیستم.	اسم	driving	رانندگی
هنگام رانندگی باید کمربند ایمنی خود را ببندید.	اسم مرکب	seat belt	کمربند ایمنی
او خیلی جوک‌های بامزه بلد است.	اسم	joke	جوک
وقتی جوان بودم می‌خواستم تا ابد زنده بمانم.	صفت/ اسم	young; young person	جوان
او به سؤال من پاسخ خوبی داد.	اسم	question	سؤال (سؤالات)
ورزش برای سلامتی لازم است.	اسم	sport	ورزش
تختی یک کشتی گیر بسیار محبوب بود.	اسم مرکب	wrestler	کشتی گیر
برای بچه‌ها پدرانشان همیشه قهرمان هستند.	اسم/ صفت	hero	قهرمان
پهلوان‌ها بسیار جوانمردند.	اسم/ صفت	champion	پهلوان
امروز برنامه‌ات چیست؟	اسم	programme; plan; schedule	برنامه
من قصد دارم در مسابقه دو شرکت کنم.	اسم	competition; match	مسابقه
تیم شما از تیم ما قوی‌تر است.	اسم	team	تیم
تقریباً همهٔ ایرانیان فوتبال را دوست دارند.	اسم	football	فوتبال
من طرفدار تیم پرسپولیس هستم.	اسم	fan; supporter	طرفدار

Lesson 7 ■ *What is your favourite sport?* **80**

مثال	نقش دستوری	معنی انگلیسی	لغت
دانشگاه ما یکی از بهترین دانشگاههای جهان است.	اسم	world	جهان
فرانسه در اروپاست.	اسم	Europe	اروپا
ایران در قاره آسیا قرار دارد.	اسم	Asia	آسیا
کشور مصر در آفریقا است.	اسم	Africa	آفریقا
آمریکا یکی از کشورهای وسیع جهان است.	اسم	America	آمریکا
ایران و مصر در دو قاره مختلف هستند.	اسم	continent	قاره
خانهٔ ما در کوچهٔ بهار است.	اسم	alley	کوچه
وقتی از خیابان می گذری مواظب باش.	اسم	street; avenue	خیابان
تولد من در فصل بهار است.	اسم	season	فصل
کتابخانهٔ ملی کجاست؟	صفت	national	ملی
خانهٔ ما از اینجا زیاد دور نیست.	صفت	far	دور
آیا بانک ملی نزدیک دانشگاه است؟	صفت	near	نزدیک
ببخشید، ممکن است لطفاً سیگار نکشید؟	صفت	possible	ممکن
لازم نیست این کتاب را بخرید.	صفت	necessary	لازم
بسیاری از مردم ایران سنتی هستند.	صفت	traditional	سنتی
کمال الملک یکی از نقاش های بسیار معروف ایران است.	صفت	famous; well-known	معروف
هر چه تلفن کردم شماره ات مشغول بود.	صفت	busy	مشغول
چند نفر را دعوت کردم.	صفت نامشخص	several	چند
آیا امکان دارد من هم با شما بیایم؟	فعل	to be possible	امکان داشتن
چقدر احتمال دارد برف ببارد؟	فعل	to be probable	احتمال داشتن
ببخشید می توانم اسمتان را بپرسم؟	فعل	to be able	توانستن (توان)
پاهایت را روی میز نگذار.	فعل	to let; to put	گذاشتن (گذار)
اسم ترا نمی دانم.	فعل	to know (something)	دانستن (دان)
بند کفشت را ببند. وگرنه زمین می خوری.	فعل	to close; to tie	بستن (بند)
اجازه می دهید از خودکارتان استفاده کنم؟	فعل	to allow	اجازه دادن (ده)

لغت	معنی انگلیسی	نقش دستوری	مثال
پاسخ دادن (ده)	to answer	فعل	وقتی از او سؤال کردم پاسخی نداد.
پر کردن (کن)	to fill	فعل	لطفاً این فرم ها را پر کنید.
درست کردن (کن)	to make	فعل	امشب من شام درست می کنم.
شرکت کردن (کن) در	to participate in	فعل	آیا دیروز در کلاس شرکت کردید؟
علاقه داشتن (دار) به	to be interested in	فعل	من به نقاشی خیلی علاقه دارم.
موافقت کردن (کن)	to agree	فعل	او موافقت کرد که با من بیاید.

گفتگو

فوتبال

لادن : سلام بچه ها. برنامهٔ امروزمان چیست؟
پیام: امروز به خانهٔ سینا می رویم تا باهم بازی فوتبال ایران و آمریکا را ببینیم.
لادن : چه خوب! من هم آجیل می آورم. شما ساعت چند می روید؟
پیام : ساعت ۵. اگر می خواهی می توانیم با هم برویم.
لادن : فکر بسیار خوبی است چون من ماشین ندارم و خانهٔ سینا خیلی دور است.

درک مطلب

امروز پیام و لادن به خانهٔ چه کسی می روند؟
چرا بچه ها امروز به خانهٔ سینا می روند؟
لادن چه چیزی می آورد؟
پیام ساعت چند می خواهد به خانهٔ سینا برود؟
آیا پیام ماشین دارد؟

بحث کنید و بنویسید

یک گفتگو بنویسید مانند گفتگوی فوتبال ولی در مورد دوستان خودتان و در آن یکی از برنامه های تفریحی تان را شرح دهید.

دستور

مضارع التزامی

Present subjunctive

Another tense which makes use of the present stem in Persian is the present subjunctive. Notice that the verb endings are the same as the ones used for the present tense. How- ever, in the present subjunctive, the prefix ﺏ precedes the present stem (instead of ﻣﻰ). In compound verbs, often the prefix ﺏ is dropped in written and formal Persian. The present subjunctive is used after certain control verbs and verbal phrases which express desire, will, necessity and obligation. Here are some example of verbs and expressions in Persian which require a subjunctive:

to want to: They want to go.	خواستن: آنها <u>می خواهند بروند</u>.
to be able to: I am not able to sleep.	توانستن: من <u>نمی توانم بخوابم</u>.
to let: My mother won't let me come with you.	گذاشتن: مادرم <u>نمی گذارد</u> با شما <u>بیایم</u>.
to allow: Will you allow me to sit here?	اجازه دادن: <u>اجازه می دهید</u> من اینجا <u>بنشینم؟</u>
to prefer to: I prefer to speak Persian.	ترجیح دادن: من <u>ترجیح می دهم</u> فارسی <u>صحبت کنم</u>.
it is possible: It is possible that she will call.	امکان دارد: <u>امکان دارد تلفن کند</u>.
it is possible: It is possible that it will rain.	ممکن است: <u>ممکن است</u> باران <u>بیاید</u>.
it is probable: It is probable that I will pass.	احتمال دارد: <u>احتمال دارد</u> که <u>قبول شوم</u>.
it is necessary: Is it necessary that I come too?	لازم است: آیا <u>لازم است</u> که من هم <u>بیایم؟</u>
must: You must apologize to her.	باید: <u>باید</u> از او <u>معذرت بخواهی</u>.
must not: You must not drive fast.	نباید: <u>نباید</u> تند <u>برانید</u>.
may: We may see one another.	شاید: <u>شاید</u> همدیگر را <u>ببینیم</u>.
before: Before you leave I must talk to you.	قبل از اینکه: <u>قبل از اینکه بروید باید</u> با شما <u>صحبت کنم</u>.

	تا:
in order to: I came here in order to see you.	آمدم اینجا <u>تا</u> تو را <u>ببینم</u>.
if: If you come, I will come too.	اگر: <u>اگر بیایی</u> من هم می آیم.
to doubt: I doubt he knows Persian.	شک داشتن: شک دارم فارسی <u>بلد باشد</u>.
to hope to: I hope to see her.	امیدوار بودن: <u>امیدوارم ببینمش</u>.
to be inclined to: I am not inclined to see him.	مایل بودن: <u>مایل نیستم</u> او را <u>ببینم</u>.
to intend to: I intend to go to Iran.	قصد داشتن: <u>قصد دارم</u> به ایران <u>بروم</u>.
to wish: I wish I would see you.	آرزو داشتن: <u>آرزو دارم</u> شما را <u>ببینم</u>.
to like to: I liked to read books.	دوست داشتن: <u>دوست داشتم</u> کتاب <u>بخوانم</u>.
to have to: I had to study.	مجبور بودن: <u>مجبور بودم</u> درس <u>بخوانم</u>.
to be supposed to: We are supposed to see each other.	قرار است: <u>قرار است</u> همدیگر را <u>ببینیم</u>.

It should be mentioned that the present subjunctive of the two verbs, داشتن and بودن are irregular:

بودن

باشیم	باشم
باشید	باشی
باشند	باشد

داشتن

داشته باشیم	داشته باشم
داشته باشید	داشته باشی
داشته باشند	داشته باشد

The present subjunctive is also used in Persian to express suggestions, e.g.:

Let's eat!	بخوریم!
Let's go!	برویم!
Let's read!	بخوانیم!

Lesson 7 ■ *What is your favourite sport?*   **84**

■ Past subjunctive   ماضی التزامی

The past subjunctive is constructed from the participle form of the main verb (خوانده، گفته), followed by the present subjunctive of the verb بودن. The past subjunctive is used after the expressions mentioned above to express wish, desire, possibility and necessity in the past.

امیدوارم که برای امتحان درس <u>خوانده باشید</u>.

I hope you have studied for the exam.

<u>شاید رفته باشند</u>.

They may have gone.

<u>اگر آمده باشد</u> شما را به او معرفی می کنم.

If he has come, I will introduce you to him.

■ Imperative verbs   فعل امری

The singular, informal imperative consists of the present stem of the verb plus the prefix ب. Note
that if the present stem starts with آ, a ی is added after the ب:

بخور   بنشین   بیا   بیاور

It is interesting to note that the plural imperative has the same form as the present subjunctive for
the second person plural/formal, e.g.:

بخورید   بنشینید   بیایید   بیاورید

اینجا بنشین.

Sit here!

غذایتان را بخورید.

Eat your food!

جاهای خالی در جملات زیر را با فعل مناسب پر کنید

تابستان سال آینده خانواده من می خواهند به دیدن من. . . . .(آمدن).
شاید شما او را. . . . . . . (دوست داشتن).

هنگام رانندگی، باید کمربندهایتان را . . . . (بستن).

ببخشید، می شود به من . . . . (کمک کردن)؟

شاید امشب خانه . . . . (بودن).

می توانم اینجا . . . . (نشستن)؟

قصد دارم سال آینده در کلاس های تابستانی . . . . (شرکت کردن).

من فارسی می خوانم تا شعرهای حافظ و سعدی و فردوسی و مولانا را . . . . (خواندن).

دیروز قرار بود باران . . . . (آمدن) ولی نیامد.

قبل از اینکه از کلاس . . . . (رفتن) تکلیفم را به استاد دادم.

پیش از اینکه ما با همدیگر . . . . (زندگی کردن) باید همدیگر را خوب . . . . (شناختن).

خواندن 🎧

ورزش

یکی از ورزشهای سنتی ایران کشتی است. کشتی گیران ایرانی در مسابقات جهانی شرکت می کنند. در ایران به قهرمانان کشتی پهلوان می گویند. معروف ترین پهلوان کشتی در ایران جهان پهلوان، تختی بود. بجز کشتی، مردم ایران به فوتبال نیز علاقه دارند. در کوچه های شهرهای ایران، اغلب تعدادی جوان مشغول بازی فوتبال هستند. اکثر ایرانیان طرفدار تیم ملی ایران هستند.

درست یا غلط؟

مردم ایران به ورزش کشتی علاقه دارند.

بازیکنان فوتبال درمسابقات جهانی کشتی شرکت می کنند.

در کوچه ها ایران، همیشه تعدادی جوان مشغول کشتی گرفتن هستند.

در ایران به قهرمانان کشتی پهلوان می گویند.

درک مطلب

نام یکی از ورزش های سنتی ایران چیست؟

کشتی گیران ایرانی درچه مسابقاتی شرکت می کنند؟

در ایران به چه کسی پهلوان می گویند؟

بجز کشتی ، مردم ایران از همه بیشتر به چه ورزشی علاقه دارند؟

چهار سؤال برای متن بالا بنویسید

فصلها و ماه های سال
■ Months and seasons

بهار: فروردین - اردیبهشت - خرداد
تابستان: تیر - مرداد - شهریور
پاییز: مهر - آبان - آذر
زمستان: دی - بهمن - اسفند

ماه های میلادی به فارسی

ژانویه - فوریه - مارس - آوریل - مه - ژوئن - ژوئیه - اوت - سپتامبر - اکتبر - نوامبر - دسامبر

جاهای خالی در جملات زیر را با واژه های مناسب زیر پر کنید

فکر - درست - مهر - ممکن - مهربان - متولد - فردا

مریم: مازیار شما . . . . چه ماهی هستید؟
مازیار: من متولد . . . . هستم.
مریم: آیا این درست است که متولدین مهر . . . . هستند؟
مازیار: درمورد من که حتماً . . . . است!

جاهای خالی در جملات زیر را با کلمات مناسب پر کنید

آیا تو . . . . به دیدن دوستت می روی؟

الف) دیروز   ب) پریروز
ج) دیشب   د) پس فردا

پدرم از . . . . من بسیار خوشش آمد.

الف) ایده   ب) احتمال
ج) امکان   د) مایل

او نمی تواند رانندگی کند چون خیلی . . . . است.

الف) مهربان   ب) جوان
ج) لازم   د) ممکن

کشتی یک . . . . سنتی ایران است.

الف) ورزش   ب) قهرمان

ج) پهلوان   د) مسابقه

جاهای خالی در جملات زیر را با زمان مناسب فعل پر کنید

ما سال آینده به ایران . . . . (مسافرت کردن).

تو نباید تنها به خیابان . . . . (رفتن).

باید شما به او . . . . (تلفن کردن).

احتمال دارد که مرا . . . . (شناختن).

می شود لطفاً در را . . . . (بستن)؟

شاید فردا مهمان . . . . (داشتن).

لازم است که خوب . . . . (کار کردن).

او باید استاد جدید ما . . . . (بودن).

می خواهم که در کلاس ادبیات فارسی . . . . (شرکت کردن).

تو نباید دروغ . . . . (گفتن).

در شهر چه خبره؟ 🎧

گردش در شهر

راهنمای تور: لطفاً همه جمع شین. پنج دیقه دیگه راه میافتیم.

فیلیپ: برنامه امروزمون چیه؟

راهنمای تور: اول می ریم موزه ایران باستان، بعدش می ریم موزه آبگینه. ناهارم می ریم هتل فردوسی.

فیلیپ: بعد از ظهر چی؟ موزه فرش رو کی بریم؟

راهنمای تور: فکر نکنم امروز برسیم.

فیلیپ: امیدوارم فردا بتونیم بریم.

این گفتگو را با کلمات زیر تمرین کنید

مسجد ـ نمایشگاه ـ آثار باستانی ـ کاخ ـ باغ ـ امامزاده ـ مسافرخانه ـ هتل ـ رستوران ـ چایخانه

عامیانه colloquial	کتابی literary
جمع شین	جمع شوید
امروزمون	امروزمان

colloquial عامیانه	literary کتابی
بریم	برویم
بتونیم	بتوانیم
می‌ریم	می‌رویم
ناهارم	ناهار هم
بریم	برویم
فرش رو	فرش را
دیقه	دقیقه
دیگه	دیگر
چیه	چیست

جاهای خالی را پر کنید و بعد گفتگو را در گروهتان تمرین کنید

- سلام مینا. تو خیلی خوش اندام هستی. آیا ورزش ....؟
- سلام زهرا. مرسی. بله من .... روز صبح به باشگاه می روم تا بدنسازی ....
- آیا می توانم یک روز با تو به باشگاه ....؟
- حتماً. خوشحال می شوم به تو کمک .... فردا چطور است؟
- نه فردا نمیتوانم چون باید به خانه ی مادر بزرگم ....
- خوب. پس فردا می توانی ....؟
- نه پس فردا با دوستم به رستوران ....
- هفته ی دیگر چطور؟
- هفته دیگر شاید .... به تو تلفن خواهم زد.

نگارش: با استفاده از کلمات این درس متنی در مورد محبوبترین ورزش کشورتان بنویسید و بعد آن را در گروهتان مطرح کنید.

درس هشتم

آیا شما چانه می زنید؟

بازار وکیل در شیراز
با اینکه شیراز مغازه و فروشگاههای زیادی دارد، خیلی از شیرازی ها - مثل خیلی ها در ایران - از خرید کردن در بازار لذت می برند چون دوست دارند چانه بزنند.
برای کسب اطلاعات بیشتر در مورد شیراز و بازار وکیل در اینترنت جستجو کنید.

آیا شما چانه می زنید؟
Do you haggle?

درس هشتم: آیا شما چانه می زنید؟
گفتگو: کوه
دستور: ماضی استمراری
ماضی نقلی
ماضی بعید
خواندن: چانه زدن
در شهر چه خبره؟ در تابستان

Chapter aims
Grammar:
1. More verb tenses, i.e. past continuous, present perfect, and past perfect

Situation:
1. Hanging out with friends
2. Haggling
3. Talking about summer plans

واژگان

لغت	معنی انگلیسی	نقش دستوری	مثال
صبحانه	breakfast	اسم	امروز برای صبحانه چه می خورید؟
ناهار	lunch	اسم	ناهار چه خوردی؟
عصرانه	afternoon snack	اسم	من هر روز برای عصرانه نان و پنیر می خورم.
شام	dinner	اسم	من شب ها شام نمی خورم.
نیمرو	fried egg	اسم	نیمرو می خواهی یا املت؟

درس هشتم ■ آیا شما چانه می زنید؟   91

مثال	نقش دستوری	معنی انگلیسی	لغت
چند تخم مرغ بخرم؟	اسم مرکب	egg	تخم مرغ
برای فسنجان باید مقداری گردو بخرم.	اسم	walnut	گردو
در شله زرد بادام هم می ریزم.	اسم	almond	بادام
تخمه شکستن در سالن سینما ممنوع است.	اسم	melon seeds	تخمه
در معجون، شیر و زرده تخم مرغ و گردو و بادام و نارگیل و شکر و چیزهای دیگر می ریزند.	اسم	smoothie; a strange combination	معجون
خرما میوه درخت نخل است.	اسم	dates	خرما
دماوند بزرگترین کوه ایران است.	اسم	mountain	کوه
مردم ایران کوهنوردی را دوست دارند.	اسم مرکب	mountain climbing	کوهنوردی
او مبلغ زیادی برای چاپ کتابش پرداخته است.	اسم	amount of money	مبلغ
قیمت ماشینش خیلی بالا بود.	اسم	price	قیمت
ببخشید ولی این بلوز برچسب قیمت ندارد.	اسم	price tag	برچسب قیمت
نصف کلاس غایب هستند.	اسم؛ صفت	half	نصف
از این نوع لباس خوشم نمی آید.	اسم	kind	نوع (انواع)
خیلی زود نمایشگاه کتاب از خریداران کتاب پر شد.	اسم	buyer	خریدار
ببخشید فروشنده کجاست؟	اسم	seller	فروشنده
او در یک مغازه کار می کند.	اسم	shop	مغازه
اجناس این سوپر مارکت بسیار گران هستند.	اسم	goods	اجناس
ببخشید تا میدان ونک چقدر می شود؟	اسم	town square; roundabout	میدان
تفریح من سینما رفتن است.	اسم	fun; entertainment	تفریح (تفریحات)
آداب غذا خوردن در کشورهای مختلف، متفاوت است.	اسم	customs; traditions	آداب
وکیل باید قدرت استدلال خوبی داشته باشد.	اسم	reasoning	استدلال
قدرت این دستگاه چقدر است؟	اسم	power	قدرت

Lesson 8 ■ *Do you haggle?* 92

مثال	نقش دستوری	معنی انگلیسی	لغت
نان تازه بوی خیلی خوبی می دهد.	صفت	fresh	تازه
این نان را نخور چون مانده است.	صفت	stale (of bread)	مانده
بعضی از بچه ها از کودکی مشکل سازند.	صفت	problematic; difficult (in terms of behaviour)	مشکل ساز
او آدم ساده ای است.	صفت	simple	ساده
فارسی زبان آسانی است.	صفت	easy; simple	آسان
بعضی از دانشجویان زبان عربی هم می خوانند.	ضمیر	some (of)	بعضی (از)
من و همسرم عقاید مختلفی داریم.	صفت	different; varied	مختلف
سلیقه های ما کاملاً متفاوت هستند.	صفت	different	متفاوت
ازدواج فامیلی در خانواده های سنتی ایران متداول است.	صفت	common	متداول
پدرم اموالش را بطور یکسان میان بچه هایش تقسیم کرد.	صفت	same	یکسان
روی میز ننشین.	حرف اضافه	over; on	روی
زیر میز پنهان شد.	حرف اضافه	under; below	زیر
او از پنجره به بیرون نگاه کرد.	حرف اضافه / اسم	outside	بیرون
خانهٔ او بین بانک و پارک است.	حرف اضافه	between	بین
البته که با شما می آییم!	قید	of course	البته
پارسال از اینجا رفت.	قید	last year	پارسال
من پیرارسال با او آشنا شدم.	قید	two years ago	پیرارسال
آیا تا بحال به ایران رفته ای؟	قید	so far	تا بحال
بعضی وقت ها دلم برای ایران تنگ می شود.	قید	sometimes	بعضی وقت ها
همیشه دوستت خواهم داشت.	قید	always	همیشه
اغلب او به من تلفن می زند.	قید	mostly	اغلب
به ندرت او را می بینم.	قید	rarely	به ندرت
هیچ وقت فراموشت نمی کنم.	قید	never	هیچ وقت

درس هشتم ■ آیا شما چانه می زنید؟

لغت	معنی انگلیسی	نقش دستوری	مثال
یاد . . . آمدن (آ)	to recall	فعل	یادت می آید چند سال پیش او را دیدی؟
فراموش کردن (کن)	to forget	فعل	ببخشید من نام خانوادگی شما را فراموش کرده ام.
امتحان کردن (کن)	to test; to try	فعل	باید غذای این رستوران را امتحان کنی چون خیلی خوب است.
امتحان دادن (ده)	to take an exam	فعل	فردا باید امتحان بدهیم.
امتحان گرفتن (گیر)	to give an exam	فعل	استادمان هر هفته امتحان می گیرد.
زنگ زدن (زن)	to phone	فعل	حتماً به من زنگ بزن.
خوش گذشتن (گذر) به	to have a good time	فعل	دیشب در منزل شما به ما خیلی خوش گذشت.
بد گذشتن (گذر) به	to have a bad time	فعل	امیدوارم به شما بد نگذشته باشد.
چانه زدن (زن)	to bargain	فعل	لطفاً چانه نزنید. قیمت این تابلو مقطوع است.
تخفیف گرفتن (گیر)	to get a discount	فعل	او توانست هزار تومان تخفیف بگیرد.
وجود داشتن (دار)	to exist	فعل	چهار فصل مختلف در ایران وجود دارد.
خالی کردن (کن)	to empty	فعل	لطفاً چمدان هایتان را خالی کنید.
میدان را خالی نکردن	not to give up easily	فعل	شما نباید میدان را خالی کنید.

گفتگو

کوه

شیرین: دیروز ساعت هفت صبح زنگ زدم نبودی! کجا رفته بودی؟
خسرو: با بچه ها کوه نوردی رفته بودیم.
شیرین: خوش گذشت؟
خسرو: خیلی! صبحانه نیمرو خوردیم. سهراب هم خرما آورده بود و من گردوی تازه.

شیرین: چه معجونی! من تابحال نیمرو با خرما و گردو نخورده ام.

خسرو: باید امتحان کنی.

شیرین: شاید هم خورده باشم ولی یادم نمی آید.

خسرو: هفتهٔ دیگر با ما بیا. به تو بد نخواهد گذشت.

شیرین: این هفته می خواستم با شما بیایم ولی به من نگفته بودید که به کوه می روید.

خسرو: حق با توست. من از تو معذرت می خواهم.

درک مطلب

خسرو دیروز کجا رفته بود؟

صبحانه چه خوردند؟

سهراب با خود چه آورده بود؟

خسرو چرا از شیرین معذرت خواست؟

شیرین چه چیزی یادش نمی آمد؟

بحث کنید و بنویسید

یک گفتگو بنویسید مانند گفتگوی کوه ولی درمورد تفریح مورد علاقه خودتان. آیا شما بیشتر به ورزش علاقه دارید یا به سرگرمی های دیگر؟

دستور

ماضی استمراری Past progressive tense

The past progressive in Persian is formed by adding the progressive prefix می to the past tense of the verb. This tense is used to express an action that was in progress in the past, as in:

کتاب می خریدم که به من زنگ زدید.

I was buying a book when you called me.

وقتی تو آمدی آشپزی می کردم.

I was cooking when you arrived.

This tense is also used to express a past state or habit as the "used to" construction in English, as in:

پارسال من خیلی قهوه می خوردم.

Last year, I used to drink a lot of coffee.

در ایران زندگی می کردیم.

We used to live in Iran.

In less formal Persian, in particular in the spoken language, the past tense of داشتن is used right after the subject, e.g.:

من داشتم با او صحبت می کردم که ترا دیدم.

I was talking to her when I saw you.

وقتی ما رسیدیم آنها داشتند غذا می خوردند.

When we arrived, they were eating.

پارسال این موقع شما داشتید فارسی می خواندید.

You were studying Persian this time last year.

■ Present perfect tense ماضی نقلی

In this tense, the participle form of the verb (e.g. دیده، گفته، رفته) is followed by the enclitic personal endings of بودن, e.g.:

I have gone	رفته ام
You have said	گفته ای
She has seen	دیده است
We have heard	شنیده ایم
You have been	بوده اید
They have read	خوانده اند

This tense is used when an action took place in the past, yet its effect continued to the present, e.g.:

من ناهار خورده ام.

I have eaten lunch.

شما این فیلم را دیده اید؟

Have you seen this film?

Present perfect tense is also used for an action that has taken place a number of times in the past, as in:

بارها به آنجا رفته ام.

I have gone there many times.

چند دفعه (بار) به ایران سفر کرده اید؟

How many times have you travelled to Iran?

■ Past perfect tense   ماضی بعید

In the past perfect tense in Persian, the participle form of the verb (دیده، گفته، رفته) is followed by the past tense of بودن.

I had gone	رفته بودم
You had eaten	خورده بودی
She had put on	پوشیده بود
We had sewn	دوخته بودیم
You have bought	خریده بودید
They had read	خوانده بودند

This tense is used when an action has been completed before another action in the past. The adverbial (پیش از اینکه، قبل از اینکه "before") followed by a present subjunctive verb are usually used to indicate the latter action, as in:

قبل از اینکه تو برسی من رفته بودم .

I had left home before you arrived.

پیش از اینکه به ایران سفر کند فارسی یاد گرفته بود.

Before she travelled to Iran she had already learnt Persian.

جاهای خالی در جملات زیر را با زمان مناسب فعل پر کنید

من سه بار این کتاب را ....(خواندن).
قبل از اینکه به ایران ....(رفتن) مادر بزرگم را هرگز ....(ندیدن).
من تا بحال غذای چینی..........(خوردن).
ما داشتیم..........(خوابیدن) که تلفن..............(زنگ زدن).
وقتی تو ....(آمدن) من داشتم..............(غذا پختن).

چندین بار به ایران .... (سفر کردن).

پیش از آنکه این کلاس را .... (برداشتن)، هرگز شعر فارسی .... (خواندن).

پس از آنکه دست هایتان را .... (شستن) می توانید .... (غذا خوردن).

من دو سال است که مادرم را .... (دیدن).

خواندن 🎧

چانه زدن

آداب خرید و فروش در کشورهای مختلف متفاوت است. در ایران چانه زدن بسیار متداول است. چانه زدن یعنی خریدار سعی می کند از فروشنده تخفیف بگیرد. بعضی وقتها خریدار می تواند تا بیش از نصف مبلغ را تخفیف بگیرد. در مغازه های کوچک معمولاً برچسب قیمت روی اجناس وجود ندارد و این مشکل ساز است. البته برای بعضی ها تخفیف گرفتن یک نوع تفریح است. شما باید برای تخفیف گرفتن قدرت استدلال خوبی داشته باشید و به این آسانی میدان را خالی نکنید.

درست یا غلط؟

برای ایرانیها تخفیف گرفتن یک جور تفریح است.

شما برای تخفیف گرفتن به قدرت استدلال نیاز ندارید.

درایران چانه زدن بسیار متداول نیست.

چانه زدن یعنی فروشنده سعی می کند ازخریدارتخفیف بگیرد.

در مغازه ها معمولاً برچسب قیمت روی اجناس وجود ندارد.

درک مطلب

آداب خرید در کشورشما چگونه است؟

در ایران معمولاً خریداران می توانند تا چه اندازه تخفیف بگیرند؟

چه چیزی برای خریداران در ایران مشکل ساز است؟

چهار سؤال برای متن بالا بنویسید

جاهای خالی را با زمان مناسب فعل پر کنید

بهتر است اتاقشان را..........(تمیز کردن).

ناگهان اسمتان را.............(فراموش کردن).

هر وقت فیلم هندی...............(دیدن)..............(گریه کردن).

دیشب هوا بسیار سرد.........(بودن) و من نتوانستم.........(خوابیدن).

آنها دیروز از ما.......(پرسیدن) پارسال چطور به ایران.......(سفر کردن).

وقتی در ایران.........(زندگی کردن) می خواستم همیشه در ایران.........(ماندن).

آنها . . . .(ممکن بودن) او را . . . .(دوست داشتن).

آیا تو . . . .(ترجیح دادن) امروز . . . .(آمدن) یا فردا؟

به پرسش های زیر پاسخ دهید

کلاس ما ساعت چند شروع می شود؟

شما در چه سالی فارغ التحصیل می شوید؟

شما چطور با همسرتان آشنا شدید؟

شما متولد چه سال و ماهی هستید؟

شما دوست دارید در آینده چه کار کنید؟

شما مشغول چه فکری هستید؟

گفتگوی زیر را کامل کنید

سام: الو.

احمد: . . . .

سام: سلام. منم سام.

احمد: . . . .

سام: خوبم. تو چطوری؟

احمد: . . . .

سام: خبری نیست. تو چی؟

احمد: . . . .

سام: فکر خوبیست.

احمد: . . . .

افعال را مرور کنیم!

فعل امری

لطفاً در را . . . .(بستن).

مادرم به من گفت: امروز ساعت پنج به خانه . . . .(آمدن).

ماضی استمراری

ما همیشه به این پارک .... (آمدن).

هر وقت به فروشگاه میرفتم او را .... (دیدن).

ماضی نقلی

من تا بحال او را .... (دیدن).

او چند بار به آمریکا .... (رفتن).

ماضی بعید

ما قبل از جنگ آنجا را .... (دیدن).

او قبل از ساعت هشت منزل را .... (ترک کردن).

التزامی

باید از او .... (معذرت خواستن).

احتمال دارد که دیروز خانه را .... (خالی کردن).

در شهر چه خبره؟ 🎧

در تابستان

پوپک : سینا جون امسال تابستون کجا می رین؟ دوباره می رین شمال؟

سینا: نه. بابام می خاد ما رو ببره فرانسه که زبان تمرین کنیم.

پوپک : خوش به حالتون. کاش منم می تونستم همراتون بیام. ما امسال تابستون هیچ جا نمی ریم.

سینا: ایشالا سال دیگه!

این گفتگو را با کلمات زیر تمرین کنید

پاکستان- آمریکا- عربستان- انگلیس- آلمان- روسیه- قبرس- یونان- ایتالیا- اسپانیا- کانادا- ژاپن- برزیل- مکزیک

عامیانه colloquial	کتابی literary
می رین	می روید
می خاد	می خواهد
بیام	بیایم
ببره	ببرد
می تونستم	می توانستم
نمی ریم	نمی رویم
ایشالا	انشاء الله
مارو	ما را
حالتون	حالتان
همراتون	همراهتان
تابستون	تابستان
منم	من هم
دیگه	دیگر

جاهای خالی را پر کنید و بعد گفتگو را در گروهتان تمرین کنید

- سلام جناب. قیمت این بلوز .... است؟
- قابل شما ...... ندارد.
- خیلی ممنون.
- دویست هزار و سیصد و چهل و هشت تومان. ولی برای شما دویست هزار تومان.
- دو........ می برم. یکی سفید و .... قهوه ای.
- از همین مدل یا از یک مدل......... .
- نه هر دو از همین .... باشند لطفاً.
- بفرمایید.

نگارش: با استفاده از واژگان این درس متنی درباره ی آداب مردم کشوتان بنویسید و سپس در گروهتان در مورد آن بحث کنید.

درس نهم
شما به چه اعتقاد دارید؟

کلیسای وانک در جلفای اصفهان

کلیسای وانک یکی از زیباترین کلیساهای ارمنی در ایران است. ارامنهٔ بسیاری در محلهٔ جلفا زندگی می کنند. برای کسب اطلاعات بیشتر در مورد جلفای اصفهان و ارامنهٔ ایران در اینترنت جستجو کنید.

Lesson 9 ■ What do you believe in? 102

شما به چه اعتقاد دارید؟

What do you believe in?

درس نهم: شما به چه اعتقاد دارید؟
گفتگو: واحدهای دانشگاهی
دستور: اسم
صفت شمارشی
صفت و ضمیر نامشخص
صفت اشاره
ضمیر اشاره
نشانه های معرفه و نکره
خواندن: دین
در شهر چه خبره؟ در رستوران

Chapter aims
Grammar:
1. Determiners
2. Demonstrative adjectives and pronouns
3. Definite and indefinite markers

Situation:
1. University courses and credits
2. Religion and beliefs
3. At a restaurant

واژگان

مثال	نقش دستوری	معنی انگلیسی	لغت
این ترم چند واحد برداشتی؟	اسم	course unit	واحد
این ترم درس هایم خیلی سنگین است.	اسم	term; semester	ترم

مثال	نقش دستوری	معنی انگلیسی	لغت
هفته آخر این ماه به ایران می روم.	صفت	last	آخر
به خط اول دقت کن.	صفت	first	اول
من فقط ترا دوست دارم.	قید	only	فقط
امروز دو نفر به شما تلفن زدند.	اسم	person	نفر
طبق قانون باید با کمربند ایمنی رانندگی کنید.	اسم	law; rule	قانون (قوانین)
من به هیچ کس اعتماد ندارم حتی تو.	حرف اضافه	even	حتی
عملاً تمام کارها را من انجام می دهم.	قید	practically	عملاً
تمام شب بیدار بودم.	صفت	whole; all	تمام
او آدم خوبی است.	اسم	human; person	آدم
درباره ادبیات فارسی چه می دانید؟	حرف اضافه	about; regarding	درباره
یک گفتگو بنویسید راجع به تاریخ ایران.	حرف اضافه	about; regarding	راجع به
او در مورد من سؤالاتی کرد.	حرف اضافه	about; regarding	در مورد
عقیده شما در مورد سخنان رئیس جمهور چیست؟	اسم	opinion; belief	عقیده (عقاید)
من نظری ندارم.	اسم	opinion	نظر
شما توانایی انجام این کار را دارید.	اسم	ability	توانایی
حداکثر سه روز می مانیم.	اسم	at most	حداکثر
او باید حداقل ۵۰ سالش باشد.	اسم	at least	حداقل
مسأله به این مهمی را چرا به من نگفتی؟	اسم	problem; issue	مسأله (مسائل)
بزرگ ترین مشکل شما در زندگی چیست؟	اسم	problem	مشکل (مشکلات)
پیامبر اسلام حضرت محمد است.	اسم	prophet	پیامبر/ پیغمبر
شورشیان همه جا را به آتش کشیدند.	اسم	rioter	شورشی
سپاهیان امنیت را در شهر برقرار کردند.	اسم	armed guard	سپاهی
در ایران خانم ها باید حجاب اسلامی را رعایت کنند.	اسم	hijab; veil	حجاب
رعایت قانون الزامی است.	اسم	Observance	رعایت
بیشتر مردم ایران مسلمان هستند.	صفت / اسم	Muslim	مسلمان

مثال	نقش دستوری	معنی انگلیسی	لغت
به جز مسلمانان، چند اقلیت مذهبی نیز در ایران وجود دارند.	عبارت اسمی	religious minority	اقلیت مذهبی
مسیحیان به حضرت عیسی اعتقاد دارند.	اسم	Christians	مسیحیان
بیشتر زرتشتیان در ایران و هندوستان زندگی می کنند.	اسم	Zoroastrians	زرتشتیان
کلیساهای ارامنه در اصفهان بسیار زیبا هستند.	اسم	Armenians	ارامنه
اکثر یهودیان مهاجرت کرده اند.	اسم	Jews	یهودیان = کلیمیان
بهائیان زیادی در هندوستان زندگی می کنند.	اسم	Baha'is	بهائیان
اکثر ادیان وجود خدا را تأیید می کنند.	اسم	existence	وجود
به دلیل مشکلات مالی باید مهاجرت کنیم.	عبارت اضافی	because of; due to	به دلیل
ملت این کشور دولت را انتخاب کرده اند.	اسم	Government	دولت
طبق قانون مدنی این کشور خانم ها حق رانندگی ندارند.	عبارت اسمی	civil law	قانون مدنی
همه آمدند به جز تو.	صفت/ضمیر	everybody; all	همه
چه پیر چه جوان همه به خیابان ها رفتند.	عبارت ربطی	both . . . and . . .; whether . . . or . . .	چه . . . چه . . .
برای قبول شدن در امتحانات باید خیلی درس بخوانی.	حرف اضافه	For	برای
بعضی از دانشجویان تکالیف خود را هنوز به استاد نداده اند.	ضمیر؛ صفت	Some	بعضی = برخی
هر ساله جهانگردان خارجی بیشماری برای دیدن آثار باستانی به ایران می روند.	اسم	tourist	جهانگرد
زیبایی او بی نظیر است.	اسم	beauty	زیبایی
ادبیات کهن فارسی بسیار غنی است.	صفت	old; ancient	کهن
ایرانیان به تمدن کهن سرزمین خود افتخار می کنند.	اسم	civilization	تمدن
ایران زمین در گذشته بسیار بزرگتر از ایران فعلی بود.	اسم مرکب	Ancient Iran	ایران زمین
من باید بروم نان بگیرم.	فعل	to get; to take; to hold	گرفتن (گیر)

لغت	معنی انگلیسی	نقش دستوری	مثال
برداشتن (دار)	to pick up	فعل	من پسرم را ساعت پنج و نیم از مدرسه برمی دارم.
ثبت نام کردن (کن)	to register	فعل	آیا برای ترم آینده ثبت نام کرده ای؟
دعوت کردن (کن)	to invite	فعل	چند نفر را برای تولدت دعوت می کنی؟
پیروی کردن (کن)	to follow; to abide by	فعل	مسلمانان از تعالیم اسلام پیروی می کنند.
جذب کردن (کن)	to attract; to absorb	فعل	این دانشگاه بهترین دانشجویان را جذب می کند.
مربوط بودن (به)	to pertain to	فعل	این مسأله به شما مربوط نیست.

گفتگو

واحدهای دانشگاهی

دارا: این ترم چند واحد برداشتی؟

سارا: چون سال آخرم می توانستم ۶ واحد بردارم ولی فکر کردم بهتر است ۴ واحد این ترم بگیرم و ۲ واحدهم در تابستان.

دارا: آیا دانشجویان زیادی ترم آخرشان است؟

سارا: نه. ما فقط ۵ نفر هستیم که ترم آخریم.

دارا: قوانین دانشگاه ما اجازه نمی دهد که بیشتر از ۴ واحد برداریم حتی اگر ترم آخر باشیم.

سارا: این قانون خوبی است چون عملاً گرفتن ۴ واحد تمام وقت آدم را می گیرد.

درک مطلب

سارا این ترم چند واحد برداشته است؟

چند دانشجو ترم آخرشان است؟

سارا راجع به قوانین دانشگاه چه عقیده ای دارد؟

به نظر سارا دانشجویان توانایی گرفتن حداکثر چند واحد را دارند؟

بحث کنید و بنویسید

یک گفتگو بنویسید مانند گفتگوی واحدهای دانشگاهی ولی درمورد درس های خودتان و بگوئید شما در یک ترم اجازه دارید چند واحد بردارید.

Lesson 9 ■ *What do you believe in?* 106

دستور

اسم

■ Nouns

In Persian, there are singular and plural nouns. The plural marker in Persian is generally ها, but for animate nouns (particularly for people) ان is often added instead to make them plural, e.g.:

مداد ← مدادها

زن ← زنان

Some nouns that are borrowed from Arabic, though, retain their original plural form, e.g.:

مشکل ← مشکلات

مسأله ← مسائل

It should be noted that some parts of the body of which there are two or more can also be pluralized by adding ان, e.g.:

انگشت ← انگشتان

دست ← دستان

چشم ← چشمان

بازو ← بازوان

The Arabic feminine plural marker ات can also be added to some words of Persian and Turkish origin to make them plural, e.g.:

باغ ← باغات

ده ← دهات

If the word ends in vowels /e/ and /i:/, a / ǰ / is inserted, as in:

سبزی ← سبزیجات

میوه ← میوجات

The Arabic masculine plural marker ین can be added to some words of Arabic origin, such as:

معلم ← معلمین

مهندس ← مهندسین

However, if the word ends in ی, ون is added, as in:

روحانی ← روحانیون

انقلابی ← انقلابیون

Orthographic rule

قانون املائی

As a general rule, in Persian orthography, where an animate noun ends in /a:/ or /u:/, a ی is inserted before ان to ease pronunciation, e.g.:

دانشجو ← دانشجویان
آقا ← آقایان

However, if the Persian (not Arabic) word ends in /i:/, only ان is added:

شورشی ← ان ← شورشیان
سپاهی ← ان ← سپاهیان

In addition, some nouns that end in the vowel /e/ are pluralized by removing the silent /h/ at the end and adding گان.

پرنده ← پرندگان
خزنده ← خزندگان
دیده ← دیدگان
مژه ← مژگان

Numericals

صفت شمارشی

Unlike in English, where plural numericals require plural nouns, in Persian, plural numericals are followed by singular nouns, e.g.:

a few problems	چند مشکل
several books	چندین کتاب
five men	پنج مرد[1]
two pencils	دو عدد مداد
four eggs	چهار دانه تخم مرغ
three sets of clothes	سه دست لباس
a pair of shoes	یک جفت کفش
three kilos of sugar	سه کیلو شکر
six bottles of soda	شش بطری نوشابه

Note that there is no *ezafe* between the counting word and the counted word.

[1] Note that in colloquial Persian, تا is normally inserted between the numerical and the noun, e.g.:

چند تا کیف
دو تا کتاب

Lesson 9 ■ *What do you believe in?* **108**

■ Determiners صفت و ضمیر نامشخص

In Persian, plural determiners are combined with plural nouns and singular determiners are followed by singular nouns, e.g.:

more students	دانشجویان بیشتر
fewer students	دانشجویان کمتر
all students	همهٔ دانشجویان
some days	بعضی روزها
many books	کتابهای زیاد
no one	هیچ کس
every student	هر دانشجو

Some determiners can also be combined with prepositional phrases, e.g.:

خیلی از دانشجویان

many of the students

بعضی از مردم

some of the people

بسیاری از ما

many of us

■ Demonstrative adjectives صفت اشاره

In Persian, این and آن are used before nouns as demonstrative adjectives. If the demonstrative is used before the noun, it always appears in the singular form, despite the number of the noun, e.g.:

these books این کتاب ها ← this book این کتاب
those woman آن زنان ← that woman آن زن

این کتاب به فارسی است.

This book is in Persian.

این کتابها به فارسی هستند.

These books are in Persian.

آن آقا ایرانی است.

That gentleman is Iranian.

آن آقایان ایرانی هستند.

Those gentlemen are Iranian.

◾ Demonstrative pronouns ضمیر اشاره

The demonstratives این, آن, آنها, and اینها can also be used on their own as pronouns, e.g.:

این کتاب جالبی است.

This is an interesting book.

اینها کتابهای جالبی هستند.

These are interesting books.

آنها ماشین های ما هستند.

Those are our cars.

اینها لباس های قشنگی هستند.

These are beautiful dresses.

◾ Definite and indefinite markers نشانه های معرفه و نکره

As a general rule, if the noun is indefinite, it takes the indefinite marker ی, and if it is definite, it does not have any marker, except for when it is an object, in which case, it takes the definite object marker را, e.g.:

I read a book.	من کتابی خواندم
I read the book.	من کتاب را خواندم

If the noun is modified by an adjective, either the noun or the adjective can take the indefinite marker ی, e.g.:

کتابی خوب
کتاب خوبی

However, if there is more than one adjective, the indefinite marker ی is either added to the last adjective, or else the ی is added to the noun and the adjectives are combined with و . In phrases with definite nouns, the definite object marker را is added after the last adjective, e.g.:

کتاب خوب گرانی

a good, expensive book

کتابی خوب و گران

a good, expensive book

من این شهر را دیده بودم.

I had seen this city.

من این شهر زیبا را دیده بودم.

I had seen this beautiful city.

من این شهر زیبای بزرگ را دیده بودم.

I had seen this big, beautiful city.

Generic nouns (which always appear in the singular) do not take any marker, even if they are objects, e.g.:

I write books.	من کتاب می نویسم.
He repairs cars.	او ماشین تعمیر می کند.

جملات زیر را ترجمه کنید

1. I can see a few birds in the sky.
2. Nobody knows the answer.
3. Every student should take four courses.
4. Everyone must watch this film.
5. I love sweets.
6. All came except for the professor.
7. Many students take more than four courses per term.
8. I have a lot of friends.
9. You will have a lot of money.
10. I have never loved anyone as I love you.

جاهای خالی در جملات زیر را با کلمه ای مناسب از لیست پر کنید

پرندگان - مردم - زنان - دانشجویان - نفر - پرنده

آقای تهرانی دو . . . . دارد.
همهٔ . . . . برای این درس ثبت نام کرده اند.
. . . . در ایران باید حجاب داشته باشند.
چند . . . . را دعوت کرده ای؟

خواندن

دین

بیشتر مردم ایران مسلمان هستند. البته اقلیتهای مذهبی هم در ایران وجود دارند مثل اقلیت های مسیحی، زرتشتی، بهائی و یهودی. به دلیل وجود دولت اسلامی، قوانین مدنی کشور قوانین اسلامی هستند و همهٔ مردم چه مسلمان و چه غیر مسلمان باید از این قوانین پیروی کنند. یکی از این قوانین که به زنان مربوط می شود رعایت حجاب اسلامی است. حتی جهانگردان خارجی زن نیز باید از این قانون پیروی کنند. بعضی از این جهانگردان این قانون را دوست ندارند ولی زیبایی ها و تمدن کهن ایران زمین آنها را به ایران جذب می کند.

درک مطلب

مذهب بیشتر مردم ایران چیست؟
سه اقلیت مذهبی در ایران نام ببرید.
قوانین مدنی ایران چگونه هستند؟
چه قانونی برای زنان در ایران در متن بالا ذکر شده است؟
آیا جهانگردان نیز باید از قوانین اسلامی ایران پیروی کنند؟
یکی از دلایلی که جهانگردان به ایران جذب می شوند چیست؟

اسمهای مفرد زیر را بدون استفاده از «ها» به جمع تبدیل کنید

پرنده
چشم
آقا
دانشجو
میوه

Lesson 9 ■ *What do you believe in?* **112**

جملات زیر را مرتب کنید

دوست ندارند - را - کارمندان - او.

بهترین - این - دارد - غذاها - رستوران - را.

شیرازی - ندارید - لهجهٔ - شما.

اصفهان - من - می کند - خواهر - زندگی - در.

جاهای خالی را با زمان مناسب فعل پر کنید

دارا: تومعمولاً تعطیلاتت را چطور .... (گذراندن)؟

سیما: معمولاً به خرید .... (رفتن) یا ورزش .... (کردن).

دارا: بیشتر چه ورزشی را .... (دوست داشتن)؟

سیما: من اسکی را به ورزشهای دیگر .... (ترجیح دادن).

دارا: بهترین پیستهای اسکی کجا .... (بودن) ؟

سیما: تهران و اطراف تهران بهترین پیستها را .... (داشتن). آیا تو .... (خواستن) با من بیایی؟

دارا: بله.

🎧 در شهر چه خبره؟

در رستوران

گارسون: سلام علیکم. بفرمایین!

مانا: سلام. یک میز برای دو نفر لطفاً.

گارسون: چشم! بفرمایین از این طرف.

مانا: یک میز کنار پنجره نداشتین؟

گارسون: نه متأسفانه.

مانا: غذای روزتون چیه؟

گارسون: خورش فسنجون داریم و ته چین.

مانا: به به. پس یه فسنجون و یه ته چین لطف کنین.

گارسون: رو چشم.

این گفتگو را با کلمات زیر تمرین کنید

خورش قورمه سبزی - خورش قیمه - زرشک پلو با مرغ - کباب برگ - کباب کوبیده - خورش کرفس

عامیانه colloquial	کتابی Literary
بفرمایین	بفرمایید
نداشتین	نداشتید
لطف کنین	لطف کنید
روزتون	روزتان
فسنجون	فسنجان

جاهای خالی را پر کنید و بعد گفتگو را در گروهتان تمرین کنید

- سلام علی. آیا همه مردم در ایران .... شیعه هستند؟

- نه این .... نیست. در ایران، مسلمانان سنی، مسیحیان، یهودیان، زرتشتیان، بهائیان و مردمی که به هم دیگر .... اعتقاد دارند و یا به هیچ ...... اعتقاد ندارند هم زندگی می کنند.

- ولی دین رسمی .... اسلام شیعه است. مگر نه؟

- بله درست است. چون دین اصلی ایرانیان .... از آمدن اسلام به ایران، دین زرتشتی بود، جشن های ملی ایران جشن های .... هستند.

- یعنی مردم ایران جشن های اسلامی ندارند؟

- چرا دارند. ایرانیان هم جشن های اسلامی و هم .... زرتشتی را برگزار می کنند ولی بزرگترین .... در ایران جشن نوروز است که جشنی زرتشتی است.

نگارش: با استفاده از کلمات این درس یک متن در مورد دین های رایج در کشورتان بنویسید.

درس دهم
آیا زن و مرد برابرند؟

Lesson Ten

دو زن جوان با حجاب اسلامی در میدان نقش جهان اصفهان مسجد شیخ لطف الله هم در عکس دیده می شود. میگویند که شاه عباس این مسجد زیبا را مخصوصاً برای خانم های خاندان صفوی ساخته بود. برای کسب اطلاعات بیشتر در مورد <u>حجاب اسلامی</u> در اینترنت جستجو کنید.

آیا زن و مرد برابرند؟

Are women and men equal?

درس دهم: آیا زن و مرد برابرند؟
گفتگو: اسباب کشی
دستور: حرف اضافه
ضمایر انعکاسی و تأکیدی
خواندن: تفکر سنتی
در شهر چه خبره؟ در کلاس

Chapter aims
Grammar:

1. Prepositions
2. Reflexive and emphatic pronouns

Situation:

1. Gender inequality
2. Traditional mentality
3. Moving house
4. At school

واژگان

لغت	معنی انگلیسی	نقش دستوری	مثال
بسیار خوب	all right; OK	عبارت قیدی	بسیار خوب تو هم می توانی بیایی.
تلویزیون	television	اسم	ما شب ها تلویزیون تماشا می کنیم.
بغل	beside; right next to	حرف اضافه	عکس پسرم بغل عکس من است.

مثال	نقش دستوری	معنی انگلیسی	لغت
کنار مبل یک چراغ هست.	حرف اضافه	beside	کنار
کتابخانهٔ این دانشگاه بسیار غنی است.	اسم	library; bookcase	کتابخانه
لطفاً ظرف ها را روی میز بگذار.	اسم	table	میز
ببخشید می توانم از تلفنتان استفاده کنم؟	اسم	telephone	تلفن
خیلی خسته بودم و روی تخت خواب افتادم.	اسم مرکب	bed	تخت خواب
این روزها همه کامپیوتر دارند.	اسم	computer	کامپیوتر
من همیشه سرمیز تحریرم درس می خوانم.	اسم مرکب	desk	میز تحریر
او پشت من ایستاده بود.	حرف اضافه	behind	پشت
جلو میز یک صندلی راحتی هست.	حرف اضافه	in front of	جلو
در طی این سه سالی که او را می‌شناسم حتی یک دروغ نشنیده ام.	حرف اضافه	during	در طی
روی لباسش یک طرح است به شکل نقشهٔ ایران.	حرف اضافه	as	به شکل، به صورت
شما خیلی اثاث دارید.	اسم	furniture	اثاث
می توانی در اسباب کشی کمکم کنی؟	اسم مرکب	moving	اسباب کشی
ببخشید امروز تکلیفمان چیست؟	اسم	assignment	تکلیف (تکالیف) = مشق
می توانید با صدای بلند حرف بزنید؟	اسم	voice; sound	صدا
صدای بوق ماشینم خیلی بلند است.	صفت	high; loud	بلند
موهای من کوتاه است.	صفت	short; low	کوتاه
او با عجله از کلاس بیرون رفت.	اسم	hurry; haste	عجله
این نان را با چاقو ببر.	اسم	knife	چاقو = کارد
در ایران برای غذا خوردن بیشتر از قاشق و چنگال استفاده می کنیم.	اسم	spoon	قاشق
برای خوردن سیب زمینی سرخ کرده از چنگال استفاده کن.	اسم	fork	چنگال
فکر می کنم کلیدم را گم کرده ام.	اسم	key	کلید
قفل در خانه مان خراب است.	اسم	lock	قفل
امروز جلسه داریم. پس دیر به دنبالت می آیم.	اسم	meeting	جلسه (جلسات)
پلاک شما چند است؟	اسم	house number	پلاک

Lesson 10 ■ *Are women and men equal?*   118

مثال	نقش دستوری	معنی انگلیسی	لغت
اتوبوس پر بود؟	اسم	bus	اتوبوس
دیر شده است. بهتر است تاکسی بگیریم.	اسم	taxi	تاکسی
مسافرت با قطار ارزان تر است.	اسم	train	قطار
هواپیما سریع ترین وسیلهٔ نقلیه است.	اسم	plane	هواپیما
آیا تهران مترو دارد؟	اسم	metro	مترو
من با دوچرخه سر کار می روم.	اسم	bicycle	دوچرخه
موتور خیلی خطرناک است.	اسم	motorcycle	موتور
این قوطی را چطور باز کنم؟	اسم	can	قوطی
این قوطی را با دربازکن باز کن.	اسم مرکب	can-opener	دربازکن
گاهی احساس خستگی می کنم.	قید	sometimes	گاهی
اخیراً متوجه شده ام که او بسیار لاغر شده است.	قید	lately; recently	اخیراً
من هم غذای ایرانی دوست دارم هم غذای هندی.	عبارت ربطی	both. . . and	هم . . . هم . . .
هنوز آن فیلم را ندیده ام.	قید	still; yet	هنوز
خیلی خسته ام. با وجود این می خواهم درس بخوانم.	عبارت ربطی	nevertheless	با وجود این
چگونه می توانی اخلاق بد او را تحمل کنی؟	کلمه پرسشی	how	چگونه
شکل ابرویت قشنگ است.	اسم	look; form; shape	شکل
مادر من خانه دار است.	اسم مرکب	housewife	خانه دار
بچه داری نیاز به حوصله زیادی دارد.	اسم مرکب	taking care of children	بچه داری
خانه داری معمولاً به عهده خانمهاست.	اسم مرکب	housework	خانه داری
تفکرما با هم خیلی متفاوت است.	اسم	way of thinking	تفکر
ازدواج امر مهمی است.	اسم	issue; matter	امر
بد خوابیدن قبل از امتحان امری طبیعی است.	صفت	natural	طبیعی
در اکثر کشورها فرهنگ مرد سالاری رایج است.	اسم مرکب	patriarchy	مرد سالاری
می توانید از بچهٔ من نیم ساعت مراقبت کنید؟	فعل	to keep an eye on	مراقبت کردن (کن)

مثال	نقش دستوری	معنی انگلیسی	لغت
من این اتاق را جارو کردم.	فعل	to vacuum; to sweep the floor	جارو کردن (کن)
لطفاً تو گردگیری کن و من جارو می کنم.	فعل	to dust	گردگیری کردن (کن)
آیا می توانید یک کاری برای من انجام بدهید؟	فعل	to carry out; to perform	انجام دادن (ده)
من خداوند یگانه را می پرستم.	فعل	to adore; to worship	پرستیدن (پرست)
او مرا مقصر می دانست.	فعل	to consider at fault	مقصر دانستن (دان)
کارهای خانه مرا خسته می کند.	فعل	to make tired	خسته کردن (کن)
در چه سالی به دنیا آمدی؟	فعل	to be born	به دنیا آمدن (آ)
لطفاً در را باز کن.	فعل	to open	باز کردن (کن)
من ظرف ها را می شویم و تو آنها را خشک کن.	فعل	to wash	شستن (شو)
می شود یک روز دیگر اینجا بمانید؟	فعل	to stay	ماندن (مان)
آرامگاه فردوسی در شهر توس در نزدیکی مشهد قرار دارد.	فعل	to be located	قرار داشتن (دار)

گفتگو 🎧

اسباب کشی

رضا: تلویزیون را کجا بگذارم؟

مریم: بغل کتابخانه. میز تلفن را کجا گذاشتی؟

رضا: پشت تخت خواب.

مریم: ولی بهتر است بگذاری کنار تخت خواب.

رضا: بسیار خوب. کامپیوتر را کجا بگذارم؟

مریم: روی میز تحریر آرین.

رضا: زیر میز را جارو کردی؟

مریم: بله. هم زیر میز، هم پشت میز و هم جلو آنرا جارو کردم. داخل و خارج میز را هم دستمال کشیدم.

رضا: آرین کجاست؟

مریم: بیرون. با بچهٔ همسایه دارد بازی می کند.

Lesson 10 ■ *Are women and men equal?*

درک مطلب

مریم و رضا دارند چه کار می کنند؟
مریم کجاها را جارو کرده است؟
آرین دارد چه کار می کند؟

بحث کنید و بنویسید

آخرین باری که اسباب کشی کردید کی بود؟ مشکلات اسباب کشی چیست؟

دستور

■ Prepositions | حرف اضافه

In Persian, prepositions are of several types: time, place, direction, means and manner, instrument, and accompaniment. As in English, a noun is placed after a preposition.

Time	زمان
after three o'clock	بعد از ساعت سه
before winter	قبل از زمستان
in June[1]	در ماه ژوئن
in the summer	در تابستان
in 1975	در سال ۱۹۷۵
on time	سر ساعت
during the summer	درطول تابستان
in two hours' time	در عرض دو ساعت
for three hours	برای سه ساعت
Place	مکان
in Canada	در کانادا
at the table	سر میز

[1] Note that the preposition در is often omitted in such time phrases.

in class	در کلاس
on Jordan Street	در خیابان جردن
at 20 Jahan Street	در خیابان جهان، پلاک ۲۰
between the table and the chair	بین میز و صندلی
among my friends	میان دوستانم
behind the door	پشت در
next to the tree	کنار درخت
from here	از اینجا
to there	تا آنجا
to school	به مدرسه
in front of the shop	جلو مغازه
on the wall	روی دیوار
Means and manner	**حالت**
by bus	با اتوبوس
in a loud voice	با صدای بلند
with a Turkish accent	با لهجه ترکی
Carefully	با دقت
without a doubt	بدون شک
through her	از طریق او
in a hurry	با عجله
without a sound	بی صدا
Instrument	**وسیله**
with a knife	با کارد
with a key	با کلید
with a can-opener	با دربازکن
Accompaniment	**همراهی**
with my friend	با دوستم
together with my family	همراه با خانواده ام
together with my father	همراه پدرم

Lesson 10 ■ Are women and men equal?   **122**

Note that some prepositions in Persian can also function as nouns, e.g.:

آن کنار یک مرد ایستاده است.

A man is standing over there.

در این بین خداحافظی کرد و رفت.

In the meantime, he said goodbye and left.

مدادم این زیر افتاده است.

My pencil has fallen under here.

جاهای خالی در جملات زیر را با حرف اضافهٔ مناسب پر کنید

ما ساعت هشت . . . . این اتاق جلسه داریم.

وقتی تلفن زنگ زد او . . . . عجله بیرون رفت.

اکثر دانشجویان . . . . اتوبوس . . . . دانشگاه می آیند.

آرین . . . . ماه اکتبر . . . . دنیا آمده است.

خانهٔ ما . . . . خیابان زعفرانیه است.

آنها . . . . خیابان گاندی پلاک ۸ زندگی می کنند.

ما ساعت ۵ . . . . اینجا قرار داریم.

. . . . کریسمس مدرسه ها دو هفته تعطیلند.

من . . . . او . . . . شما آشنا شدم.

. . . . عشق زندگی بی معنی است.

ضمایر انعکاسی و تأکیدی

■ **Reflexive and emphatic pronouns**

Persian has reflexive and emphatic pronouns, which are identical in terms of form. The reflexive pronoun acts as the object of the sentence, and it refers to the same entity as the subject. Look at these examples:

I saw myself in the mirror.	<div dir="rtl">من خودم را در آیینه دیدم.</div>
He likes himself.	<div dir="rtl">او خودش را دوست دارد.</div>
You know yourself better.	<div dir="rtl">تو خودت را بهتر می شناسی.</div>

The emphatic pronoun is used to emphasize the subject and is placed immediately after the subject, e.g.:

I wrote my homework myself.	<div dir="rtl">من خودم تکالیفم را نوشتم.</div>
You said it yourself.	<div dir="rtl">تو خودت گفتی.</div>

Note that in Persian the subjective pronoun (من، تو، او) is frequently dropped in these sentences.

جاهای خالی را با ضمیر انعکاسی یا تأکیدی مناسب پر کنید

شما . . . . خواستید بروید.

من . . . . ماشینم را می شویم.

او . . . . را می پرستد.

پدر و مادرم . . . . را مقصر می دانند.

تو . . . . را خیلی خسته می کنی.

خواندن 🎧

تفکر سنتی

در ایران خیلی از خانواده ها به شکل سنتی زندگی می کنند. یعنی مرد سر کار می رود و زن در خانه می ماند و خانه داری و بچه داری می کند. اخیراً خیلی از زن و شوهرهای جوان کارهای خانه را بین خودشان تقسیم می کنند زیرا هم مرد و هم زن خارج از خانه کار می کنند. با این وجود تفکر اکثر مردم هنوز سنتی است و مرد سالاری را امری طبیعی می دانند.

درک مطلب

در ایران معمولاً خانواده ها به چه شکلی زندگی می کنند؟

اغلب چه کسی از بچه مراقبت می کند؟

چرا خیلی از زن و شوهرهای جوان دیگر به شکل سنتی زندگی نمی کنند؟

مردسالاری یعنی چه؟

جاهای خالی را با زمان فعل مناسب پر کنید

او چانه می زند تا . . . . (تخفیف گرفتن).

من هنوز کارهایم را . . . . (انجام دادن).

وقتی که به مهمانی رسیدم همهٔ مهمان ها . . . . (آمدن).

وقتی پدرم آمد ما داشتیم . . . . (چانه زدن).

کلید روی قفل نبود. شاید برادرم آن را روی میز . . . . (گذاشتن).

قبل از اینکه به خانه . . . . می خواهم نان بگیرم (رفتن).

مادرم فردا به من . . . . (زنگ زدن).

سارا دارد اتاق را . . . . (جارو کردن).

لطفاً از بچه ها خوب .... (مراقبت کردن).
او درخانه نبود. احتمال دارد که به دانشگاه .... (رفتن).
بعد از اینکه غذایم را .... تکالیفم را انجام می دهم (خوردن).
آنها شاید دیشب به مادر بزرگ .... (تلفن کردن).
شما نباید او را .... (مقصر دانستن).

جملات زیر را به فارسی ترجمه کنید

1. I eat my lunch with a spoon and fork.
2. I saw her myself at the cinema last night.
3. Next to the table there is a chair, and on the table there is a lamp.
4. I got to know Moluk through Maryam.
5. They don't want to go to school by car.
6. I made the coffee myself.
7. We were all sitting at the table when Golnaz arrived.
8. They were standing in front of the shop looking at the shoes.
9. Without a doubt this is the best kebab I have ever eaten!
10. I have milk and sugar with my coffee.
11. He finished two pizzas in three minutes.
12. She is famous to be religious among her friends.
13. You must do your homework with a ballpoint pen, not with a pencil.
14. Iran is between Turkey and Pakistan.
15. He was born in 1971 and passed away in 2019 at the age of 48.

در شهر چه خبره؟

در کلاس

رعنا: سلام کامران. درس خوندی؟
کامران: نه خیلی. تو چی؟
رعنا: من تاریخ اسلام رو یه نیگایی کردم ولی ادبیات رو اصلاً!
کامران: من لای هیچ کدومش رو باز نکردم.
رعنا: می خای یه خلاصه از تاریخ اسلام رو بهت بگم؟
کامران: آره! دمت گرم!

این گفتگو را با کلمات زیر تمرین کنید

درس دادن - درس خواندن - امتحان گرفتن - امتحان دادن - امتحان میان ترم - امتحان پایان ترم - تقلب کردن - سخنرانی کردن - امتحان شفاهی - امتحان کتبی

عامیانه colloquial	کتابی literary
درس خوندی	درس خوانده ای
تو چی؟	تو چطور؟
نیگایی	نگاهی
تاریخ اسلام رو	تاریخ اسلام را
ادبیات رو	ادبیات را
هیچ کدومش رو	هیچ کدامش را
یه	یک
می خوای	می خواهی
بهت	به تو
بگم	بگویم
آره	بله

جاهای خالی را پر کنید و بعد گفتگو را در گروهتان تمرین کنید

- سلام .... قاضی. می خواهم .... شوهرم طلاق بگیرم.
- چرا خواهر؟ مگر خرجتان .... نمی دهد؟
- چرا می دهد ولی ما .... تفکرمان با هم خیلی .... است.
- این که دلیل خوبی نیست. شوهرتان باید موافق .... که شما را طلاق بدهد.
- ولی او نمی خواهد مرا طلاق دهد و .... زن دوم بگیرد.
- بله این حق مرد است که چهار .... بگیرد.
- ولی این عادلانه .... چرا زن و مرد نباید .... برابر داشته باشند؟
- حق با شماست خواهر ولی در .... کشور دنیا حقوق زن و مرد .... است؟

نگارش: با استفاده از کلمات این درس یک متن در مورد برابری زن و مرد بنویسید.

Lesson Eleven

درس یازدهم

تخت جمشید کجاست؟

قسمتی از مجموعهٔ سلطنتی باستانی تخت جمشید
تخت جمشید حدوداً پانصد سال قبل از میلاد توسط پادشاهان هخامنشی ساخته شد. برای کسب اطلاعات بیشتر در مورد <u>تخت جمشید</u> و دوره <u>هخامنشی</u> در اینترنت جستجو کنید.

تخت جمشید کجاست؟

Where is Persepolis?

درس یازدهم: تخت جمشید کجاست؟
گفتگو: خرید
دستور: عبارت وصفی
خواندن: مراکز جهانگردی
در شهر چه خبره؟ در پستخانه

Chapter aims
Grammar:
1. Adjectival clauses

Situation:
1. Shopping
2. Touristic sites
3. At the post office

واژگان

لغت	معنی انگلیسی	نقش دستوری	مثال
شلوار	trousers	اسم	چه شلوار قشنگی پوشیدی!
شلوار جین	jeans	اسم	ببخشید این شلوار جین چند است؟
ویترین	shop window	اسم	لطفاً آن کفش پاشنه بلند سفیدی را که پشت ویترین است بیاورید.
اندازه	size	اسم	این کفش اندازه من نیست.
خرید	shopping	اسم	خانم ها اکثراً از خرید لذت می برند.
کدام	which	کلمه پرسشی	کدام را می خواهی؟ آیا این را بیاورم؟
پر رنگ	dark-coloured	صفت	روسری من از روسری تو پررنگ تر است.

درس یازدهم ■ تخت جمشید کجاست؟   129

مثال	نقش دستوری	معنی انگلیسی	لغت
چشمان او قهوه ای کم رنگ است.	صفت	light-coloured	کم رنگ
وطن من ایران است.	اسم	home country	وطن
بچه ها خیلی باهوش هستند.	صفت	clever	باهوش
اولین اختراع بشر چه بود؟	اسم	humankind	بشر
ایران بناهای تاریخی بسیاری دارد. به این دلیل مورد توجه جهانگردان است.	عبارت ربطی	that's why	به این دلیل
هرساله هزاران نفر برای حج به مکه می روند.	قید	every year; yearly	هر ساله
متأسفانه این بیماری در سراسر دنیا شایع شده است.	عبارت اسمی	all over the world	سراسر دنیا
بناهای تاریخی بسیاری در شیراز و اطراف آن قرار دارند.	عبارت اسمی	historical buildings	بناهای تاریخی
مقبره سعدی در شیراز قرار دارد.	اسم	tomb	مقبره (مقابر)
آرامگاه بابا طاهر عریان در همدان است.	اسم	tomb	آرامگاه
حافظ یکی از بزرگترین شاعران ایران است.	اسم	poet	شاعر (شعرا)
خیلی از شهرهای ایران دیدنی های جالبی دارند.	اسم	sights	دیدنی ها
خصوصیت ویژه شما چیست؟	صفت	special	ویژه
این فیلم مثل فیلمی است که دیشب دیدم.	حرف اضافه	like	مثل
غار علی صدر در نزدیکی همدان است.	اسم	cave	غار
بالأخره زمستان تمام شد و بهار فرا رسید.	قید	finally	بالأخره
آرزوی من این است که روزی دور دنیا سفر کنم.	حرف اضافه	around	دور
ما شاء الله! چه خوشگل شدی!	عبارت تعجبی	Wow! (lit. What God wills!)	ما شاء الله!
آیا شما متأهل هستید؟	صفت	married	متأهل
من مجرد هستم. شما چطور؟	صفت	single	مجرد
آیا درست است که اجداد انسان اولیه میمون بوده اند؟	اسم	monkey	میمون
لطفاً کارت شناسایی تان را نشان دهید.	فعل	to show	نشان دادن (ده)
لطفاً بچه هایتان را به این مهمانی نیاورید.	فعل	to bring	آوردن (آور)

مثال	نقش دستوری	معنی انگلیسی	لغت
این رنگ خیلی به شما می آید.	فعل	to suit someone	به کسی آمدن (آ)
از رفتار او تعجب کردم.	فعل	to be surprised	تعجب کردن (کن)
امیدوارم از حرف هایم ناراحت نشده باشی.	فعل	to be upset	ناراحت شدن (شو)
من روزهای جمعه خرید می کنم.	فعل	to shop	خرید کردن (کن)
لطفاً سر راهت کمی شیرینی بخر.	فعل	to buy	خریدن (خر)
بالأخره توانستم ماشینم را بفروشم.	فعل	to sell	فروختن (فروش)
هفتهٔ پیش یک نامه برایت فرستادم. آیا به دستت رسید؟	فعل	to send	فرستادن (فرست)
ایران دارای منابع طبیعی بسیاری است.	فعل	to have	دارا بودن (باش)
کلاهت را بپوش. هوا سرد است.	فعل	to wear	پوشیدن (پوش)
ما خاطرات خوب را خیلی زود فراموش می کنیم.	فعل	to forget	فراموش کردن (کن)
هنوز آن روزها را به یاد دارم.	فعل	to remember	به یاد داشتن (دار)
لطفاً بایستید. چراغ قرمز است.	فعل	to stop; to stand	ایستادن (ایست)
ببخشید. می توانم کنار شما بنشینم؟	فعل	to sit	نشستن (نشین)
او مرا در شرایط بدی ترک کرد .	فعل	to leave; to abandon	ترک کردن (کن)
پسرم یاد گرفته است که به بزرگترها احترام بگذارد.	فعل	to learn	یاد گرفتن (گیر)
می شود لطفاً به من دوچرخه سواری یاد بدهید؟	فعل	to teach	یاد دادن (ده)
میمون ها خیلی خوب از آدم تقلید می کنند.	فعل	to imitate	تقلید کردن (کن)
من در کنکور قبول شدم.	فعل	to pass	قبول شدن (شو)
او در امتحان رانندگی رد شد.	فعل	to fail	رد شدن (شو)

گفتگو

خرید

خریدار: لطفاً آن شلوار جینی را که پشت ویترین است به من نشان بدهید.
فروشنده: کدام را؟ آبی پررنگ را می خواهید یا آبی کم رنگ را؟
خریدار: لطفاً آبی پررنگ را بیاورید.

درس یازدهم ■ تخت جمشید کجاست؟   131

فروشنده: چه سایزی می پوشید؟

خریدار: سایز ۴۰.

فروشنده: ما شاء الله! به شما نمی آید سایزتان ۴۰ باشد! شما به نظر لاغرتر می آیید.

خریدار: خیلی ممنون!

درک مطلب

خریدار کدام شلوار جین را می خواهد ببیند؟

چرا فروشنده تعجب می کند؟

چه چیزی خریدار را خوشحال می کند؟

فروشنده در مورد خریدار چه فکری می کند؟

بحث کنید و بنویسید

یک گفتگو بنویسید مانند گفتگوی خرید ولی درمورد خودتان. تصور کنید که در یک کفش فروشی هستید و می خواهید یک جفت کفش بخرید.

دستور

▣ Relative clauses   عبارت وصفی

A relative clause is used to modify a noun in a sentence. This noun can either be the subject or object. The relative marker ی is added to the noun that is being modified, which is then followed by که. If the modified noun is a direct object, را is inserted between the noun and که, e.g.:

مردی که آنجا ایستاده است فارسی می خواند.

The man who is standing over there is studying Persian.

I know the man who is standing there.	مردی را که آنجا ایستاده است می شناسم.
The book that you gave me is excellent.	کتابی که به من دادی عالیست.
I like the book you gave me very much.	کتابی را که به من دادی خیلی دوست دارم.

خانه ای را که بیست سال در آن زندگی کرده بودیم ترک کردیم.

We left the house in which we had lived for 20 years.

مسجدی که روبروی خانهٔ ماست خیلی قدیمی است.

The mosque, which is opposite our house, is very old.

جملات زیر را به فارسی ترجمه کنید

1. Do you know the lady who is wearing black jeans?
2. I haven't yet read the letter you sent me.
3. The bird which is singing is very pretty.
4. The man who was here yesterday will return today.
5. I gave the book that I bought yesterday to my friend.
6. The university at which we study is famous in the world.
7. I like the pen with which you wrote this letter.
8. The man with whom I live is my husband.
9. I will never forget the summer when I met you.
10. The city where he lived all his life is in the north of the country.

جملات زیر را با «که» به هم ربط دهید

آن بچه گریه میکند. آن بچه گرسنه است.
کیوان دانشجوی دانشگاه تهران است. او چند زبان می داند.
غذای خوشمزه ای دیشب خوردیم. آن را بپز.
تهران خیلی شلوغ است. تهران پایتخت ایران است.

خواندن

مراکز جها نگردی

ایران دارای یکی از کهن ترین تمدن ها است و به این دلیل هر ساله عده بسیاری از سراسر جهان به ایران می آیند تا بناهای تاریخی و مقابر شعرا و دیگر مراکز جهانگردی را از نزدیک ببینند. هر یک از شهر های ایران دیدنی های ویژه ای دارد مثل آرامگاه فردوسی که در شهر طوس خراسان است، ارگ بم که در استان کرمان است، غار علی صدر که نزدیک همدان است، بیستون که نزدیک کرمانشاه است، سی و سه پل که در اصفهان است و تخت جمشید، آرامگاه حافظ و مقبره سعدی که همه در استان فارس هستند.

درک مطلب

چرا هر ساله عده ای از ایران دیدن می کنند؟
چند بنای تاریخی در ایران را نام ببرید.

غار علی صدر کجاست؟

استان فارس چه دیدنی هایی دارد؟

جملات زیر را کامل کنید

من آقایی را که ....

آن خانمی که ....

نامه ای را که ....

ما خانه ای را که ....

دانشجویان استادی را که ....

شهری که ....

جملات زیر را به فارسی ترجمه کنید

1. Come sit here. I want to show you this film which is about the poets of Iran.
2. The trousers you bought for yourself last week suit you.
3. I was surprised by the things you told me.
4. We learned most of the grammatical points that our professor taught us.
5. The letter that they sent to me upset me.
6. I am reading the book that you wrote in 2015.
7. I cannot forget the lies that he told me.
8. The street on which we parked our car is the next one.
9. The gulf which is in the South of Iran is called the Persian Gulf.
10. Yesterday, I sent her the letter I had written last week.

در شهر چه خبره؟

در پستخانه

سروین: سلام جناب. می خواستم این بسته رو به کانادا بفرستم.

کارمند پستخانه: توش چیه؟ کتابه؟

سروین: بله سه تا کتابه. واسه پسرعموم دارم می فرستم.

کارمند پستخانه: می خاین با پست هوایی بفرستین یا زمینی؟

سروین: کدومش ارزونتره؟

کارمند پستخانه: معلومه خانم! زمینی دیگه!

سروین: چند روزه می رسه؟

کارمند پستخانه: چند روز نه! چند هفته! یه سه هفته ای طول می کشه.

Lesson 11 ■ *Where is Persepolis?*   **134**

این گفتگو را با کلمات زیر تمرین کنید

تمبر - پاکت نامه - صندوق پستی - پست سفارشی - گیرنده - فرستنده

عامیانه colloquial	کتابی Literary
توش	در آن
عموم	عمویم
می خاین	می خواهید
بفرستین	بفرستید
کدومش	کدامش
رو	را
ارزونتره	ارزانتر است
دیگه	دیگر
معلومه	معلوم است
چیه	چیست
واسه	برای
کتابه	کتاب است
می رسه	می رسد
یه	یک
طول می کشه	طول می کشد

جاهای خالی را پر کنید و بعد گفتگو را در گروهتان تمرین کنید

–   سلام آرش. این تابستان من برای اولین .... با خانواده ام به ایران می روم.

–   سلام نازنین. چه خوب. حتماً .... شما خیلی .... خواهد گذشت. به .... شهرها خواهید رفت؟

–   خانواده ی پدرم شیرازی هستند پس ما اول به شیراز می رویم ولی قرار .... به اصفهان، یزد، کاشان، کرمان و تهران هم برویم.

–   نمی دانستم که پدرت .... شیراز است. خانواده مادرت .... هستند؟

–   آنها اهل تهران هستند .... همگی در لوس آنجلس زندگی می کنند.

–   چه جالب. برای همین است که .... لوس آنجلس، تهرانجلس می گویند!

نگارش: با استفاده از کلمات این درس یک متن در مورد جاهای دیدنی کشورتان بنویسید.

Lesson Twelve

درس دوازدهم

موسیقی پاپ بهتر است یا سنتی؟

چند عدد سی دی موسیقی سنتی ایرانی
استاد محمدرضا شجریان و استاد شهرام ناظری از معروفترین و محبوبترین خوانندگان سنتی کشور هستند.
برای کسب اطلاعات بیشتر در مورد محمدرضا شجریان و شهرام ناظری در اینترنت جستجو کنید.

Lesson 12 ■ *Is pop music better or traditional music?*

موسیقی پاپ بهتر است یا سنتی؟

Is pop music better or traditional music?

درس دوازدهم: موسیقی پاپ بهتر است یا سنتی؟
گفتگو : خواننده مورد علاقه
دستور: عبارت قیدی
عبارت غیر شخصی
خواندن: آموزش و پرورش
در شهر چه خبره؟ در مطب دکتر

Chapter aims
Grammar:
1. Different adverbial clauses
2. Conditional sentences
3. Impersonal constructions

Situation:
1. Music
2. Educational system
3. At the doctor's office

واژگان

مثال	نقش دستوری	معنی انگلیسی	لغت
او برای امتحان سراسری خیلی درس می خواند.	عبارت اسمی	nationwide examination	امتحان سراسری
امشب به کنسرت شجریان می آیی؟	اسم	concert	کنسرت
من از موسیقی پاپ خوشم نمی آید.	عبارت اسمی	pop music	موسیقی پاپ
من عاشق موسیقی سنتی هستم.	عبارت اسمی	traditional music	موسیقی سنتی
خواننده ی مورد علاقه ات کیست؟	اسم	singer; reader	خواننده

درس دوازدهم ■ موسیقی پاپ بهتر است یا سنتی؟ 137

مثال	نقش دستوری	معنی انگلیسی	لغت
رنگ مورد علاقهٔ من آبی است.	صفت	favourite	مورد علاقه
دفعهٔ بعد که می آیی لطفاً کتاب مرا هم بیاور.	عبارت قیدی	next time	دفعهٔ بعد
نتیجهٔ امتحانت چه شد؟	اسم	result	نتیجه (نتایج)
بگذار یک داستان خنده دار برایت تعریف کنم.	صفت	funny	خنده دار
سیستم آموزشی ایران شبیه سیستم آموزشی فرانسه است.	عبارت اسمی	educational system	سیستم آموزشی
دانش آموزان به طور منظم در صف ایستادند.	صفت	orderly; organized	منظم
دخترم به پیش دبستانی می رود.	اسم مرکب	pre-school	پیش دبستانی
دبستان در ایران شش سال است.	اسم	primary school	دبستان
دانش آموزان دبیرستانی خود را برای کنکور آماده می کنند.	اسم	high school	دبیرستان
هیچ وقت از خانم ها سنشان را سؤال نکن.	اسم	age	سن (سنین)
در پایان نامه اسم خودت را بنویس و امضاء کن.	اسم	end	پایان
تنها با داشتن دیپلم نمی توانی کار پیدا کنی.	اسم	high school diploma	دیپلم
کنکور بسیار سخت است.	اسم	university entrance examination	کنکور
کل کلاس غایبند.	اسم	whole	کل
این فیلم بر اساس رمان صادق هدایت ساخته شده است.	عبارت اضافی	based on	براساس
رتبهٔ شما در کنکور چه بود؟	اسم	rank	رتبه
رشتهٔ من مطالعات اسلامی است.	اسم	field of study	رشته
او در دفتر یک روزنامه کار می کند.	اسم	newspaper	روزنامه
از رفتار خشن او گریه ام گرفت.	فعل	to burst into tears	گریه . . . گرفتن (گیر)
از جوک او خنده ام گرفت.	فعل	to burst into laughter	خنده . . . گرفتن (گیر)
آیا از خطاطی خوشت می آید؟	فعل	to like	خوش . . . آمدن (آ) از

Lesson 12 ■ Is pop music better or traditional music? 138

مثال	نقش دستوری	معنی انگلیسی	لغت
دیشب دیر آمدم و روی مبل خوابم برد.	فعل	to fall asleep	خواب . . . بردن (بر)
یادم رفت قرصم را بخورم.	فعل	to forget	یاد . . . رفتن (رو)
یادم است همیشه می گفت صدای مرا دوست دارد.	فعل	to recall	یاد . . . بودن
من از غذای چرب بدم می آید.	فعل	to dislike	بد . . . آمدن (آ) از
پنجره را باز کن. خیلی گرمم است.	فعل	to feel hot	گرم . . . بودن
می شود بخاری را روشن کنی؟ خیلی سردم است.	فعل	to feel cold	سرد . . . بودن
کی درست را تمام می کنی؟	فعل	to finish	تمام کردن (کن)
نمی دانم کدام رشته را انتخاب کنم.	فعل	to choose	انتخاب کردن (کن)
کتاب شما کی چاپ شد؟	فعل	to be published	چاپ شدن (شو)
چقدر طول می کشد که از خانه به دانشگاه بروی؟	فعل	to last	طول کشیدن (کش)
خبر ترور نخست وزیر را در رسانه ها اعلان کردند.	فعل	to announce	اعلان کردن (کن)
آنها در دانشگاه پذیرفته شدند.	فعل	to be admitted	پذیرفته شدن (شو)

گفتگو

خوانندهٔ مورد علاقه

مهیار: می خواهی با هم به کنسرت گروه آریان برویم؟
میترا: من از موسیقی پاپ خوشم نمی آید. چرا نرویم کنسرت شجریان؟
مهیار: من همیشه در کنسرتهای موسیقی سنتی خوابم می برد.
میترا: یادم می آید پارسال وقتی به کنسرت شهرام ناظری رفتیم نه تنها بدت نیامد بلکه خیلی هم خوشت آمد!
مهیار: بله یادم هست ولی گروه مورد علاقهٔ من آریان است.
میترا: خیلی خوب. ولی دفعهٔ بعد باید با من به کنسرت شجریان بیایی!

درک مطلب

گروه مورد علاقهٔ مهیار کدام است؟
مهیار از چه نوع موسیقی ای خوشش می آید؟

پارسال که مهیار و میترا به کنسرت شهرام ناظری رفتند آیا از کنسرت خوششان آمد؟

شجریان چه نوع خواننده ای است؟

بحث کنید و بنویسید

یک گفتگو بنویسید مانند گفتگوی بالا ولی درمورد خواننده ی مورد علاقهٔ خودتان. بگویید از چه نوع موسیقی ای خوشتان می آید.

دستور

■ Adverbial clauses

عبارت قیدی

Adverbial clauses are added to the main clause to express time, place, manner, contrast, reason, intention, etc. Look at the following sentences where the adverbial clauses are underlined:

من ایران را دوست دارم <u>چون وطنم است.</u>

I love Iran <u>because it is my homeland.</u>

<u>وقتی که زبان دومی یاد می گیری</u> باهوش تر می شوی.

<u>When you learn a second language</u>, you become smarter.

او <u>همانطوری که پدرش صحبت می کند</u> حرف می زند.

He speaks <u>in the same manner as his father does.</u>

<u>اگر چه کمی دیر است</u>، با شما می آیم.

<u>Although it is a bit late</u>, I will come with you.

<u>هر کجا تو بخواهی</u> می روم.

I will go <u>wherever you want me to.</u>

من خیلی درس می خوانم <u>تا اینکه در امتحان قبول شوم.</u>

I study hard <u>so that I can pass the test.</u>

Lesson 12 ■ *Is pop music better or traditional music?*   **140**

Conditional sentences   جملات شرطی

Conditional clauses are another type of adverbial clause, which express condition. Conditional clauses are normally introduced in Persian by اگر.

Possible conditionals (present or future condition)

Possible conditionals can take the present subjunctive in the *if-clause*,[1] e.g.:

اگر بروی من هم می روم.

If you go, I will go too.

اگر بیایی او را خواهی دید.

If you come, you will see him.

Possible conditionals (past condition)

Possible conditionals can also take the past subjunctive in the *if-clause*, e.g.:

اگر نرفته باشد او را می بینیم.

If he has not gone, we will see him.

اگر قول داده باشد عمل خواهد کرد.

If he has promised, he will do it.

Impossible conditionals

Impossible conditionals can take the past progressive tense or the past perfect in the *if-clause*, e.g.:

اگر می رفت من هم می رفتم.

If he had gone, I would have gone too.

---

[1] The present subjunctive can be replaced by the simple past, especially in spoken Persian, e.g.:

اگر آمد ما هم می رویم.

If he comes, we will go too.

درس دوازدهم ∎ موسیقی پاپ بهتر است یا سنتی؟ 141

اگر کمک خواسته بودی کمکت می کردم.

If you had asked for help, I would have helped you.

اگر برف آمده بود روی زمین نشسته بود.

If it had snowed, it would have covered the ground.

اگر می دانستم نرفته بودم.

If I had known, I would not have gone.

∎ Impersonal constructions عبارت غیر شخصی

In impersonal constructions, the verbal part is not conjugated in accordance with the subject. The verbal part always appears in the third person singular. However, the nonverbal part of these constructions is followed by the pronominal suffix which agrees with the subject of the sentence.

Read the sentences below in which the impersonal constructions are underlined, and then translate them into English:

من از فیلم هندی <u>خوشم می آید</u>.
من از سیر <u>بدم می آید</u>.
<u>تو یادت نمی آید</u> او را اولین بار کجا دیده ای؟
من شماره تلفنت <u>یادم نیست</u>.
تو اگر <u>گرمت شد</u> می توانی پنجره را باز کنی.
ما تلویزیون تماشا می کردیم که <u>خوابمان برد</u>.
وقتی خبر را به او دادم، <u>گریه اش گرفت</u>.
شما اگر <u>خوابتان می آید</u> بروید بخوابید!
آنها از حرف مسخره اش <u>خنده شان گرفت</u>.

There are additional impersonal constructions in Persian, such as می توان, می شود and باید, all of which are followed by the past stem of the main verb. Look at the examples below:

می توان گفت که ایران کشوری غنی است.

One can say that Iran is a rich country.

می شود به او اعتماد کرد.

One can trust him.

باید قبول کرد که مرگ امری طبیعی است.

One must accept that death is something natural.

جاهای خالی را با افعال مناسب پر کنید

من از رنگ آبی .... (خوش آمدن).

دیر بود و پسرم زود .... (خواب بردن).

جوک هایی که او گفت خیلی خنده دار بود و همهٔ ما .... (خنده گرفتن).

بعد از اینکه بستنی خوردم .... (سرد شدن).

.... که در ماشین را قفل کنم (یاد رفتن).

غلط های جملات زیر را درست کنید

اگر می توانم به موقع ویزا می گیرم با شما به ایران آمده باشم.

ما آن دانشجوی مصری ای که تو با او مکاتبه داری دیدیم.

پولی را که به من دادید زیاد بودند.

اگر دروغ خواهی گفت به تو اطمینان نخواهم کرد.

می توانید ما را با خودت می برید؟

آنها پسرها در این دانشگاه ادبیات های فارسی می خواند.

اگر او را دوست داشته باشی با او ازدواج کرده بودی.

آنها قرار است فردا با همه دانشجویان کلاس فارسی آنها به موزه خواهند رفت.

من با مادر و پدر من زندگی می کنند.

کتابی را که دیروز از کتابفروشی بخرم جدید است.

خواندن

آموزش و پرورش

سیستم آموزشی در مدارس ایران بسیار منظم است. بچه ها در سن ۵ سالگی به پیش دبستانی می روند. آنها از ۶ سالگی تا ۱۲ سالگی به مدت ۶ سال به دبستان می روند. پس از دبستان، برای مدت ۶ سال به دبیرستان می روند. پس از تمام کردن دبیرستان، در ۱۸ سالگی، در کنکور که یک امتحان سراسری در کل کشور است شرکت می کنند. این امتحان بسیار سخت است بنابراین دانش آموزان باید بسیار درس بخوانند. سپس آنها بر اساس رتبه شان در کنکور می توانند انتخاب رشته کنند. پس از مدتی، در اینترنت نتایج کنکور اعلان می شود. این روز بهترین روز برای آنهایی است که در دانشگاه پذیرفته شده اند و بدترین روز برای آنهایی است که نتوانسته اند پذیرفته شوند.

درک مطلب

دورهٔ دبستان در ایران چند سال طول می کشد؟
دانش آموزان در چه سنی به دبیرستان می روند؟
چرا دانش آموزان باید برای کنکور بسیار درس بخوانند؟
شرط ورود به دانشگاه چیست؟
کنکور چیست؟
روز اعلان نتایج کنکور چه روزی است؟

جاهای خالی را با زمان مناسب فعل پر کنید

وقتی که به خانه رسیدی همهٔ ما شام .... (خوردن).
پس فردا ما درس شانزدهم را .... (خواندن).
اگر او به این زودی .... (خوابیدن- منفی)می توانستیم با هم به سینما .... (رفتن).
یکسال است که او را .... (دیدن- منفی).
دو روز بود که من .... (خندیدن - منفی).
پدر و مادرم هفتهٔ آینده به ایران .... (سفر کردن).
کلاس ما هنوز .... (تمام شدن).
ما خیلی خوش شانس هستیم چون هرگز .... (مریض شدن).
من از ایدهٔ شما .... (خوش ... آمدن- منفی).
آنها دیروز از داستان او .... (گریه ... گرفتن).
مادرم از فیلم دیشب خیلی .... (خوش ... آمدن).
لطفاً پالتوی سارا را بده. او خیلی .... (سرد ... بودن).
شما دیشب خسته بودید و زود .... (خواب ... بردن).
امیدوارم برادرم با نمرهٔ عالی .... (قبول شدن).
اگر باران .... (آمدن) نمی توانیم به پارک .... (رفتن).
اگر این فیلم را قبلاً .... (دیدن- منفی) امشب با هم به سینما .... (رفتن).
اگر زودتر به من .... (گفتن) می توانستم برای تولدش کیک .... (پختن).
اگر آنها دروغ .... (گفتن) .... (تنبیه شدن).

در شهر چه خبره؟

در مطب دکتر

دکتر: خب مشکلتون چیه خانوم؟
نازگل: گلوم درد می کنه و سرم.

دکتر : چند روزه؟

نازگل: چاهار روزه ولی امروز حالم خیلی بدتره. حالت تهوع هم دارم.

دکتر : دراز بکشین اینجا تا فشار خونتون رو بگیرم.

نازگل: فکر می کنین جدیه؟ آخه من باردارم.

دکتر : نه یه سرما خوردگی جزئیه. این قرصا رو هر شیش ساعت با مایعات فراوون بخورین حالتون خوب می شه. جای نگرانی نیست.

این گفتگو را با کلمات زیر تمرین کنید

معده درد - دندان درد - پادرد - کمردرد - خونریزی - شربت - تب ـ درجه - کپسول - آمپول - قطره

عامیانه colloquial	کتابی literary
خب	خوب
خانوم	خانم
قرصارو	قرص ها را
فراوون	فراوان
درد می کنه	درد میکند
روزه	روز است
جدیه	جدی است
شیش	شش
بخورین	بخورید
حالتون	حالتان
خونتون رو	خونتان را
گلوم	گلویم
مشکلتون	مشکلتان
چیه	چیست
می شه	می شود
بدتره	بدتر است
جزئیه	جزئی است
می کنین	می کنید
دراز بکشین	دراز بکشید

جاهای خالی را پر کنید و بعد گفتگو را در گروهتان تمرین کنید

- سلام مهسا جان. .... چندمی عزیزم؟
- سلام خاله مریم. سال آخر دبیرستانم. امسال باید تصمیم .... چه رشته ای .... دانشگاه بخوانم.
- به چه موضوعی علاقه ....؟
- به ادبیات فارسی خیلی .... دارم ولی پدر و مادرم می خواهند من پزشکی و یا مهندسی ....
- به نظر من، اگر رشته ای .... که دوست داری بخوانی، بیشتر موفق می شوی.
- من .... شما کاملاً موافقم. می شود لطفاً .... پدر و مادرم در این مورد صحبت ....؟
- حتماً مهسا جان! .... باشی عزیزم.
- ممنون خاله مریم.

نگارش: با استفاده از واژگان این درس یک متن بنویسید و در آن سیستم آموزشی کشورتان را با سیستم آموزشی ایران مقایسه کنید. بعد آنرا در گروهتان بحث کنید.

Lesson Thirteen

درس سیزدهم

دانشگاه شما چه نوع دانشگاهی است؟

مدرسهٔ مادرشاه یا مدرسهٔ چهار باغ اصفهان

امروزه طلبه ها در مدارس علمیه یا حوزه های علمیه تحصیل می کنند. قبل از تأسیس دارالفنون (اولین دانشگاه ایران) در سال ۱۸۵۱ میلادی هیچ دانشگاهی در ایران وجود نداشت و محصلین برای ادامهٔ تحصیل به حوزه های علمیه ویا اروپا می رفتند. برای کسب اطلاعات بیشتر در مورد <u>دارالفنون</u> در اینترنت جستجو کنید.

Lesson 13 ■ *What kind of university is your university?*

دانشگاه شما چه نوع دانشگاهی است؟

What kind of university is your university?

درس سیزدهم: دانشگاه شما چه نوع دانشگاهی است؟
گفتگو: اداره پلیس
دستور: مجهول
خواندن: انواع دانشگاه
در شهر چه خبره؟ در کتابفروشی

Chapter aims
Grammar:
1. Passive constructions

Situation:
1. Different kinds of universities
2. At the police station
3. At the bookstore

واژگان

لغت	معنی انگلیسی	نقش دستوری	مثال
ضبط صوت	tape recorder	اسم مرکب	اگر ضبط صوت داشتم می توانستم سخنرانی استاد را ضبط کنم.
لاستیک زاپاس	spare tyre	عبارت اسمی	آخ پنچر شدیم! لاستیک زاپاس داری؟
گزارش	Report	اسم	طبق گزارش این خبرگزاری بی سوادی در ایران کاهش یافته است.
کتبی	Written	صفت	من امتحان کتبی را به شفاهی ترجیح می‌دهم.
شفاهی	Oral	صفت	من در امتحان شفاهی قبول می شوم.

درس سیزدهم ■ دانشگاه شما چه نوع دانشگاهی است؟ 149

مثال	نقش دستوری	معنی انگلیسی	لغت
چند درصد از دانش آموزان مدرسهٔ شما در کنکور قبول شدند؟	اسم	Percent	درصد
دزد توانست فرار کند.	اسم	Thief	دزد
تا بحال هیچ سرقتی در خیابان ما صورت نگرفته است.	اسم	Theft	سرقت
هر روزه عدهٔ زیادی در این کشور جان خود را از دست می دهند.	قید	Daily	هر روزه
صدها نفر در آن درگیری کشته شدند.	صفت شمارشی	hundreds	صدها
دانشگاه دولتی شهریه ندارد.	عبارت اسمی	state university	دانشگاه دولتی
امروز اتوبوس و مترو مجانی است.	صفت	Free	مجانی = رایگان
ببخشید ولی پول کافی همراهم نیست.	اسم	Money	پول
شهریهٔ دانشگاه شما چقدر است؟	اسم	tuition fee	شهریه
ورود به دانشگاه در ایران بسیار مشکل است.	اسم	entering; entrance	ورود
امتحان پایان ترم بسیار سخت بود.	صفت	hard; difficult	سخت
او تو را دوست دارد اما نه به اندازه من.	عبارت اضافی	not as much as...	نه به اندازهٔ ...
شهریهٔ دانشگاه مکاتبه ای زیاد نیست.	عبارت اسمی	correspondence university	دانشگاه مکاتبه ای
از طریق علی با زینب آشنا شدیم.	عبارت اضافی	through; via	از طریق
آیا با دوستان دبیرستانت هنوز مکاتبه داری؟	اسم	correspondence	مکاتبه
افرادی که مشکل قلبی دارند نباید امروز بیرون بروند چون آلودگی هوا بسیار بالا است.	اسم	person; individual	فرد (افراد)
من به این رشته خیلی علاقمند بودم.	صفت	interested	علاقمند
او تحصیلاتش را در دانشگاه مک گیل به پایان برد.	اسم	education; studies	تحصیلات
آیا شما تحصیلات عالی دارید؟	عبارت اسمی	higher education	تحصیلات عالی
آیا قصد دارید به تحصیلاتتان ادامه دهید؟	فعل	to continue	ادامه دادن (ده)
سعی کن رفتارت را تغییر بدهی.	فعل	to try; to attempt	سعی کردن (کن)
دوچرخهٔ مرا دزدیده اند.	فعل	to steal	دزدیدن (دزد)
آیا کیفت را پیدا کردی؟	فعل	to find	پیدا کردن (کن)
هرگونه مورد مشکوکی را گزارش کنید.	فعل	to report	گزارش کردن (کن)

Lesson 13 ■ *What kind of university is your university?*

لغت	معنی انگلیسی	نقش دستوری	مثال
وجود داشتن (دار)	to exist	فعل	می دانی دایناسورها چند میلیون سال پیش وجود داشته اند؟
وارد شدن (شو)	to enter	فعل	در باز شد و او وارد شد.
موفق شدن (شو)	to succeed	فعل	آنها موفق شدند در جنگ پیروز شوند.
سرقت کردن (کن)	to rob	فعل	این بانک را سرقت کردند.

گفتگو

ادارۀ پلیس

افسر پلیس: بسیار خوب بگو ببینم چه شده؟
مرجان: چیزهای ماشینم سرقت شده.
افسر پلیس: چه چیزهایی سرقت شده؟
مرجان: ضبط صوت و لاستیک زاپاس.
افسر پلیس: باید یک گزارش کتبی بنویسید و چیزهایی را که سرقت شده نام ببرید.
مرجان: چشم جناب. معمولاً چند درصد احتمال دارد که دزد پیدا بشود؟
افسر پلیس: چقدر سؤال می کنید! مگر فقط ماشین شماست که سرقت شده؟! هرروز صدها سرقت مثل این به ما گزارش می شود.

درک مطلب

به نظر شما چرا مرجان به ادارۀ پلیس رفته است؟
به نظر شما آیا آنجا محله ای امن است؟
رفتار افسر پلیس با مرجان چطور است؟
مرجان باید چه بنویسد؟

دستور

مجهول ■ Passive constructions

In Persian the passive construction is used when the agent (the doer of the action) is not mentioned, e.g.:

هزاران نفر کشته شدند.

Thousands of people were killed.

درس سیزدهم ■ دانشگاه شما چه نوع دانشگاهی است؟   151

هیچ چیز دیده نمی شود.

Nothing can be seen.

To form a passive construction, the participle form of the main verb (e.g. گفته, خورده) is combined with the conjugated form of شدن. In transitive compound verbs (where the verbal part is normally دیدن or خوردن , شدن), to form a passive, the verbal part is normally replaced by (کردن or زدن).

پدرش او را تنبیه کرد.

His father punished him.

او تنبیه شد.

He was punished.

من هیچوقت او را کتک نمی زنم.

I never beat him.

او هیچوقت کتک نمی خورد.

He is never beaten.

واردات این محصول به اقتصاد ایران صدمه زده است.

The import of this product has damaged Iran's economy.

اقتصاد ایران صدمه دیده است.

Iran's economy has been damaged.

جملات زیر را از معلوم به مجهول تبدیل کنید

سربازان دشمن تعداد زیادی از غیر نظامیان را کشتند.
من هیچ دانشجویی را رد نکردم.
روزنامه نگاران مطالب مهم بسیاری نوشته اند.
آیا مشقهایت را تمام کرده ای؟
استاد مرا بعنوان نماینده کلاس انتخاب کرد.

خواندن

انواع دانشگاه

در ایران چهار نوع دانشگاه وجود دارد: دانشگاه دولتی که مجانی است و ورود به آن سخت است، دانشگاه آزاد که شهریه ای است و ورود به آن مشکل است، اما نه به اندازهٔ دانشگاه دولتی، دانشگاه مکاتبه ای که پولی است و از طریق اینترنت و مکاتبه است و دانشگاه شبانه که پولی است و برای افرادی است که در طول روز کار می کنند.

هر سال عدهٔ زیادی از جوانان ایرانی در کنکور شرکت می کنند و کمتر از نیمی از آنها موفق به ورود به دانشگاه می شوند. جوانان ایرانی به تحصیلات عالی بسیار علاقمند هستند و سعی می کنند تحصیلات خود را در دانشگاه های داخل کشور و یا خارج از کشور ادامه دهند.

درک مطلب

چند نوع دانشگاه در ایران وجود دارد؟
چرا هر ساله عده زیادی از جوانان ایرانی در کنکور شرکت می کنند؟
چرا همهٔ جوانان ایرانی به دانشگاه راه پیدا نمی کنند؟
آیا شما به تحصیلات عالی علاقه دارید؟ چرا؟

جاهای خالی را با زمان مناسب فعل پر کنید

(بعضی از افعال داخل پرانتز باید از معلوم به مجهول تبدیل شوند.)

پارسال که در ایران . . . . (بودن)، کیفم . . . . (گم کردن).
فکر نمی کنم که او هرگز در آن شهر . . . . (زندگی کردن).
دیروز دانشجویان زیادی در امتحان . . . . (رد شدن).
اگر در تهران . . . . (بودن) هر هفته به بازار . . . . (رفتن).
من دیشب دیر به خانه . . . . (برگشتن) و تا ۲ نصف شب . . . . (خواب بردن - منفی).
اگر قبلاً آن کتاب را . . . . (خواندن) موضوع آنرا . . . . (دانستن).
این اتاق بسیار زیبا . . . . (تزئین شدن).
من از آن پارک خیلی . . . . (خوش آمدن) و همیشه به آنجا . . . . (رفتن).
فردا . . . . (توانستن) با هم به آنجا . . . . (رفتن).
این نامه ها چند وقت پیش . . . . (نوشتن).
وقتی شما آمدید من . . . . (رفتن).
قبل از آن مهمانی ما او را هرگز . . . . (دیدن).
این لباسها همه . . . . (اتو کردن).

پیش از آنکه به ایران بروم فیلم ایرانی زیاد . . . . (دیدن).

لطفاً زیاد . . . .(سؤال کردن- منفی).

مواظب باش رنگی نشوی. این دیوار تازه . . . . (رنگ شدن).

برادرم هنوز . . . . (ثبت نام کردن).

شما کی فارغ التحصیل . . . . (شدن)؟

در شهر چه خبره؟ 🎧

در کتابفروشی

کتاب فروش: بفرمایین.

تبسم: فرهنگ انگلیسی به فارسی دارین؟

کتاب فروش: بله داریم، جیبی باشه، یه جلدی باشه، چند جلدی باشه؟

تبسم: فرقی نداره. جدیدترینش رو می خوام.

کتاب فروش: این یکی از همه جدیدتره ولی این یکی کامل تره.

تبسم: دانشجوها کدوم رو بیشتر می خرن؟

کتاب فروش: این یکی که کاملتره.

تبسم: پس منم همون رو می خرم.

این گفتگو را با کلمات زیر تمرین کنید

رمان- بیوگرافی- طنز - اتوبیوگرافی- فیلمنامه- کتابهای درسی- دائرة المعارف- لغتنامه

عامیانه colloquial	کتابی literary
بفرمایین	بفرمایید
دارین	دارید
باشه	باشد
جدیدتره	جدیدتر است
کاملتره	کامل تر است
یه	یک
نداره	ندارد
جدیدترینش رو	جدیدترینش را
کدوم رو	کدام را

عامیانه colloquial	کتابی literary
همون رو	همان را
می خام	می خواهم
منم	من هم
می خرن	می خرند

جاهای خالی را پر کنید و بعد گفتگو را در گروهتان تمرین کنید

– سلام استاد. آیا نسخه جدید کتابتان چاپ .... است؟

– سلام پرویز جان. هنوز نه. قرار است ماه آینده منتشر ....

– چه خوب. در چاپ جدید چه چیزهایی عوض .... است؟

– تا جایی که ممکن بود، غلط های تایپی درست شد و چند قسمت هم به هر درس اضافه ....

– استاد آیا می دانید که این کتاب در چندین دانشگاه در آمریکا و اروپا و ...... در ایران تدریس می شود؟

– نه نمی دانستم! ممنون که اطلاع .... امیدوارم ...... خواندن کتاب لذت ....

– ممنون استاد. خداحافظ.

نگارش: با استفاده از کلمات این درس یک متن در مورد انواع دانشگاه در کشورتان بنویسید.

درس چهاردهم

مجرد هستید یا متأهل؟

Lesson Fourteen

یک زن و شوهر جوان ایرانی در حیاط خانه ای قدیمی در شهر کاشان
طبق تازه ترین آمار میانگین سن ازدواج برای زنان در ایران ۲۳ سال است و برای مردان ۲۶ سال.
برای کسب اطلاعات بیشتر در مورد آمار ازدواج در ایران در اینترنت جستجو کنید.

Lesson 14 ■ Are you single or married? 156

مجرد هستید یا متأهل؟

Are you single or married?

درس چهاردهم: مجرد هستید یا متأهل؟
گفتگو: هدیه تولد
خواندن: ازدواج به سبک سنتی
دستور: مرکب سازی
مشتقات
کلمات ربط
در شهر چه خبره؟ سفر

Chapter aims
Grammar:
1. Compounds and derivatives
2. Conjunctions

Situation:
1. Birthday gift
2. Traditional marriage
3. Travelling

واژگان

مثال	نقش دستوری	معنی انگلیسی	لغت
روز مادر برای مادرم گل خریدم.	اسم	flower	گل
هدیهٔ تولدت را بعداً برایت می‌آورم.	اسم	present; gift	هدیه
تولد شما در چه ماهی است؟	اسم	birth; birthday	تولد
تولدت مبارک! امیدوارم به همهٔ آرزوهایت برسی.	عبارت	Happy birthday!	تولدت مبارک!

درس چهاردهم ■ مجرد هستید یا متأهل؟   157

مثال	نقش دستوری	معنی انگلیسی	لغت
من سلیقۀ تو را در تزئین خانه دوست دارم.	اسم	taste	سلیقه
از طرف من به خانواده ات سلام برسان.	عبارت اضافی	on behalf of	از طرف
من اطلاعات کافی در این مورد ندارم.	صفت	enough	کافی
قیمت‌ها از سال گذشته تاحالا ده برابرشده‌اند.	عبارت وصفی	ten times	ده برابر
بابا جان! یک کم بیشتر مواظب باش!	عبارت تعجبی	O my God!	بابا جان!
من از آدم های خسیس اصلاً خوشم نمی آید.	صفت	stingy	خسیس
اگر دست و دل باز باشی دوستان بیشتری خواهی داشت.	صفت مرکب	generous	دست و دل باز
او آرزو دارد ازدواج کند.	اسم	marriage	ازدواج
عروسی آنها بسیار مجلل بود.	اسم	wedding	عروسی
سبک این نویسنده طنزگونه است.	اسم	style	سبک
مراسم عقد در خانه خودمان برگزار شد.	اسم	ceremonies; rituals	مراسم
کشورهای غربی از نظر صنعت بسیار پیشرفته اند.	صفت / اسم	western; westerner	غربی
اقوام مادرم همه در خرمشهر زندگی می کنند.	اسم	relatives	اقوام
او از آشنایان پدرم بود.	اسم	acquaintance	آشنا
هر روز باید امر خیری انجام داد تا بهتر زندگی کرد.	اسم	a good deed	امر خیر
ابتدا تخم مرغ ها را بزنید وسپس آرد و شیر را اضافه کنید.	قید/اسم	firstly; beginning	ابتدا
معمولاً دخترها به خواستگاری پسرها نمی روند.	اسم	asking for a girl's hand in marriage	خواستگاری
او به همراه پسرش به خانه ام آمد.	عبارت اضافی	together with	به همراه
دسته گل عروس بسیار زیباست.	اسم مرکب	bouquet of flowers	دسته گل
نامزدی آنها بطور ساده برگزار شد.	اسم	engagement	نامزدی
دوران استبداد به سر رسید و زمان آزادی فرا رسید.	اسم	period	دوران
آیا آنها زوج خوشبختی هستند؟	اسم	a married couple	زوج

لغت	معنی انگلیسی	نقش دستوری	مثال
اتفاق	event	اسم	یک اتفاق ساده می تواند سرنوشت فرد را تغییر دهد.
برگزار شدن (شو)	to be held	فعل	امسال کنفرانس زبان و ادبیات فارسی در این شهر برگزار می شود.
نامزد شدن (شو)	to be nominated; to get engaged	فعل	او نامزد ریاست جمهوری شد.
موافق بودن	to agree	فعل	آیا شما با عقاید من موافقید؟
گم کردن (کن)	to lose	فعل	من کیف پولم را گم کرده ام.
پیشنهاد کردن (کن)	to recommend	فعل	من به آنها پیشنهاد کردم که کمتر صحبت کنند و بیشتر عمل کنند.
فرق کردن (کن)	to change (intransitive)	فعل	ایران از پنج سال گذشته خیلی فرق کرده است.
وقت گرفتن (گیر)	to make an appointment	فعل	پیش از رفتن به پزشک باید وقت بگیرید.
اعتقاد داشتن (دار)	to believe in	فعل	آیا به معجزه اعتقاد دارید؟
عقد کردن (کن)	to marry	فعل	می توانیم امسال عقد کنیم و سال آینده عروسی کنیم.
شرح دادن (ده)	to explain	فعل	لطفاً در مورد پیشینهٔ کارتان به طور مختصر شرح دهید.
توضیح دادن (ده)	to explain	فعل	ببخشید می شود لطفاً این موضوع را کمی بیشتر توضیح دهید؟
به دست کردن (کن)	to wear on one's hand	فعل	حلقه اش را به دستش کرد.

گفتگو

هدیهٔ تولد

علی: امروز تولد خانمم است. نمی دانم چه هدیه ای برای او بگیرم.
رویا: گل بگیر همهٔ خانمها گل دوست دارند.
علی: سلیقهٔ من خوب نیست. تو این ده هزار تومان را بگیر و از طرف من برای او گل بخر.
رویا: این پولی که تو می دهی کافی نیست. باید ده برابرش کنی!
علی: خیلی خوب. پس، هزار تومانی را که به تو دادم بده.

رویا: بابا جان تو چقدر خسیسی. آدم باید برای خانمش دست و دلباز باشد.

علی: من خیلی هم دست و دلبازم! خوب، این صد هزار تومان را بگیر ولی مواظب باش گم نشود.

درک مطلب

امروز تولد کیست؟

آیا به نظر شما علی خسیس است؟ چرا؟

رویا به علی پیشنهاد می کند برای تولد خانمش چه بگیرد؟

چه کسی برای خانم علی گل می خرد؟

بحث کنید و بنویسید

یک گفتگو بنویسید مانند گفتگوی هدیهٔ تولد ولی درمورد تولد یکی از دوستانتان. شما تولدتان را چطور جشن می گیرید.

خواندن 🎧

ازدواج به سبک سنتی

مراسم سنتی ازدواج در ایران با مراسم ازدواج در کشورهای غربی فرق میکند. معمولاً دختر و پسر به هم معرفی می شوند. اقوام و آشنایان این کار را امری خیر می دانند. ابتدا خانوادهٔ پسر از خانوادهٔ دختر وقت می گیرند و به خواستگاری دختر می روند. در روز خواستگاری، پسر به همراه خانواده اش با یک دستهٔ گل به خانهٔ دختر می روند، دختر برای آنها چای می آورد و با پسر و خانواده اش آشنا می شود. اگر هر دو خانواده موافق باشند، دختر و پسر با هم نامزد می شوند. نامزدی رسوم ویژهٔ خود را دارد. جشن نامزدی جشن نسبتاً کوچکی است که در خانهٔ دختربرگزار می شود و دختر و پسر حلقه ای به دست همدیگر می کنند. خیلی ها اعتقاد دارند که دوران نامزدی بهترین دوران زندگی یک زوج است. پس از دوران نامزدی، دو خانواده روزی را برای عقد تعیین می کنند. جشن عروسی بعد از عقد و معمولاً در خانهٔ پسر برگزار می شود و جشن بزرگی است. عروس و داماد این روز را همراه با خانواده، اقوام، دوستان و آشنایانشان جشن می گیرند.

درک مطلب

اکثر زوج های سنتی چطور با هم آشنا می شوند؟

مراسم خواستگاری را شرح دهید.

فرق نامزدی با عقد چیست؟

چه وقت دختر و پسر به دست همدیگر حلقه می کنند؟

Lesson 14 ■ *Are you single or married?*   **160**

دستور

■ Compounding

مرکب سازی

Compounding is a common way of forming words in Persian, and many words you will encounter in Persian are compounds where two or more words are combined to form a new word, e.g.:

کتابخانه (کتاب + خانه)

Compound verbs are very common in Persian, e.g.:

کتاب خواندن (کتاب + خواندن)

Note that compound verbs outnumber simple verbs in Persian. Compound verbs contain a verbal part and a nonverbal part. The verbal part is chosen from a limited list of verbs. The simple verbs most commonly used as the verbal component in compound verbs in Persian are:

(to have)	(to give)	(to eat)	(to be)	(to close)	(to take)	(to throw)	(to fall)	(to bring)
داشتن	دادن	خوردن	بودن	بستن	بردن	انداختن	افتادن	آوردن
(to get)	**(to pass)**	**(to draw)**	**(to do)**	**(to become)**	**(to hit)**		**(to go)**	**(to come)**
...	گرفتن	گذشتن	کشیدن	کردن	شدن	زدن	رفتن	آمدن

The nonverbal part of a compound verb can be either:

(1) a noun (گریه کردن in گریه)
(2) an adjective or past participle (خسته شدن in خسته)
(3) a prepositional phrase (به دنیا آمدن in به دنیا)
(4) an adverbial (برداشتن in بر)
(5) a complex nominal (سر و کار داشتن in سر و کار)

Even borrowed words can combine with the above verbs to make new compound words in Persian, such as:

ایمیل زدن
چت کردن
کلیک کردن

Verbal nouns (which can be used as either adjectives or nouns) are often formed from compound verbs in Persian, where the nonverbal part is added to the present stem of the verbal component, e.g.:

درس خواندن > درس خوان (صفت)

داستان نوشتن > داستان نویس (اسم)

پناه جستن > پناه جو (اسم)

Verbal nouns can often also be formed from the present stem of verbs, e.g.:

گفتن > گو > گویش

رفتن > رو > روش

دیدن > بین > بینش

خوردن > خور > خورش

Active participles can sometimes also be formed from the present stem by adding نده e.g.:

خواندن > خوان > خواننده

شنیدن > شنو > شنونده

فرستادن > فرست > فریسنده

نوشتن > نویس > نویسنده

■ Derivatives   مشتقات

The smallest meaningful units in a language are called morphemes. One word may consist of one or more morphemes. Derivatives are words that are derived from other words by combining two or more morphemes. Derivational morphemes are added to other words and often change the part of speech of the word, e.g.:

بزرگ (صفت) + ی ← بزرگی (اسم)

بزرگ (صفت) + وار ← بزرگوار (صفت) + ی ← بزرگواری (اسم)

خشم (اسم) + گین ← خشمگین (صفت)

غم (اسم) + ناک ← غمناک(صفت)

مهر (اسم) + بان ← مهربان (صفت) + ی ← مهربانی (اسم)

جدول زیر را کامل کنید. سپس با استفاده از فرهنگ لغات، کلمات مرکب و مشتقات بیشتری به جدول اضافه کنید

صفت	اسم	فعل
نوشته	نویسنده	نوشتن
	خشم	

صفت	اسم	فعل
مکا تبه ای		
	تشنگی	
تصادفی		
	نوشتار	
	آشنایی	
باهوش		
		ترسیدن
		خسته بودن
دانا		

▇ Conjunctions   کلمـات ربط

Conjunctions are words that connect two words, two phrases, two clauses, two sentences, and even two paragraphs. Conjunctions include coordinate conjunctions (e.g. *and, but,* etc.), correlative conjunctions (e.g. *both ..... and . . . .; either ..... or .... ,* etc.), subordinate conjunctions (e.g. *when, if, because, since, so that,* etc.) and conjunctive adverbs (e.g. *however, furthermore, consequently,* etc.).

معنی کلمات ربطی را که زیرشان خط کشیده شده درفرهنگ لغات پیدا کنید و سپس جملات زیر را کامل کنید

من فارسی می خوانم <u>چون</u> . . . .

ایران نفت دارد <u>بنابراین</u> . . . .

<u>اگرچه</u> او را می شناسم . . . .

<u>علی رغم</u> مشکلا ت اقتصادی . . . .

امروز کار نمی کنم <u>لذا</u> . . . .

ایران کشوری غنی است <u>زیرا</u> . . . .

<u>با وجودیکه</u> خیلی درس خوانده بودم . . . .

واژگان این درس مشکل است <u>از اینرو</u> . . . .

بخاطر کم آبی در ایران .....
به دلیل بحران اقتصادی .....
من این فیلم را دیده ام ولی .....
می خواهم به ایران بروم تا .....
مستقیم برانید و بعد .....
من امروز خیلی کار دارم به علاوه .....
از مادرت بپرس که آیا .....
ویزایمان را گرفتیم اما .....
زبان فارسی از ریشهٔ هند و اروپائی است بر خلاف .....
در اشعار حافظ عشق به شیراز نمایان است چرا که .....
شهر یزد شهری کویری است به همین دلیل .....
آنقدر هوا گرم است که .....
امتحان نهایی نهایی بسیار مشکل بود با این وجود .....
تهران به سرعت رشد کرده است در صورتیکه .....
یاد گرفتن زبان فارسی آسان است به این دلیل که .....
من برای امتحان پایان ترم خیلی درس خوانده ام، با این وجود .....
علاوه بر .... ، من در کتابخانه دانشگاه هم بطور پاره وقت کار می کنم.

در شهر چه خبره؟

سفر

دارا: ما فردا می ریم ترکیه.
سیما: با قطار؟
دارا: نه با هواپیما. قطار خیلی طول می کشه.
سیما: چه ساعتی پرواز می کنین؟
دارا: ساعت نه صبح ولی باید هفت صبح فرودگاه باشیم.
سیما: ترمینال پروازای خارجی می رین یا پروازای داخلی؟
دارا: پروازای خارجی. باید عوارض فرودگاه رو هم بدیم.
سیما: می دونی هر نفر چند کیلو بار می تونه داشته باشه؟
دارا: نه ولی موقع تحویل بار می فهمم.
سیما: بله ولی اون موقع باید اضافه بار هم بدی!

این گفتگو را با کلمات زیر تمرین کنید

بدون توقف- پرواز یکسره/ یکطرفه- پرواز دوسره / دوطرفه - ورود- حرکت- گذرنامه- سالن ترانزیت- سفارت - ویزا

عامیانه colloquial	کتابی Literary
می ریم	می رویم
بدیم	بدهیم
بدی	بدهی
می کنین	می کنید
می رین	می روید
پروازا	پروازها
رو	را
داشته باشه	داشته باشد
طول می کشه	طول می کشد
می تونه	می تواند
می دونی	می دانی
اون	آن

جاهای خالی را پر کنید و بعد گفتگو را در گروهتان تمرین کنید

- سلام مینا جان. می توانم .... شما بپرسم که چرا به کانادا مهاجرت ....؟

- سلام داریوش جان. بله. بیشتر .... دلیل مشکلات اقتصادی و اجتماعی مجبور شدیم ایران را ترک.........

- دلتان بیشتر برای چه چیزی .... می شود؟

- من دلم بیشتر .... دوستانم تنگ می شود. با وجود مشکلات اقتصادی، مردم ایران هنوز مهربان ترین .... دنیا هستند.

- آیا قصد دارید روزی به ایران ....؟

- بله. امیدوارم بعد از بازنشسته ....، بتوانم به ایران برگردم. می خواهم یک خانه ی کوچک .... دریای خزر بخرم تا هرروز صبح با صدای موج .... و پرندگان دریایی از خواب بیدار ....

- چه رویای زیبایی!

نگارش: با استفاده از واژگان این درس و کلمات ربط، یک متن درباره ی مراسم ازدواج در کشورتان بنویسید و بعد در گروهتان درمورد آن بحث کنید.

درس پانزدهم

چرا آنقدر تعارف می کنید؟

Lesson Fifteen

چند جلد رمان فارسی

رمان نویسی نسبت به شعر در ایران قدمت چندانی ندارد. نویسندگان ایرانی در دورهٔ قاجار در قرن نوزدهم شروع به رمان نویسی کردند. در حال حاضر تعداد رمان نویسان ایرانی چه در خود ایران چه در غربت نسبت به سی سال پیش افزایش یافته است.

برای کسب اطلاعات بیشتر در مورد رمان فارسی در اینترنت جستجو کنید.

چرا آنقدر تعارف می کنید؟

Why do you stand on ceremony?

درس پانزدهم : چرا آنقدر تعارف می کنید؟
گفتگو : بوق
دستور: افعال سببی
مروری بر زمان ها
خواندن نمایشگاه کتاب
در شهر چه خبره؟ تعارف

Chapter aims
Grammar:

1. Causative verbs
2. Review of verb tenses

Situation:

1. At a book exhibit
2. ta'arof

واژگان

لغت	معنی انگلیسی	نقش دستوری	مثال
بوق	horn (of a car)	اسم	رانندگان ایرانی عادت به بوق زدن دارند.
مسیر	way; route	اسم	ببخشید مسیر شما کدام طرف است؟
تعمیرگاه	mechanic's; repairshop	اسم	باید ماشینم را به تعمیرگاه ببرم.
مخصوصاً	especially	قید	همهٔ شهر های ایران زیبا هستند مخصوصاً شهر های شمالی.
نمایشگاه کتاب	book fair	عبارت اسمی	نمایشگاه کتاب در این محل برگزار می شود.

درس پانزدهم ■ چرا آنقدر تعارف می کنید؟   167

مثال	نقش دستوری	معنی انگلیسی	لغت
از غرفهٔ صنایع دستی ایران دیدن کنید.	اسم	stand; stall	غرفه
شمار بازدید کنندگان به یک میلیون نفر رسید.	اسم	visitor	بازدید کننده (بازدید کنندگان)
محققان بسیاری دربارهٔ تاریخچهٔ زبان فارسی نوشته اند.	اسم	scholar	محقق (محققان)
کی به دیدار من می آیید؟	اسم	visit	دیدار
آیا به کتب علمی علاقه داری؟	عبارت اسمی	academic books	کتب علمی
قرار است کتب درسی عوض شوند.	عبارت اسمی	text books	کتب درسی
موضوع تز شما چیست؟	اسم	subject	موضوع (موضوعات)
نشریات داخلی و خارجی در این غرفه یافت می شوند.	اسم	journal; newsletter	نشریه (نشریات)
صنایع دستی اصفهان معروف است.	عبارت اسمی	handicrafts	صنایع دستی
نرخ پوند چند است؟	اسم	exchange rate	نرخ
از کجا می توانم ارز تهیه کنم؟	اسم	foreign currency	ارز
شرکت های دولتی از دولت یارانه دریافت می کنند.	صفت	state; government (adjective)	دولتی
سرگرمی او خیاطی است.	اسم	hobby	سرگرمی
خوابم نمی برد. احتیاج به قرص خواب دارم.	عبارت اسمی	sleeping pill	قرص خواب
از فیلم های ترسناک اصلاً خوشم نمی آید.	صفت	scary; frightening	ترسناک
یک ساعت طول کشید تا تکلیفم را بازنویسی کنم.	اسم مرکب	rewriting	بازنویسی
آیا چیزی برای نوشیدن میل دارید؟	فعل	to drink	نوشیدن (نوش)
بچه ها از تاریکی می ترسند.	فعل	to be scared	ترسیدن (ترس)
برای رسیدن به اهدافت باید خیلی تلاش کنی.	فعل	to achieve; to arrive at	رسیدن (رس) (به)
آب در ۱۰۰ درجه سانتیگراد می جوشد.	فعل	to boil (intransitive)	جوشیدن (جوش)
می شود لطفاً مرا به خانه ام برسانید؟	فعل	to give somebody a ride; to deliver sth.	رساندن (رسان)
آیا مایلید با هم قهوه بخوریم؟	فعل	to like to; to want to	مایل بودن

لغت	معنی انگلیسی	نقش دستوری	مثال
پیاده رفتن (رو)	to go on foot	فعل	من اخیراً پیاده سر کار می روم.
مطمئن بودن	to be sure	فعل	آیا مطمئنی که باران نمی آید؟
تعارف کردن (کن)	to be very polite; to stand on ceremony	فعل	ایرانیان عادت دارند زیاد تعارف کنند.
مزاحم شدن (شو)	to bother someone	فعل	ببخشید مزاحم شما شدم.
باور کردن (کن)	to believe	فعل	باور کنید راست می گویم.
تبدیل کردن (کن)	to exchange; to transform	فعل	کجا می توانم دلارهایم را تبدیل کنم؟
منتشر کردن (کن)	to publish	فعل	او کتابهای زیادی منتشر کرده است.
به نمایش گذاشتن (گذار)	to put on display	فعل	تعدادی از تابلوهایش را به نمایش گذاشت.
عرضه شدن (شو)	to be displayed	فعل	نشریات داخلی و خارجی در این فروشگاه عرضه می شوند.
حواس... بودن	to pay attention	فعل	حواست هست داری چه کار می کنی؟

گفتگو

بوق

آرمین: کجا می روی؟ من می رسانمت.
مهسا: نه. مایلم پیاده بروم. متشکرم.
آرمین: تعارف نکن! تو در مسیرم هستی.
مهسا: مطمئنی؟ مزاحمت نمی شوم؟
آرمین: نه. باور کن. خیلی هم خوشحال می شوم.
مهسا: بوق ماشینت مرا ترساند.
آرمین: خیلی معذرت می خواهم . باید ماشینم را به تعمیرگاه ببرم. صدای بوقش خیلی بلند است.
مهسا: دقیقاً. مخصوصاً اگر حواست نباشد و یک نفر پشتت سه بار بوق بزند!

درک مطلب

چرا آرمین می خواهد مهسا را برساند؟
چرا مهسا ترسید؟

ماشین آرمین چه مشکلی دارد؟

تعارف یعنی چه؟

بحث کنید و بنویسید

یک گفتگو بنویسید مانند گفتگوی بوق ولی در مورد یکی از خنده دارترین اتفاقاتی که برای شما پیش آمده است.

دستور

افعال سببی
■ Causative verbs

In causative constructions the subject causes the object to do something. Note the difference between the position of subject, object and verb in these sentences:

They laughed.   آنها خندیدند.
She made them laugh.   او آنها را خنداند.
The water boiled.   آب جوشید.
I boiled the water.   من آب را جوشاندم.

In Persian, to form causative verbs, the suffix اندن is often added to the present stem of the simple verb, e.g.:

ترسیدن ← ترس + اندن ← ترساندن
خوردن ← خور + اندن ← خوراندن
نوشیدن ← نوش + اندن ← نوشاندن
خوابیدن ← خواب + اندن ← خواباندن
جوشیدن ← جوش + اندن ← جوشاندن
پوشیدن ← پوش + اندن ← پوشاندن
خندیدن ← خند + اندن ← خنداندن

افعال جملات زیر را به افعال سببی تبدیل کنید و جملات را بازنویسی کنید

او از فیلمهای ترسناک می ترسد.

من با نصف قرص خواب می خوابم.

بچه ها از جوک های خنده دار خندیدند.

او روی صورتش روبنده می پوشد.

وقتی دخترم بچه بود روی زانوهایم می نشست.

خواندن

نمایشگاه کتاب

هر ساله در اردیبهشت ماه نمایشگاه بزرگ کتاب در تهران برگزار می شود. در این نمایشگاه کتابهای مختلفی از سراسر دنیا به نمایش گذاشته می شوند. دانشجویان و محققان بسیاری برای دیدار و خرید کتب علمی و درسی به این نمایشگاه می روند. کتابهای گوناگون بر اساس موضوع در غرفه های این نمایشگاه عرضه می شوند. نمایشگاه کتاب از نمایشگاه های دیگر، بازدید کنندگان بیشتری دارد. بجز کتاب، می توان نشریات و صنایع دستی نیز در این نمایشگاه خرید. دانشجویان می توانند کتابهای منتشر شده در کشور های غربی را با نرخ ارز پایین تر خریداری کنند. کتاب خواندن یکی از محبوب ترین سرگرمی های ایرانیان است.

درک مطلب

چه نوع کتاب هایی در نمایشگاه کتاب به نمایش گذاشته می شود؟
بجز کتاب چه چیزهای دیگری در این نمایشگاه فروخته می شود؟
چرا دانشجویان مایلند از این نمایشگاه کتاب بخرند؟
آیا در کشور شما این گونه نمایشگاه ها برگزار می شوند؟

مروری بر زمان ها ■ A review of verb tenses

Past[1]

1. **Simple past:** This tense is used to express an action completed in the past, which is often accompanied by a past time expression, e.g.:

دیروز به پارک رفتم.

I went to the park yesterday.

2. **Past progressive:** This tense is used to express an action that was in progress in the past when another action interrupted it, e.g.:

وقتی تو زنگ زدی من داشتم به پارک می رفتم.

I was going to the park when you called me.

---

[1] The verb tenses are reviewed here in the order they are presented in the book.

The past progressive is also used for past habitual actions, e.g.:

همیشه به آن کافه می رفتیم.

We always used to go to that café.

3. **Past perfect:** This tense is used when an action happened before another action in the past, e.g.:

قبل از اینکه تو زنگ بزنی من به پارک رفته بودم.

I had gone to the park before you called me.

Present

1. **Simple present:** The simple present is used when expressing the following:

    a. Habit

    I drink tea every morning.

من هر روزصبح چای می خورم.

    b. Fact

ایرانیان زیاد چای می خورند.

    Iranians drink tea a lot.

    c. Extended action

من هفت سال است که در منتریال زندگی می کنم.

    I have lived in Montreal for seven years.

2. **Present progressive:** This tense is used to express an action that is taking place at the moment of speaking, e.g.:

من دارم درس می خوانم.

I am studying.

3. **Present perfect:** This tense is used to express an action that took place in the past, but its effect has remained until now, e.g.:

من صبحانه خورده ام.

I have (already) eaten breakfast.

او این فیلم را سه بار دیده است.

He has seen this film three times.

Future

1. **Simple future:** This tense is often used to express an action in the future. In Persian, the simple present is commonly used to express a future action, e.g.:

امشب درس می خوانم.

I will study tonight.

2. **Formal or emphatic future:** There is another (less common) way of forming the future tense in Persian that is often more emphatic and which is more frequently used in the written language, e.g.:

تابستان به ایران خواهم رفت.

I will go to Iran in the summer.

او را هیچ وقت نخواهی دید.

You will never see him.

■ Subjunctive

1. **Present subjunctive:** The present subjunctive is used after certain verbs and expressions that variously indicate wish, desire, intent, obligation, doubt; e.g.:

شاید سال دیگر به ایران بروم.

I may go to Iran next year.

نمی توانم آن کار را بکنم.

I cannot do that.

قبل از اینکه بیایی تلفن بزن.

Call before you come.

2. Past subjective: The past subjunctive is used in the same way as the present subjunctive but for past actions; e.g.:

شاید به پارک رفته باشد.

He might have gone to the park.

باید رسیده باشند.

They must have arrived.

اگر دروغ گفته باشی،هرگز تو را نخواهم بخشید.

If you have lied, I will never forgive you.

جاهای خالی را با زمان مناسب فعل پر کنید

او هفته ی گذشته (هفته ی پیش) با دوستش به سینما .... (رفتن).

آنها دیروز ساعت چهارونیم تلویزیون .... (تماشا کردن).

من دیشب نام آن فیلم .... (یاد آمدن).

وقتی وارد کلاس شدم، او داشت درس سوم را .... (تدریس کردن).

من از برف .... (بد آمدن).

قبل از آنکه (پیش از آنکه) به ایران .... (رفتن)، خانه شان را خریده بودند.

بعد از آنکه (پس از آنکه) الفبای فارسی را .... (یاد گرفتن)، نوشتن آن را شروع کردید (شروع به نوشتن آن کردید).

ما هرروز در کافه تریا .... (ناهارخوردن).

تو خیلی .... (کارکردن).

او شلوار آبی .... (پوشیدن).

من زمان ها را چندین بار به شما .... (درس دادن).

ما هنوز اصفهان را .... (دیدن).

من از سال ۲۰۰۶ در مسکو .... (زندگی کردن).

من یک ماه دیگر کتاب را .... (تمام کردن).

تو در امتحان .... (قبول شدن).

تو می خواهی در امتحان .... (قبول شدن).

من باید کمتر .... (غذا خوردن).

باید بیشتر .... (درس خواندن).

شاید از کانادا .... (رفتن).

Lesson 15 ■ *Why do you stand on ceremony?* 174

ممکن است (که) شما را .... (شناختن).
غیرممکن است (که) شما را .... (شناختن) چون شما خیلی عوض شده اید.
شاید به مدرسه .... (رفتن).
شاید مریض .... (بودن).
باید از کلاس .... (رفتن) چون کیفش اینجا نیست.
اگر کتاب را .... (خواندن)، زمان ها را یاد می گیرید (یاد خواهید گرفت).
اگر کتاب را خوانده باشید، جواب ها را .... (دانستن).
اگر یک پرنده .... (بودن)، پرواز می کردم.
اگر شما را دیده بودم، .... (رفتن).
این کتاب باید .... (خواندن) چون داخلش خیلی یادداشت هست.
دانشجویان به هم .... (معرفی کردن) چون اسم همدیگر را می دانستند.
روزنامه ها هر روز (روزانه) .... (نوشتن).
کیک در یخچال است و هنوز توسط هیچ کسی .... (خوردن).
اگر پنجره ها .... (شکستن)، شما تنبیه می شدید.
امتحان توسط استاد .... (نوشتن).

در شهر چه خبره؟

تعارف

رضا: سلام شهلا خانوم. رضام.
شهلا: به! آقا رضا! قربون شما! همین الآن داشتم به شما و بابا فکر می کردم.
رضا: محبت دارین شما. آقای دکتر خوبن؟ با زحمتای ما چطورین؟ چقدر دیشب بهتون زحمت دادیم.
شهلا: اختیار دارین رضا جون. این حرفا چیه. چه زحمتی. لطف کردین تشریف آوردین. ما که از زیارت شما و آقای مهندس سیر نمی شیم.
رضا: شما محبت دارین. مهندس می خواس با آقای دکتر صحبت کنه. تشریف دارن؟
شهلا: بله. گوشی دستتون.
رضا: قربون شما. خدافظ.

این گفتگو را با کلمات زیر تمرین کنید

چشم شما روشن - چشم ما روشن- پیشکش- قابلی ندارد- دست شما درد نکند- مبارک باشد- انشاالله. مرحمت فرمودید- مرحمت شما زیاد- نوش جان- امری نیست؟- خسته نباشید- سلامت باشید- خواهش میکنم- استدعا می کنم

عامیانه colloquial	کتابی literary
دارین	دارید
حرفا	حرفها
جون	جان
دستتون	دستتان
خانوم	خانم
بهشان	بهشان
بهتون	به شما
قربون	قربان
خوبن	خوب هستند
خوبین	خوبید
چطورین	چطورید
اختیار دارین	اختیار دارید
لطف کردین	لطف کردید
تشریف آوردین	تشریف آوردید
محبت دارین	محبت دارید
سیر نمی شیم	سیر نمی شویم
می خواس	می خواست
کنه	کند
داره	دارند
چیه	چیست
خدافظ	خداحافظ
رضام	رضا هستم
زحمتا	زحمتها

جاهای خالی را پر کنید و بعد گفتگو را در گروهتان تمرین کنید

– سلام امیر. دیروز به یک تئاتر کمدی رفتیم و بازیگران خیلی ما را ....

– سلام مانی. ما .... عکس شما به سینما رفتیم و مثل بیشتر فیلمهای ایرانی، غم انگیز بود و ما را ....

Lesson 15 ■ *Why do you stand on ceremony?* 176

– من از فیلمهایی که مرا می گریانند خوشم .... ولی از فیلمهایی که مرا بترسانند خیلی .... می آید.

– من از فیلمهای ترسناک اصلاً لذت نمی برم چون وقتی بچه بودم پدرم به زور مرا کنار خود .... تا این جور فیلمها را ببینیم.

– پس خاطره ی خوبی از فیلمهای .... نداری؟

– نه به هیچ وجه!

نگارش: با استفاده از واژگان این درس یک متن درمورد کتاب و کتاب خوانی و بطور کلی صنعت کتاب بنویسید. سپس آن را در گروهتان مطرح نمایید.

واژگان (به ترتیب الفبای فارسی)

Persian–English Glossary

آب	water
آب میوه	fruit juice
آباد	habitable; populated, flourishing
آبلیمو	lemon juice
آبی	blue
آتش	fire
آتش بازی	fireworks
آثار باستانی	ancient ruins or artifacts
آجیل	nuts
آخ	ouch
آخر	last; end
آخر هفته	weekend
آخرین	last
آداب	customs; traditions
آدم	human; person
آرامگاه	tomb
آرد	flour
آرزو داشتن (دار)	to wish
آزادی	freedom
آسان	easy
آسایش	comfort
آسیا	Asia

Persian–English Glossary   178

acquaintance	آشنا
to become acquainted with	آشنا شدن (شو) با
Africa	آفریقا
Mr; gentleman	آقا (آقایان)
Germany	آلمان
German	آلمانی
pollution	آلودگی
air pollution	آلودگی هوا
to prepare	آماده کردن (کن)
statistics	آمار
injection	آمپول
America	آمریکا
that	آن
there	آنجا
so much/many . . . that	آنقدر .... که ....
those; they	آنها
iron	آهن
song	آواز
to bring	آوردن (آور)
hanging (adj.)	آویزان
future	آینده
mirror	آیینه
firstly; beginning	ابتدا
eternity	ابد
not at all	ابداً
eyebrow	ابرو
room	اتاق
event	اتفاق (اتفاقات)
actually	اتفاقاً
to iron	اتو کردن (کن)

bus	اتوبوس
autobiography	اتوبیوگرافی
furniture	اثاث (اثاثیه)
to allow	اجازه دادن (ده)
to have permission to	اجازه داشتن (دار)
stove	اجاق
to respect	احترام گذاشتن (گذار)
to be probable	احتمال داشتن (دار)
need	احتیاج (احتیاجات)
feeling	احساس (احساسات)
invention	اختراع (اختراعات)
manners; morals	اخلاق
latest; most recent	اخیر
lately; recently	اخیراً
to continue	ادامه دادن (ده)
continuing education; further education	ادامۀ تحصیل
literature	ادبیات
foreign currency	ارز
cheap	ارزان
Armenian	ارمنی (ارامنه)
Europe	اروپا
to destroy	از بین بردن (بر)
over	از روی
on behalf of	از طرف
through, via	از طریق
marriage	ازدواج
family marriage (where the bride and groom's families are related)	ازدواج فامیلی
that is why	ازینرو
horse	اسب

moving house	اسباب کشی
Spain	اسپانیا
professor	استاد (استادان)
province	استان
oppression	استبداد
exception	استثناء
reasoning	استدلال
to use	استفاده کردن (کن)
banknote	اسکناس
skiing	اسکی
Islam	اسلام
Islamic Studies	اسلام شناسی
first name	اسم
Esfahan (a city in central Iran)	اصفهان
not at all	اصلاً
main	اصلی
excess baggage	اضافه بار
to be added	اضافه شدن (شو)
to add	اضافه کردن (کن)
information	اطلاعات
to inform	اطلاع دادن
to trust	اطمینان کردن (کن) به
to believe in	اعتقاد داشتن (دار) به
to have confidence in	اعتماد داشتن (دار) به
to rely upon	اعتماد کردن (کن) به
to announce	اعلان کردن (کن)
mostly	اغلب
to fall	افتادن (افت)
to be proud of	افتخار کردن (کن)
to increase	افزایش یافتن (یاب)

officer	افسر
economics	اقتصاد
economic	اقتصادی
religious minority	اقلیت مذهبی
relatives	اقوام
ocean	اقیانوس
most	اکثر
if	اگر
now	الآن
of course	البته
Alborz (mountain range north of Tehran)	البرز
required; necessary	الزامی
alphabet	الفبا
but; although	اما
Emirates	امارات
local shrine	امامزاده
end of semester exam	امتحان پایان ترم
to take an exam	امتحان دادن (ده)
driving test	امتحان رانندگی
nationwide examination	امتحان سراسری
oral exam	امتحان شفاهی
written exam	امتحان کتبی
to test; to try	امتحان کردن (کن)
to give an exam	امتحان گرفتن (گیر)
mid-semester exam	امتحان میان ترم
final exam	امتحان نهایی
issue; matter	امر (امور)
a good deed	امر خیر
today	امروز
this year	امسال

Persian–English Glossary   182

tonight	امشب
to sign	امضاء کردن (کن)
to be possible	امکان داشتن (دار)
omelette	املت
security	امنیت
to hope	امیدوار بودن
pomegranate	انار
to choose	انتخاب کردن (کن)
to carry out; to perform	انجام دادن (ده)
size	اندازه
human	انسان
revolution	انقلاب
revolutionary	انقلابی (انقلابیون)
finger	انگشت (انگشتان)
England	انگلیس
grapes	انگور
he; she	او
first	اول
First	اولین
state	ایالت (ایالات)
Italy	ایتالیا
idea	ایده
ancient Iran	ایران باستان
Persian Empire; the pre-modern Iranian world	ایران زمین
Iranian Studies	ایران شناسی
to stop; to stand	ایستادن (ایست)
this	این
here	اینجا
together	با هم
O my God!	بابا جان!

stand; stall	باجه
almond	بادام
aubergine (egg plant)	بادمجان
pregnant	باردار
to open	باز کردن (کن)
visitor	بازدید کننده
retired	بازنشسته
rewriting	بازنویسی
arm	بازو (بازوان)
game	بازی
to play	بازی کردن (کن)
actor/actress	بازیگر
ancient	باستان
gym	باشگاه، ورزشگاه
garden	باغ (باغات)
finally	بالاخره
funny; cute	بامزه
bank	بانک
clever	باهوش
despite the fact that	باوجودیکه
to believe	باور کردن (کن)
must	باید
childhood	بچگی
child; baby	بچه
taking care of children	بچه داری
crisis	بحران
heater; radiator	بخاری
for the sake of	بخاطر
section	بخش
to forgive; to bestow	بخشیدن (بخش)

bad	بد
to have a bad time	بد گذشتن (گذر) به
unlucky (e.g. number)	بد یمن
to dislike	بد . . . آمدن (آ) از
worse	بدتر
worst	بدترین
body building	بدنسازی
non-stop	بدون توقف
equal	برابر
brother	برادر
based on	براساس
for	برای
price tag	برچسب قیمت
unlike	برخلاف
withdrawal	برداشت
to pick up	برداشتن (دار)
Brazil	برزیل
to snow	برف آمدن (آ)
to snow	برف باریدن (بار)
to set up	برقرار کردن (کن)
leaf	برگ
to be held	برگزار شدن (شو)
to return	برگشتن (گرد)
programme plan; schedule	برنامه
rice (uncooked)	برنج
to cut	بریدن (بر)
goat	بز
to close; to tie	بستن (بند)
ice cream	بستنی
very	بسیار

all right; OK	بسیار خوب
human beings; man	بشر
plate	بشقاب
bottle	بطری
after	بعد
afternoon	بعد از ظهر
afterwards	بعداً
some	بعضی
sometimes	بعضی وقت ها
as	بعنوان
beside; right next to	بغل
to know how to; to know (e.g. languages)	بلد بودن
high; loud	بلند
ticket	بلیت
on this basis; therefore	بنابراین
historical buildings	بناهای تاریخی
port	بندر (بنادر)
in addition to	به اضافهٔ
that's why	به این دلیل
to set on fire	به آتش کشیدن (کش)
to finish something	به پایان بردن (بر)
to be published	به چاپ رسیدن (رس)
to wear on one's hand	به دست کردن (کن)
because of; due to	به دلیل
to come after someone	به دنبال کسی آمدن (آ)
to be born	به دنیا آمدن (آ)
by force	به زور
to come to an end	به سر رسیدن (رس)
quickly	به سرعت
as	به صورت

Persian–English Glossary

in addition to	به علاوه
to be on someone's shoulders	به عهد ﺓ کسی بودن
except for	به غیر از
to suit someone	به کسی آمدن (آ)
on time	به موقع
rarely	به ندرت
to put on display	به نمایش گذاشتن (گذار)
together with	به همراه
for that very reason	به همین دلیل
not at all	به هیچ وجه
to remember	به یاد داشتن (دار)
Baha'i	بهائی (بهائیان)
spring	بهار
better	بهتر
best	بهترین
large Muslim cemetery in South Tehran	بهشت زهرا
without	بدون
kiss	بوسه
horn (of a car)	بوق
illiteracy	بی سوادی
meaningless	بی معنی
unique	بی نظیر
awake	بیدار
to wake up	بیدار شدن (شو)
outside	بیرون
innumerable	بیشمار
between	بین
nose	بینی
biography	بیوگرافی
footache	پا درد

king	پادشاه
paragraph	پاراگراف
last year	پارسال
park	پارک
part-time	پاره وقت
passport	پاسپورت
answer	پاسخ
to answer	پاسخ دادن (ده)
envelope	پاکت
Pakistan	پاکستان
winter coat	پالتو
end	پایان
capital city	پایتخت
to cook	پختن (پز)
father	پدر
grandfather	پدربزرگ
to be admitted	پذیرفته شدن (شو)
feather	پَر
full	پُر
dark-coloured	پر رنگ
to fill	پر کردن (کن)
flag	پرچم
to adore; to worship	پرستیدن (پرست)
bird	پرنده (پرندگان)
seagull	پرنده دریایی
return flight	پرواز دوسره /دوطرفه
to fly	پرواز کردن (کن)
one-way flight	پرواز یکسره / یطرفه
international flights	پروازهای خارجی
domestic flights	پروازهای داخلی

Persian–English Glossary 188

butterfly	پروانه
to jump	پریدن (پر)
the day before yesterday	پریروز
withered	پژمرده
medicine	پزشکی
after	پس از
the day after tomorrow	پس فردا
surface mail	پست زمینی
registered mail	پست سفارشی
airmail	پست هوایی
post office	پستخانه
boy; son	پسر
cousin (maternal uncle's son)	پسر دایی
cousin (maternal aunt's son)	پسرخاله
cousin (paternal aunt's son)	پسرعمه
cousin (paternal uncle's son)	پسرعمو
behind	پشت
bridge	پل
house number	پلاک
rice (cooked)	پلو
police	پلیس
Thursday	پنج شنبه
window	پنجره
puncture	پنچر
to be hidden	پنهان شدن (شو)
cheese	پنیر
champion	پهلوان
to wear	پوشیدن (پوش)
money	پول
pound sterling	پوند

to go on foot	پیاده رفتن (رو)
prophet	پیامبر
screw; bend (in the road)	پیچ
to twist; to turn (in a car)	پیچیدن (پیچ)
to find	پیدا کردن (کن)
old (of people)	پیر
the year before last	پیرارسال
victorious	پیروز
to follow, to abide by	پیروی کردن (کن)
old age	پیری
ski piste	پیست اسکی
before	پیش از
pre-university college	پیش دانشگاهی
preschool	پیش دبستانی
in advance	پیشاپیش
developed; advanced	پیشرفته
to recommend	پیشنهاد کردن (کن)
background	پیشینه
theatre	تئاتر
until; so that	تا
so far	تا بحال
summer	تابستان
painting; sign	تابلو
crown	تاج
to play the tar	تارزدن (زن)
history	تاریخ
historical	تاریخی
darkness	تاریکی
fresh	تازه
taxi	تاکسی

Thai	تایلندی
to establish	تأسیس کردن (کن)
to confirm	تأیید کردن (کن)
fever	تب
to exchange; to transform	تبدیل کردن (کن)
to study	تحصیل کردن (کن)
education; studies	تحصیلات
graduate studies	تحصیلات عالی
to tolerate; to put up with	تحمل کردن (کن)
airport check-in desk	تحویل بار
to submit; to hand in	تحویل دادن (ده)
Persepolis	تخت جمشید
bed	تخت خواب
discount	تخفیف
to get a discount	تخفیف گرفتن (گیر)
egg	تخم مرغ
dried melon seeds	تخمه
to teach	تدریس کردن
wet	تر
physical education	تربیت بدنی
to prefer	ترجیح دادن (ده)
mourning ceremony	ترحیم
to frighten someone	ترساندن (ترسان)
scary; frightening	ترسناک
to be scared	ترسیدن (ترس)
pickles	ترشی (ترشیجات)
to leave; to abandon	ترک کردن (کن)
Turkish	ترکی
Turkey	ترکیه
term, semester	ترم

terminal	ترمینال
assassination	ترور
thesis	تز
to decorate	تزئین کردن (کن)
to encourage	تشویق کردن (کن)
to imagine	تصور کردن (کن)
demonstration	تظاهرات
to be very polite	تعارف کردن (کن)
to be surprised	تعجب کردن (کن)
number; quantity	تعداد
to recount; to speak highly of	تعریف کردن (کن)
closed (temporarily); pl. holidays	تعطیل (تعطیلات)
teaching; tenet	تعلیم (تعالیم)
mechanic's	تعمیرگاه
changing the oil in a car	تعویض روغن
to change something	تغییر دادن (ده)
fun; entertainment	تفریح (تفریحات)
way of thinking; mentality	تفکر (تفکرات)
approximately	تقریباً
to divide	تقسیم کردن (کن)
to cheat	تقلب کردن (کن)
to imitate	تقلید کردن (کن)
assignment; homework	تکلیف (تکالیف)
to strive	تلاش کردن (کن)
bitter	تلخ
telephone	تلفن
to phone	تلفن زدن (زن)
TV	تلویزیون
to watch	تماشا کردن (کن)
whole; all	تمام

to finish	تمام کردن (کن)
full-time	تمام وقت
stamp	تمبر
civilization	تمدن
to practice	تمرین کردن (کن)
lazy	تنبل
to punish	تنبیه کردن
spicy; quick	تند
statue	تندیس
to prepare	تهیه کردن (کن)
you (informal sing.)	تو
ability	توانایی
to be able	توانستن (توان)
ball	توپ
berry	توت
mulberry	توت سفید
by; by means of	توسط
to explain	توضیح دادن (ده)
birth; birthday	تولد
Happy birthday!	تولدت مبارک!
toman (ten rials)	تومان
blade	تیغ
team	تیم
second	ثانیه
record	ثبت
to register	ثبت نام کردن (کن)
a third	ثلث
broom	جارو
to vacuum; to sweep the floor	جارو کردن (کن)
interesting	جالب

sociology	جامعه شناسی
to die	جان خود را از دست دادن (ده)
ancestor	جد (اجداد)
to become separated	جدا شدن (شو)
new	جدید
to attract; to absorb	جذب کردن (کن)
partial; particular	جزئی
to search	جستجو کردن (کن)
celebration	جشن
to celebrate	جشن گرفتن (گیر)
box	جعبه
geography	جغرافیا
pair	جفت
volume (of a series of books)	جلد
meeting	جلسه (جلسات)
in front of	جلو
to gather	جمع شدن (شو)
Friday	جمعه
sentence	جمله (جملات)
Sir (used before a name to show respect)	جناب
gender; pl. goods	جنس (اجناس)
war	جنگ
The Imposed War (the Iran-Iraq War)	جنگ تحمیلی
south	جنوب
world	جهان
tourist	جهانگرد
effort	جهد
young; young person	جوان
chivalrous	جوانمرد
chick	جوجه

Persian–English Glossary · 194

to boil (intransitive)	جوشیدن (جوش)
joke	جوک
pocket (adjective)	جیبی
to be published	چاپ شدن (شو)
knife	چاقو
to bargain	چانه زدن (زن)
teahouse	چایخانه
left	چپ
umbrella	چتر
why?	چرا؟
lamp	چراغ
traffic light	چراغ راهنمایی
since; because	چرا که
greasy	چرب
to stick something	چسباندن (چسبان)
eye	چشم (چشمان)
how; in what way	چطور
beetroot	چغندر
how much	چقدر
cheque	چک
travellers' cheque	چک پول
how	چگونه
rice and kebab	چلوکباب
suitcase	چمدان
lawn	چمن
several	چند
what day of the week?	چند شنبه؟
so much; so	چندان
fork	چنگال
what	چه

in what way; what type of	چه جور
what	چه چیزی
who	چه کسی
both . . . and . . . ; whether ..... or	چه ... چه ...
crossroads	چهارراه
Wednesday	چهارشنبه
last Tuesday night of the year	چهارشنبه سوری
since, because	چون
because	چونکه
to set (a table); to pluck (a flower)	چیدن (چین)
thing	چیز
to have something on someone	چیزی همراه کسی بودن
Chinese	چینی
Hafiz (celebrated 14th-century poet)	حافظ
the "present tense or time; state, condition"	حال
state of being	حال (احوال)
nausea	حالت تهوع
pulses	حبوبات
definitely	حتماً
even	حتی
Hajj (pilgrimage to Mecca)	حج
hijab, veil	حجاب
at least	حداقل
at most	حداکثر
approximately; around	حدوداً
letter (of the alphabet)	حرف (حروف)
to speak	حرف زدن (زن)
swear word	حرف زشت
movement	حرکت
savings account	حساب پس انداز

Persian–English Glossary

current account	حساب جاری
a title used before the names of prophets or of very respected individuals	حضرت
fence	حفاظ
preservation	حفظ
to memorize	حفظ کردن
salary; law (the subject); rights	حق (حقوق)
wedding ring	حلقه
halva	حلوا
epic	حماسه
to pay attention	حواس کسی بودن
patience	حوصله
pool (in a courtyard)	حوض
towel	حوله
yard	حیاط
outside; abroad	خارج
foreign; pl. memoirs	خارجی
memory	خاطره (خاطرات)
dust; earth	خاک
mole; beauty spot	خال
pure	خالص
maternal aunt	خاله
to empty	خالی کردن (کن)
raw; immature	خام
important family; dynasty	خاندان
Mrs; Ms; Miss; lady; wife	خانم
house	خانه
housewife	خانه دار
housework	خانه داری
Middle East	خاورمیانه

news	خبر
news agency	خبرگزاری
goodbye	خداحافظ
God	خداوند
service	خدمت (خدمات)
broken; ruined; spoilt	خراب
to break into small pieces	خرد کردن (کن)
dates	خرما
shopping	خرید
to shop	خرید کردن (کن)
buyer; customer	خریدار
to buy	خریدن (خر)
reptile	خزنده (خزندگان)
to make tired	خسته کردن (کن)
stingy	خسیس
to dry sth	خشک کردن (کن)
rough; violent	خشن
particular characteristic	خصوصیت (خصوصیات)
line; handwriting; style of calligraphy	خط (خطوط)
calligraphy	خطاطی
danger	خطر (خطرات)
dangerous	خطرناک
summary	خلاصه
pilot	خلبان
to make someone laugh	خنداندن
to burst into laughter	خنده. . . گرفتن (گیر)
funny	خنده دار
to feel sleepy	خواب . . . آمدن (آ)
to fall asleep	خواب . . . بردن (بر)
to sleep	خوابیدن (خواب)

asking for a woman's hand in marriage	خواستگاری
to want	خواستن (خواه)
to study; to read; to recite; to sing	خواندن (خوان)
singer; reader	خواننده (خوانندگان)
sister	خواهر
well; good	خوب
self; own	خود
biro	خودکار
to eat	خوردن (خور)
stew	خورش
nice; happy	خوش
to like	خوش . . . آمدن (آ) از
to have a good time	خوش گذشتن (گذر) به
Lucky you!	خوشا به حالتان!
physically fit	خوش اندام
fortunate	خوشبخت
happy	خوشحال
Pleased to meet you!	خوشوقتم!
bleeding	خونریزی
street; avenue	خیابان
cucumber	خیار
sewing	خیاطی
very; many	خیلی
a kind of traditional Iranian puppet theatre	خیمه شب بازی
encyclopaedia	دائرة المعارف = دانشنامه
inside	داخل
affluent; possessing	دارا
to have	دارا بودن
story	داستان
to have	داشتن (دار)

wise	دانا
to know something	دانستن (دان)
university student	دانشجو (دانشجویان)
university	دانشگاه
state university	دانشگاه دولتی
correspondence university	دانشگاه مکاتبه ای
a grain of something (e.g. rice)	دانه
dinosaur	دایناسور
maternal uncle	دایی
primary school	دبستان
high school	دبیرستان
girl; daughter	دختر
cousin (maternal aunt's daughter)	دختر خاله
cousin (maternal uncle's daughter)	دختر دایی
cousin (paternal aunt's daughter)	دختر عمه
cousin (paternal uncle's daughter)	دختر عمو
in	در
to fail	در . . . رد شدن (شو)
to pass	در . . . قبول شدن (شو)
during	در طیِ
about	در موردِ
to discuss something (with someone)	در میان گذاشتن (گذار) با
about	دربارهٔ
can-opener	دربازکن
class; degree; level	درجه
tree	درخت (درختان)
to be painful	درد کردن (کن)
lesson	درس (دروس)
to study	درس خواندن (خوان)
to teach	درس دادن (ده)

right; correct	درست
to make	درست کردن (کن)
percent	درصد
whereas	درصورتیکه
to take into account	درنظر گرفتن (گیر)
greeting; Hello	درود
to lie	دروغ گفتن (گو)
sea	دریا
lake	دریاچه
to receive	دریافت کردن (کن)
thief	دزد
to steal	دزدیدن (دزد)
fortress	دژ
hand	دست (دستان)
cooking	دست پخت
generous	دست و دل باز
piece of machinery; appliance	دستگاه
bouquet of flowers	دسته گل
order; command	دستور (دستورات)
enemy	دشمن
to invite	دعوت کردن (کن)
office; notebook	دفتر (دفاتر)
next time	دفعهٔ بعد
to pay particular attention	دقت کردن (کن)
minute	دقیقه (دقایق)
heart; stomach	دل
to miss someone	دل تنگ شدن (شو)
toothache	دندان درد
dentist	دندانپزشک
village	ده (دهات)

ten times	ده برابر
decade	دهه
medicine	دوا
bicycle	دوچرخه
cycling	دوچرخه سواری
around	دور
far	دور
period	دوران
to like	دوست داشتن (دار)
Monday	دوشنبه
government	دولت (دول)
state; government (adjective)	دولتی
high school diploma	دیپلم
visit	دیدار
to see	دیدن (بین)
to visit	دیدن کردن (کن)
sights	دیدنی ها
eye	دیده (دیدگان)
late	دیر
yesterday	دیروز
last night	دیشب
religion	دین (ادیان)
demon	دیو
sweetcorn	ذرت
to be mentioned	ذکر شدن (شو)
president	رئیس جمهور
regarding	راجع به
to tell the truth; to be right	راست گفتن (گو)
driving	رانندگی
to drive	رانندگی کردن (کن)

driver	راننده
path; way; road	راه
to set off	راه افتادن (افت)
junior high school	راهنمایی
widespread; common	رایج
a quarter	ربع
rank	رتبه
to give somebody a ride	رساندن (رسان)
media outlets	رسانه ها
restaurant	رستوران
custom	رسم (رسوم)
formal, official	رسمی
to achieve; to arrive at	رسیدن (رس) به
field of study	رشته
to grow	رشد کردن (کن)
observance	رعایت
to abide by	رعایت کردن (کن)
behaviour	رفتار
novel	رمان
colour	رنگ
fox	روباه
face veil	روبنده
cleric	روحانی (روحانیون)
day	روز
newspaper	روزنامه
journalist	روزنامه نگار
village	روستا
headscarf	روسری
Russian language	روسی
Russia	روسیه

to turn on	روشن کردن (کن)
oil	روغن
olive oil	روغن زیتون
over; on	روی
dream	رویا
presidency	ریاست جمهوری
to spill; to pour	ریختن
tiny; fine	ریز
root	ریشه
language	زبان
linguistics	زبان شناسی
to hit	زدن
Zoroastrian	زرتشتی (زرتشتیان)
yellow	زرد
barberry	زرشک
ugly	زشت
to fall over	زمین خوردن (خور)
woman; wife	زن
to live	زندگی کردن (کن)
to survive	زنده ماندن (مان)
to phone	زنگ زدن (زن)
a married couple; an even number	زوج
beautiful	زیبا
beauty	زیبایی
under; below	زیر
because	زیرا
to live	زیستن (زی)
Japan	ژاپن
Japanese	ژاپنی
dew	ژاله

to ask	سؤال کردن (کن)
building	ساختمان
to build	ساختن (ساز)
simple	ساده
hour; o'clock; watch	ساعت (ساعات)
when (at what time)	ساعت چند
year	سال
salad	سالاد
transit hall	سالن ترانزیت
screening (of a film)	سانس
green	سبز
vegetable	سبزی (سبزیجات)
style	سبک
armed guard	سپاهی
shield	سپر
long-term savings account	سپرده بلند مدت
short-term savings account	سپرده کوتاه مدت
then; afterwards	سپس
star	ستاره (ستارگان)
hard; difficult	سخت
word	سخن (سخنان)
speech	سخنرانی
to give a speech	سخنرانی کردن (کن)
all over the world	سراسر دنیا
soldier	سرباز
to feel cold	سرد . . . بودن
headache	سردرد
land	سرزمین
whenever possible (i.e. there's no rush)	سرفرصت
theft	سرقت

to steal	سرقت کردن (کن)
to go to work	سرکار رفتن (رو)
vinegar	سرکه
hobby	سرگرمی
having a cold	سرما خوردگی
destiny	سرنوشت
cypress	سرو
to be engaged in	سروکارداشتن با (دار)
quick	سریع
to try; to attempt	سعی کردن (کن)
embassy	سفارت
to travel	سفرکردن (کن)
table cloth	سفره
Haft Sin (Noruz table setting)	سفره هفت سین
white	سفید
coin	سکه
dog	سگ
hello	سلام
health	سلامتی
dynasty	سلسله
royal	سلطنتی
taste (aesthetic)	سلیقه
sumac	سماق
on the left	سمت چپ
on the right	سمت راست
age	سن (سنین)
traditional	سنتی
Tuesday	سه شنبه
supermarket	سوپر مارکت
question	سؤال (سؤالات)

Persian–English Glossary

CD	سی دی
black	سیاه
potato	سیب زمینی
chip; fried potato	سیب زمینی سرخ کرده
noun, garlic; adjective full (with food)	سیر
circus	سیرک
educational system	سیستم آموزشی
to smoke	سیگارکشیدن (کش)
cinema	سینما
cheerful	شاد
poet	شاعر (شعرا)
dinner; evening meal	شام
shah	شاه
maybe; perhaps	شاید
common; widespread	شایع
dignity; matter	شأن (شئون)
night; evening	شب
Good night!	شب بخیر!
similar to	شبیه
brave	شجاع
conditions; circumstances	شرایط
sherbet	شربت
biography	شرح حال
to explain	شرح دادن (ده)
east	شرق
company	شرکت
to participate in	شرکت کردن (کن) در
to begin (intransitive)	شروع شدن (شو)
to begin (transitive)	شروع کردن (کن)
noble	شریف

to wash	شستن (شوی)
chess	شطرنج
poem; poetry	شعر (اشعار)
profession; job	شغل
oral	شفاهی
to doubt	شک داشتن (دار)
sugar	شکر
shape, look, appearance; form	شکل
blossom	شکوفه
loose	شل
a kind of traditional rice pudding	شله زرد
trousers	شلوار
jeans	شلوار جین
busy; crowded	شلوغ
you (plural; formal singular)	شما
number (amount)	شمار
north	شمال
candle	شمع
to know	شناختن (شناس)
Saturday	شنبه
to hear	شنیدن (شنو)
city; town	شهر
tuition fee	شهریه
martyr	شهید (شهدا)
salty	شور
rioter	شورشی
husband	شوهر
milk	شیر
Shiraz (a city in Iran)	شیراز
sweet	شیرین

Persian–English Glossary   **208**

sweet pastries	شیرینی
morning	صبح
Good morning!	صبح بخیر!
breakfast	صبحانه
to speak	صحبت کردن (کن)
desert; plain	صحرا
correct	صحیح
hundreds	صد
voice; sound	صدا
shell	صدف
line; queue	صف (صفوف)
handicrafts	صنایع دستی
chair	صندلی
armchair	صندلی راحتی
PO Box	صندوق پستی
industry	صنعت (صنایع)
to take place	صورت گرفتن (گیر)
confiscation; retention	ضبط
tape recorder	ضبط صوت
to record	ضبط کردن (کن)
a kind of drum	ضرب
harm	ضرر
pronoun	ضمیر
according to; in accordance with	طبق
floor; level	طبقه (طبقات)
tabla	طبل
countryside; nature	طبیعت
natural	طبیعی
plan	طرح
side	طرف (اطراف)

fan, supporter	طرفدار
gold	طلا (طلاجات)
divorce	طلاق
Muslim seminary student	طلبه (طلاب)
satire	طنز
satirical	طنزگونه
parrot	طوطی
stormy	طوفانی
to last	طول کشیدن (کش)
dish	ظرف (ظروف)
within a few hours	ظرف چند ساعت
victory	ظفر
noon	ظهر
habit	عادت
fair	عادلانه
in love; lover	عاشق
phrase	عبارت (عبارات)
amazing	عجب
hurry; haste	عجله
strange	عجیب
number	عدد (اعداد)
number	عده
Arabia	عربستان
Arabic	عربی
to be displayed	عرضه شدن (شو)
bride	عروس
wedding	عروسی
angry	عصبانی
late afternoon	عصر
Good afternoon!	عصر بخیر!

Persian–English Glossary 210

afternoon snack	عصرانه
muscle	عضله
great; magnificent	عظیم
to marry	عقد کردن (کن)
opinion; belief	عقیده
photo	عکس
interested	علاقمند
to be interested in	علاقه داشتن (دار) به
in addition	علاوه بر این
political science	علوم سیاسی
despite	علی رغم
to act; to operate	عمل کردن (کن)
practically	عملاً
paternal aunt	عمه
paternal uncle	عمو
public	عمومی
deep	عمیق
airport taxes	عوارض فرودگاه
to change	عوض کردن (کن)
gift given at Noruz	عیدی
glasses	عینک
cave	غار
absent	غایب
double chin	غبغب
west	غرب
western; westerner	غربی
stand; stall	غرفه
sunset	غروب
sad (things)	غم انگیز
sad (people)	غمگین

rich	غنی
civilian	غیر نظامی (غیر نظامیان)
graduate	فارغ التحصیل
distance	فاصله
last name	فامیلی
to arrive	فرا رسیدن (رس)
to flee; to escape	فرار کردن (کن)
to forget	فراموش کردن (کن)
France	فرانسه
abundant	فراوان
odd number	فرد
person; individual	فرد (افراد)
tomorrow	فردا
to send	فرستادن (فرست)
sender	فرستنده
carpet	فرش
difference	فرق
to change (intransitive)	فرق کردن (کن)
form	فرم
culture; dictionary	فرهنگ
to sell	فروختن (فروش)
airport	فرودگاه
shop	فروشگاه
seller	فروشنده
a stew made with chicken, pomegranate syrup, and walnuts	فسنجان
blood pressure	فشارخون
season; chapter	فصل (فصول)
current; present	فعلی
only	فقط

thought	فکر (افکار)
philosophy	فلسفه
to die	فوت کردن (کن)
football	فوتبال
film	فیلم
film script	فیلمنامه
mushroom	قارچ
continent	قاره
spoon	قاشق
judge	قاضی
law; rule	قانون (قوانین)
civil law	قانون مدنی
Cyprus	قبرس
graveyard	قبرستان
bill; note	قبض (قبوض)
BC	قبل از میلاد
before	قبل از اینکه
previously; already	قبلاً
to be accepted; to pass (an exam)	قبول شدن (شو)
power	قدرت
age (ancientness); antiquity	قدمت
old (of things)	قدیمی
to be arranged	قرار بودن
to be located	قرار داشتن (دار)
pill	قرص
sleeping pill	قرص خواب
red	قرمز
century	قرن (قرون)
beautiful	قشنگ
to intend to	قصد داشتن (دار)

train	قطار
North Pole	قطب شمال
drop (e.g., eyedrop)	قطره (قطرات)
lock	قفل
heart	قلب (قلوب)
canary	قناری
cube sugar	قند
hero	قهرمان
a stew made with red meat and herbs	قورمه سبزی
can	قوطی
to promise	قول دادن (ده)
strong	قوی
price	قیمت
fixed price	قیمت مقطوع
a stew made with red meat and split peas	قیمه
palace	کاخ
work	کار
to work	کار کردن (کن)
identity card	کارت شناسایی
employee	کارمند
paper	کاغذ
enough	کافی
computer	کامپیوتر
completely	کاملاً
Canada	کانادا
to reduce (intransitive)	کاهش پیدا کردن (کن)
kebab made from lamb or beef steak	کباب برگ
kebab made from lamb or beef mince	کباب کوبیده
dove; pigeon	کبوتر
great	کبیر

capsule	کپسول
copy	کپی
textbook	کتاب درسی (کتب درسی)
academic book	کتاب علمی (کتب علمی)
library; bookcase	کتابخانه
written	کتبی
kettle	کتری
inscription	کتیبه
multiplicity	کثرت
crooked	کج
where	کجا
Where are you from?	کجایی هستید؟
bald	کچل
which	کدام
celery	کرفس
butter	کره
Christmas	کریسمس
to receive	کسب کردن (کن)
to kill	کشتن (کش)
ship	کشتی
wrestling	کُشتی
wrestler	کشتی گیر
country	کشور
shoe	کفش
high-heel shoes	کفش پاشنه بلند
shroud	کفن
all	کل
class	کلاس
exhausted	کلافه

واژگان (به ترتیب الفبای فارسی)   215

hat	کلاه
key	کلید
church	کلیسا
water shortage	کم آبی
light-coloured	کم رنگ
bow	کمان
cupboard	کمد
seat belt	کمربند ایمنی
backache	کمردرد
help	کمک
to ask for help	کمک خواستن (خواه)
to help	کمک کردن (کن)
beside	کنار
concert	کنسرت
conference; lecture	کنفرانس
university entrance examination	کنکور
old	کهن
short, low	کوتاه
alley	کوچه
mountain	کوه
mountain climbing	کوه نوردی
desert (adj)	کویری
when	کی
who	کی
bag; handbag	کیف
kilo	کیلو
sometimes	گاهی
chalk	گچ
to let, to put	گذاشتن (گذار)

Persian–English Glossary 216

passport	گذرنامه
to pass	گذشتن (گذر)
past	گذشته
expensive	گران
to dust	گردگیری کردن (کن)
walnut	گردو
to get; to take; to hold	گرفتن (گیر)
to feel hot	گرم . . . بودن
group	گروه
to make someone cry	گریاندن
to cry	گریه کردن (کن)
to burst into tears	گریه . . . گرفتن (گیر)
a kind of nougat	گز
report	گزارش
to report	گزارش کردن (کن)
to search for; to become	گشتن (گرد)
conversation; dialogue	گفتگو
to say; to tell	گفتن (گو)
flower	گل
throat	گلو
lost	گم
to lose	گم کردن (کن)
treasure	گنج
sparrow	گنجشک
calf, veal	گوساله
polo ball	گوی
receiver; addressee	گیرنده
necessary	لازم
spare tyre	لاستیک زاپاس

thin	لاغر
brag	لاف
tulip	لاله
lip	لب
clothes	لباس
moment	لحظه (لحظات)
that's why	لذا
to enjoy	لذت بردن (بر) از
delicious	لذیذ
please	لطفاً
word	لغت (لغات)
encyclopaedia	لغتنامه
stork	لک لک
accent	لهجه
Polish	لهستانی
tablet (i.e. of stone)	لوح (الواح)
spoiled (person)	لوس
bath sponge	لیف
we	ما
mother	مادر
grandmother	مادربزرگ
snake	مار
yoghurt	ماست
Wow! (lit. What God wills)	ماشاء الله
car	ماشین
possession	مال (اموال)
financial	مالی
to stay	ماندن (مان)
stale (e.g. bread)	مانده

Persian–English Glossary 218

month; moon	ماه
monthly	ماهیانه
liquid	مایع (مایعات)
to like to; to want to	مایل بودن
blessed	مبارک
sofa	مبل
amount of money	مبلغ (مبالغ)
unfortunately	متأسفانه
married	متأهل
common	متداول
metro; subway	مترو
Thank you	متشکرم
different	متفاوت
text	متن (متون)
varied; diverse	متنوع
to realise	متوجه شدن (شو)
example	مثال
like	مثل
triangle	مثلث
free	مجانی
to be forced to; to have to	مجبور بودن
single	مجرد
majestic	مجلل
collection; complex	مجموعه
kindness; love	محبت
beloved	محبوب
modest	محجوب
student	محصل (محصلین)
protected; secure	محفوظ
scholar	محقق (محققین)

free (in terms of will)	مختار
brief	مختصر
different; varied	مختلف
especially	مخصوصاً
pencil	مداد
help	مدد
school	مدرسه (مدارس)
management	مدیریت
ceremonies; rituals	مراسم
to keep an eye on	مراقبت کردن (کن)
to pertain to	مربوط بودن به
patriarchy	مردسالاری
people	مردم
anthropology	مردم شناسی
dead	مرده
border	مرز
thanks	مرسی
chicken	مرغ
centre	مرکز (مراکز)
death	مرگ
ill	مریض
to bother someone	مزاحم شدن (شو)
farm	مزرعه
eyelash	مژه (مژگان)
copper	مس
competition; match	مسابقه (مسابقات)
running race	مسابقه دو
to travel	مسافرت رفتن (رو)
inn; motel	مسافرخانه
problem; issue	مسأله (مسائل)

straight; straight on	مستقیم
mosque	مسجد (مساجد)
Friday or congregational mosque	مسجد جامع
Muslim	مسلمان
to brush one's teeth	مسواک زدن (زن)
Christ	مسیح
Christian	مسیحی (مسیحیان)
way; route	مسیر
busy	مشغول
homework; calligraphic exercises	مشق
problem	مشکل (مشکلات)
problematic; difficult	مشکل ساز
suspicious	مشکوک
Egypt	مصر
Egyptian	مصری
contents	مضمون
studies	مطالعات
Islamic Studies	مطالعات اسلامی
topic	مطلب (مطالب)
to be sure	مطمئن بودن
manifestation	مظهر (مظاهر)
miracle	معجزه (معجزات)
smoothie	معجون
stomach ache	معده درد
to apologize to	معذرت خواستن (خواه) از
to introduce	معرفی کردن (کن)
famous, well-known	معروف
teacher	معلم (معلمین)
architecture	معماری
usual; customary	معمول

usually	معمولاً
meaning	معنی (معانی)
shop	مغازه
article; essay	مقاله (مقالات)
to compare	مقایسه کردن (کن)
tomb	مقبره (مقابر)
an amount of	مقداری
to consider at fault	مقصر دانستن (دان)
correspondence	مکاتبه (مکاتبات)
place	مکان (اماکن)
Mexico	مکزیک
Mecca	مکه
nation; people	ملت (ملل)
locust	ملخ
national	ملی
possible	ممکن
forbidden	ممنوع
thanks; grateful	ممنون
I	من
natural resources	منابع طبیعی
appropriate	مناسب
to publish	منتشر کردن (کن)
home	منزل (منازل)
secretary	منشی
orderly; organized	منظم
prohibition	منع
wave	موج
to emigrate	مهاجرت کردن (کن)
kindness	مهر
kind	مهربان

important	مهم
guest	مهمان
party	مهمانی
engineer	مهندس (مهندسین)
electrical engineer	مهندس الترونیک
construction engineer	مهندس ساختمان
chemical engineer	مهندس شیمی
civil engineer	مهندس عمران
mechanical engineer	مهندس مکانیک
engineering	مهندسی
hair	مو
to be careful	مواظب بودن
to agree	موافق بودن
to agree	موافقت کردن (کن)
motorcycle	موتور
to be the centre of attention	مورد توجه بودن
favourite	مورد علاقه
museum	موزه
music	موسیقی
pop music	موسیقی پاپ
traditional (Iranian) music	موسیقی سنتی
mouse; rat	موش
topic; subject	موضوع (موضوعات)
to succeed	موفق شدن (شو)
time; moment	موقع (مواقع)
wax	موم
average	میانگین
nail	میخ
town square; roundabout	میدان (میادین)
not to give up	میدان را خالی نکردن

table	میز
desk	میز تحریر
to want to	میل داشتن
million	میلیون
monkey	میمون
fruit	میوه (میوجات)
to be upset	ناراحت شدن (شو)
penetrating	نافذ
suddenly	ناگهان
name	نام
to mention	نام بردن (بر)
to be nominated	نامزد شدن (شو)
engagement	نامزدی
letter	نامه
bread	نان
lunch	ناهار
must not	نباید
result	نتیجه (نتایج)
prime minister	نخست وزیر
palm tree	نخل
exchange rate	نرخ
narcissus	نرگس
near	نزدیک
compared to	نسبت به
copy	نسخه
breeze	نسیم
to show	نشان دادن (ده)
to make someone sit	نشاندن
journal; newsletter	نشریه (نشریات)
to sit	نشستن (نشین)

half	نصف
military	نظامی
opinion	نظر (نظرات)
oil	نفت
person (counting word)	نفر
painting	نقاشی
cash	نقد
map	نقشه
look	نگاه
to look at	نگاه کردن (کن)
worry	نگرانی
to keep	نگه داشتن (دار)
damp	نم
to pray (the obligatory prayer)	نماز خواندن (خوان)
visible	نمایان
exhibition; fair	نمایشگاه
book fair	نمایشگاه کتاب
representative	نماینده (نمایندگان)
number	نمره
salt	نمک
new	نو
Noruz (Iranian New Year)	نوروز
soft drink	نوشابه
to write	نوشتن (نویس)
to drink	نوشیدن (نوش)
kind; type	نوع (انواع)
grandchild	نوه
writer	نویسنده (نویسندگان)
whale	نهنگ
to need	نیاز داشتن (دار)

half	نیم
midnight	نیمه شب
fried egg	نیمرو
bench	نیمکت
course unit	واحد
to enter	وارد شدن (شو)
to deposit	واریز کردن (کن)
word	واژه (واژگان)
existence	وجود
to exist	وجود داشتن (دار)
sport	ورزش
entry	ورود
middle	وسط
extensive	وسیع
means of transport	وسیلهٔ نقلیه
home country	وطن
time	وقت (اوقات)
to make an appointment	وقت گرفتن (گیر)
when	وقتی که
lawyer; member of parliament	وکیل (وکلا)
if not	وگرنه
but	ولی
shop window	ویترین
to get a visa	ویزا گرفتن (گیر)
special	ویژه
emigration; hijra	هجرت
Achaemenid	هخامنشی
never	هرگز
crescent	هلال
peach	هلو

Persian–English Glossary 226

each other	همدیگر
India	هندوستان
Indian	هندی
art	هنر
at the time of	هنگام
still; yet	هنوز
weather	هوا
airplane	هواپیما
nowhere	هیچ جا
no one	هیچ کس
never	هیچ وقت
memory; remembrance	یاد
to teach	یاد دادن
to learn	یاد گرفتن
note (written)	یادداشت
fridge	یخچال
same	یکسان
Sunday	یکشنبه
one-way	یکطرفه
unique	یگانه
Jew	یهودی (یهودیان)
Greece	یونان

واژگان (به ترتیب الفبای انگلیسی)

English–Persian Glossary

ability	توانایی
about	در مورد؛ دربارهٔ
absent	غایب
abundant	فراوان
accent	لهجه
according to; in accordance with	طبقِ
Achaemenid	هخامنشی
acquaintance	آشنا
actor/actress	بازیگر
actually	اتفاقاً
affluent; possessing	دارا
Africa	آفریقا
after	بعد؛ پس از؛ بعد از
afternoon	بعد از ظهر
afternoon snack	عصرانه
afterwards	بعداً
age	سن (سنین)
age (ancientness)	قدمت
air pollution	آلودگی هوا
airmail	پست هوایی
airplane	هواپیما
airport	فرودگاه

English–Persian Glossary 228

airport taxes	عوارض فرودگاه
all	کل
all over the world	سراسر دنیا
all right; OK	بسیار خوب
alley	کوچه
almond	بادام
alphabet	الفبا
America	آمریکا
amount	مقدار
amount of money	مبلغ (مبالغ)
ancestor	جد (اجداد)
ancient	باستان
ancient ruins	آثار باستانی
angry	عصبانی
answer	پاسخ؛ جواب
anthropology	مردم شناس
appropriate	مناسب
approximately	تقریباً؛ حدوداً
Arabia	عربستان
Arabic	عربی
architecture	معماری
arm	بازو (بازوان)
armchair	صندلی راحتی
armed guard	سپاهی
Armenian	ارمنی (ارامنه)
around	دور
art	هنر
article; essay	مقاله (مقالات)
as	بعنوان
Asia	آسیا

assassination	ترور
assignment; homework	تکلیف (تکالیف)
at least	حداقل
at most	حداکثر
aubergine (egg plant)	بادمجان
aunt (maternal)	خاله
aunt (paternal)	عمه
autobiography	اتوبیوگرافی
average	میانگین
awake	بیدار
backache	کمردرد
background	پیشینه
bad	بد
bag; handbag	کیف
Baha'i	بهائی (بهائیان)
bald	کچل
ball	توپ
bank	بانک
banknote	اسکناس
barberry	زرشک
based on	براساس
bath sponge	لیف
BC	قبل از میلاد
beautiful	زیبا
beautiful (of things)	قشنگ
beauty	زیبایی
because	چونکه
because	زیرا
because of; due to	به دلیل
bed	تخت خواب

beetroot	چغندر
before	پیش از قبل از (اینکه)
behaviour	رفتار
behind	پشتِ
beloved	محبوب
bench	نیمکت
berry	توت
beside	کنار
beside; right next to	بغل
best	بهترین
better	بهتر
between	بین
bicycle	دوچرخه
bill; slip (of paper)	قبض
biography	بیوگرافی؛ شرح حال
bird	پرنده (پرندگان)
biro	خودکار
birth; birthday	تولد
bitter	تلخ
black	سیاه
blade	تیغ
bleeding	خونریزی
blood	خون
blood pressure	فشارخون
blossom	شکوفه
blue	آبی
body building	بدنسازی
book fair	نمایشگاه کتاب
border	مرز

bottle	بطری
bouquet of flowers	دسته گل
bow	کمان
box	جعبه
boy; son	پسر
brag	لاف
brave	شجاع
Brazil	برزیل
bread	نان
breakfast	صبحانه
breeze	نسیم
bride	عروس
bridge	پل
brief	مختصر
broken; ruined; spoilt	خراب
broom	جارو
brother	برادر
building	ساختمان
bus	اتوبوس
busy (crowded)	شلوغ
busy (occupied)	مشغول
but	ولی ؛ اما
butter	کره
butterfly	پروانه
buyer; customer	خریدار
by; by means of	توسطِ
by force	به زور
calf; veal	گوساله
calligraphy	خطاطی

English–Persian Glossary 232

can	قوطی
Canada	کانادا
canary	قناری
candle	شمع
can-opener	دربازکن
capital city	پایتخت
capsule	کپسول
car	ماشین
carpet	فرش
cash	نقد
cave	غار
CD	سی دی
celebration; festival	جشن
celery	کرفس
centre	مرکز (مراکز)
century	قرن (قرون)
ceremonies; rituals	مراسم
chair	صندلی
chalk	گچ
champion (i.e. in wrestling)	پهلوان
cheap	ارزان
cheerful	شاد
cheese	پنیر
chemical engineer	مهندس شیمی
cheque	چک
chess	شطرنج
chick	جوجه
chicken	مرغ
child; baby	بچه

childhood	بچگی
Chinese	چینی
chip; fried potato	سیب زمینی سرخ کرده
chivalrous	جوانمرد
Christ	مسیح
Christian	مسیحی (مسیحیان)
Christmas	کریسمس
church	کلیسا
cinema	سینما
circus	سیرک
city; town	شهر
civil engineer	مهندس عمران
civil law	قانون مدنی
civilian (i.e. non-military)	غیر نظامی (غیر نظامیان)
civilization	تمدن
class	کلاس
class; degree; level	درجه
cleric	روحانی (روحانیون)
clever	باهوش
closed (temporarily); pl. holidays	تعطیل (تعطیلات)
clothes	لباس
coin	سکه
cold (temperature)	سرد
cold (illness)	سرما
collection	مجموعه
colour	رنگ
comfort; ease	آسایش
common	شایع؛ متداول، رایج
company	شرکت

English–Persian Glossary   234

compared to	نسبت به
competition; match	مسابقه (مسابقات)
completely	کاملاً
computer	کامپیوتر
concert	کنسرت
conditions; circumstances	شرایط
conference; lecture	کنفرانس
confiscation; retention	ضبط
construction engineer	مهندس ساختمان
contents	مضمون
continent	قاره
continuing education	ادامهٔ تحصیل
conversation; dialogue	گفتگو
cooking	آشپزی
copper	مس
copy	کپی، نسخه
correct	صحیح
correspondence	مکاتبه (مکاتبات)
country	کشور
countryside; nature	طبیعت
course unit	واحد
cousin (maternal aunt's daughter)	دختر خاله
cousin (maternal aunt's son)	پسر خاله
cousin (maternal uncle's daughter)	دختر دایی
cousin (maternal uncle's son)	پسر دایی
cousin (paternal aunt's daughter)	دختر عمه
cousin (paternal aunt's son)	پسر عمه
cousin (paternal uncle's daughter)	دختر عمو
cousin (paternal uncle's son)	پسر عمو
crescent	هلال

crisis	بحران
crooked	کج
crossroads	چهارراه
crown	تاج
cube sugar	قند
cucumber	خیار
culture; dictionary	فرهنگ
cupboard	کمد
current account	حساب جاری
current; present	فعلی
custom	رسم (رسوم)
customs; traditions	آداب
cycling	دوچرخه سواری
cypress tree	سرو
Cyprus	قبرس
damp	نم
danger	خطر
dangerous	خطرناک
dark-coloured	پر رنگ
darkness	تاریکی
dates	خرما
day	روز
dead	مرده
death	مرگ
decade	دهه
deep	عمیق
definitely	حتماً
delicious	لذیذ
demon	دیو
demonstration	تظاهرات

English–Persian Glossary 236

dentist	دندانپزشک
desert	کویر؛ صحرا
desk	میز تحریر
despite	علی رغم
despite the fact that	با وجودیکه
destiny	سرنوشت
developed	پیشرفته
dew	ژاله
difference	فرق
different; varied	متفاوت؛ مختلف
dignity; matter	شأن
dinner	شام
dinosaur	دایناسور
discount	تخفیف
dish	ظرف (ظروف)
distance	فاصله
divorce	طلاق
dog	سگ
double chin	غبغب
dove; pigeon	کبوتر
dream	رویا
dried melon seeds	تخمه
driver	راننده
driving	رانندگی
driving test	امتحان رانندگی
drop	قطره (قطرات)
during	در طیِ
dust; earth	خاک
dynasty	سلسله
each other	همدیگر

east	شرق
easy	آسان
economic	اقتصادی
economics	اقتصاد
education; studies	تحصیلات
educational system	سیستم آموزشی
effort	جهد
egg	تخم مرغ
Egypt	مصر
Egyptian	مصری
electrical engineer	مهندس الکترونیک
embassy	سفارت
emigration; hijra	هجرت
Emirates	امارات
employee	کارمند
encyclopaedia	دائرة المعارف؛ دانشنامه
end	پایان
enemy	دشمن
engagement	نامزدی
engineer	مهندس (مهندسین)
engineering	مهندسی
England	انگلیس؛ انگلستان
enough	کافی
entry	ورود
envelope	پاکت
epic	حماسه
equal	برابر
especially	مخصوصاً
eternity	ابد
Europe	اروپا

English–Persian Glossary

even	حتی
event	اتفاق (اتفاقات)
exam	امتحان
example	مثال
except for	به غیر از به جز
exception	استثناء
excess baggage	اضافه بار
exchange rate	نرخ
exhausted	کلافه
exhibition; fair	نمایشگاه
exile; diaspora	غربت
existence	وجود
expensive	گران
extensive	وسیع
eye	چشم (چشمان) ؛ دیده (دیدگان)
eyebrow	ابرو (ابروان)
eyelash	مژه (مژگان)
fair	عادلانه
family	خانواده؛ فامیل
family name; surname	نام خانوادگی؛ فامیلی
famous; well-known	معروف
fan; supporter	طرفدار
far	دور
farm	مزرعه (مزارع)
father	پدر
favourite	مورد علاقه
feather	پر
feeling	احساس (احساسات)
fence	حفاظ
fever	تب

field of study	رشته
film	فیلم
film script	فیلمنامه
final exam	امتحان نهایی
finally	بالاخره
financial	مالی
finger	انگشت (انگشتان)
fire	آتش
fireworks	آتش بازی
first	اول؛ اولین
first name	اسم، نام
firstly; beginning	ابتدا
fixed price	قیمت مقطوع
flag	پرچم
floor; level	طبقه
flour	آرد
flower	گل
footache	پا درد
football	فوتبال
for	برای
forbidden	ممنوع
foreign	خارجی
foreign currency	ارز
fork	چنگال
form	فرم
formal, official	رسمی
fortress	دژ؛ قلعه
fortunate	خوشبخت
fox	روباه
France	فرانسه

English–Persian Glossary

free	مجانی
free (in terms of will)	مختار
freedom	آزادی
fresh	تازه
Friday	جمعه
Friday or congregational mosque	مسجد جامع
fridge	یخچال
fried egg	نیمرو
fruit	میوه (میوجات)
fruit juice	آب میوه
full	پر
full-time	تمام وقت
fun; entertainment	تفریح (تفریحات)
funny	خنده دار؛ بامزه
furniture	اثاث (اثاثیه)
future	آینده
game	بازی
garden	باغ (باغات)
garlic; (noun) (adj.) full (with food)	سیر
generous	دست و دل باز
geography	جغرافیا
German	آلمانی
Germany	آلمان
gift	کادو؛ هدیه
girl; daughter	دختر
glasses	عینک
goat	بز
God	خداوند؛ خدا
gold	طلا (طلاجات)
Good afternoon! (late afternoon)	عصر بخیر!

Goodbye!	خداحافظ!
Good morning!	صبح بخیر!
Good night!	شب بخیر!
goods	اجناس
government; state	دولت (دول)
graduate	فارغ التحصیل
graduate studies	تحصیلات عالی
grandchild	نوه
grandfather	پدربزرگ
grandmother	مادربزرگ
grapes	انگور
graveyard	قبرستان
greasy	چرب
great; magnificent	کبیر ؛ عظیم
Greece	یونان
green	سبز
greeting	درود
group	گروه
guest	مهمان
gym	باشگاه، ورزشگاه
habit	عادت (عادات)
habitable; populated	آباد
hair	مو
Hajj (pilgrimage to Mecca)	حجّ
half	نصف ؛ نیم
halva	حلوا
hand	دست (دستان)
handicrafts	صنایع دستی
hanging (adj.)	آویزان
happy	خوشحال

English	Persian
Happy birthday!	تولدت مبارک!
hard; difficult	سخت
harm	ضرر
hat	کلاه
he; she	او
headache	سردرد
headscarf	روسری
health	سلامتی
heart; stomach	قلب؛ دل
heater; radiator	بخاری
hello	سلام
help	مدد؛ کمک
here	اینجا
hero	قهرمان
high school	دبیرستان
high school diploma	دیپلم
high; tall; loud	بلند
high-heel shoes	کفش پاشنه بلند
hijab; veil	حجاب
historical	تاریخی
history	تاریخ
hobby	سرگرمی
home; house	خانه؛ منزل (منازل)
homeland	وطن
homework; calligraphic exercises	مشق
horn (of a car)	بوق
horse	اسب
hour; watch	ساعت (ساعات)
house number	پلاک
housewife	خانه دار

housework	خانه داری
how	چگونه
how many	چند
how much	چقدر
how; in what way	چطور
human	انسان
human beings	بشر
human; person	آدم
hundred	صد
hurry; haste	عجله
husband	شوهر
I	من
ice cream	بستنی
idea	ایده
identity card	کارت شناسایی
if	اگر
if not	وگرنه
ill	مریض؛ بیمار
illiteracy	بی سوادی
illness	مریضی؛ بیماری
important	مهم
in	در
in addition to	به اضافۀ؛ به علاوه
in advance	پیشاپیش
in front of	جلو
India	هندوستان
Indian	هندی
industry	صنعت (صنایع)
information	اطلاعات
injection	آمپول

English–Persian Glossary

inn; motel	مسافرخانه
innumerable	بیشمار
inscription	کتیبه
inside	داخل
interested	علاقمند
interesting	جالب
international	بین المللی
invention	اختراع (اختراعات)
Iranian Studies	ایران شناسی
iron	آهن
Islam	اسلام
Islamic Studies	مطالعات اسلامی، اسلام شناسی
issue; matter	امر (امور)
Italy	ایتالیا
Japan	ژاپن
Japanese	ژاپنی
jeans	شلوار جین
Jew	یهودی (یهودیان)
joke	جوک
journal; newsletter	نشریه (نشریات)
journalist	روزنامه نگار
judge	قاضی
junior high school	راهنمایی
kebab	کباب
kettle	کتری
key	کلید
kilo	کیلو
kind	مهربان
kind; type	نوع (انواع)
kindness	مهر؛ مهربانی؛ محبت

king	پادشاه
kiss	بوسه
knife	چاقو؛ کارد
lake	دریاچه
lamp; light	چراغ
land	سرزمین
language	زبان
last	آخر؛ آخرین
last name	فامیلی
last night	دیشب
last year	پارسال
late	دیر
late afternoon	عصر
lately	اخیراً
latest; most recent	اخیر
law; rule	قانون (قوانین)
lawn	چمن
lawyer; member of parliament	وکیل (وکلا)
lazy	تنبل
leaf	برگ
left	چپ
lemon	لیمو
lesson	درس (دروس)
letter	نامه
letter (of the alphabet)	حرف (حروف)
library; bookcase	کتابخانه
light-coloured	کم رنگ
like; similar to	مثلِ؛ شبیهِ
line; handwriting; style of calligraphy	خط (خطوط)
line; queue	صف (صفوف)

linguistics	زبان شناسی
lip	لب
liquid	مایع (مایعات)
literature	ادبیات
local	محلی
lock	قفل
locust	ملخ
look	نگاه
loose	شل
lost	گم
love	عشق
lover; in love	عاشق
lunch	ناهار
majestic	مجلل
main	اصلی
management	مدیریت
manifestation	مظهر
manners; morals	اخلاق
map	نقشه
marriage	ازدواج
married	متأهل
martyr	شهید (شهدا)
maybe; perhaps	شاید
meaning	معنی (معانی)
meaningless	بی معنی
Mecca	مکه
mechanic	تعمیرگاه
mechanical engineer	مهندس مکانیک
media outlets	رسانه ها
medicine	دارو، پزشکی

meeting	جلسه (جلسات)
memory	خاطره (خاطرات)
memory; remembrance	یاد
metro	مترو
Mexico	مکزیک
middle	وسط
Middle East	خاورمیانه
midnight	نیمه شب
mid-semester exam	امتحان میان ترم
military	نظامی
milk	شیر
million	میلیون
minute	دقیقه (دقایق)
miracle	معجزه (معجزات)
mirror	آیینه
modest	محجوب
mole; beauty spot	خال
moment	لحظه (لحظات)
Monday	دوشنبه
money	پول
monkey	میمون
month; moon	ماه
monthly	ماهیانه
morning	صبح
mosque	مسجد (مساجد)
most	اکثر
mostly	اغلب
mother	مادر
motorcycle	موتور
mountain	کوه

English–Persian Glossary   248

mountain climbing	کوه نوردی
mouse; rat	موش
movement	حرکت
moving house	اسباب کشی
Mr.; gentleman	آقا (آقایان)
Mrs; Ms; Miss; lady; wife	خانم
mulberry	توت
multiplicity	کثرت
muscle	عضله (عضلات)
museum	موزه
mushroom	قارچ
music	موسیقی
Muslim	مسلمان (مسلمانان)
Muslim seminary student	طلبه (طلاب)
must	باید
must not	نباید
nail	میخ
name	نام
narcissus	نرگس
nation; people	ملت (ملل)
national	ملی
natural	طبیعی
natural resources	منابع طبیعی
nausea	حالت تهوع
near	نزدیک
necessary	لازم
need	احتیاج (احتیاجات)
never	هیچ وقت؛ هرگز
nevertheless	با وجود این
new	جدید؛ نو

news	خبر
news agency	خبرگزاری
newspaper	روزنامه
next	بعد؛ بعدی
nice; happy	خوش
night; evening	شب
no one	هیچ کس
noble	شریف
non-stop	بدون توقف
noon	ظهر
north	شمال
north pole	قطب شمال
Noruz (Iranian New Year)	نوروز
nose	بینی
not at all	ابداً، اصلاً، به هیچ وجه
note (written)	یادداشت
novel	رمان
now	الآن
nowhere	هیچ جا
number	عدد (اعداد) ؛ نمره ؛ شماره
number (e.g. a number of people)	عده
number; quantity	تعداد
nuts	آجیل
observance	رعایت
ocean	اقیانوس
odd (number)	فرد
of course	البته
office	دفتر (دفاتر)
officer	افسر
oil (e.g. cooking oil)	روغن

English–Persian Glossary 250

oil (e.g. crude oil)	نفت
old (of people)	پیر
old age	پیری
old; ancient (of things)	کهن؛ قدیمی
olive oil	روغن زیتون
omelette	املت
on behalf of	از طرف
on the left	سمت چپ
on the right	سمت راست
on this basis; therefore	بنابراین
on time	به موقع؛ سر ساعت
one-way	یکطرفه
only	فقط
opinion; belief	نظر (نظرات) ؛ عقیده (عقاید)
oppression	استبداد؛ ظلم
oral exam	امتحان شفاهی
order; command; recipe	دستور (دستورات)
orderly; organized	منظم
ouch	آخ
outside	بیرون
outside; abroad	خارج
over; above	از روی
over; on	روی
painting	نقاشی
painting; sign	تابلو
pair	جفت
Pakistan	پاکستان
palace	کاخ
palm tree	نخل
paper	کاغذ

paragraph	پاراگراف
park	پارک
parrot	طوطی
part-time	پاره وقت
partial; particular	جزئی
particular characteristic	خصوصیت (خصوصیات)
party	مهمانی
passport	پاسپورت؛ گذرنامه
past	گذشته
path; way; road	راه
patience	حوصله
patriarchy	مردسالاری
peach	هلو
pencil	مداد
penetrating	نافذ
people	مردم
percent	درصد
period	دوران
Persepolis	تخت جمشید
person (counting word)	نفر
person; individual	فرد (افراد)
philosophy	فلسفه
photo	عکس
phrase	عبارت (عبارات)
physical education	تربیت بدنی
physically fit	خوش اندام
pickles	ترشی (ترشیجات)
piece of machinery; appliance	دستگاه
pill	قرص
pilot	خلبان

English–Persian Glossary 252

place	مکان
plan	طرح
plate	بشقاب
Please	لطفاً
Pleased to meet you!	خوشوقتم!
PO Box	صندوق پستی
pocket	جیب
poem; poetry	شعر (اشعار)
poet	شاعر (شعرا)
police	پلیس
Polish	لهستانی
political party	حزب (احزاب)
political science	علوم سیاسی
pollution	آلودگی
polo	چوگان
polo ball	گوی
pomegranate	انار
pool	حوض؛ استخر
pop music	موسیقی پاپ
port	بندر
possession	مال (اموال)
possibility	امان
possible	ممکن
post office	پستخانه
potato	سیب زمینی
pound sterling	پوند
power	قدرت
practically	عملاً
pregnant	باردار؛ حامله
pre-school	پیش دبستانی

present (time)	حال
preservation	حفظ
presidency	ریاست جمهوری
president	رئیس جمهور
pre-university college	پیش دانشگاهی
previously; already	قبلاً
price	قیمت
price tag	برچسب قیمت
primary school	دبستان
prime minister	نخست وزیر
probably	احتمالاً
problem	مشکل (مشکلات)
problem; issue	مسأله (مسائل)
problematic; difficult	مشکل ساز
profession; job	شغل
professor	استاد (استادان)
programme; plan; schedule	برنامه
prohibition	منع
pronoun	ضمیر
prophet	پیامبر؛ پیغمبر
protected; secure	محفوظ
province	استان
public	عمومی
pulses	حبوبات
puncture	پنچر
pure	خالص
a quarter	ربع
question	سؤال (سؤالات)؛ پرسش
quick	سریع
quickly	به سرعت

English–Persian Glossary

rank	رتبه
rarely	به ندرت
raw; immature	خام
reasoning	استدلال
receiver; addressee	گیرنده
record	ثبت
red	قرمز
regarding	راجع به
relatives	اقوام
religion	دین (ادیان)
religious minority	اقلیت مذهبی
report	گزارش
report to	گزارش کردن (کن)
representative	نماینده (نمایندگان)
reptile	خزنده (خزندگان)
required; necessary	الزامی
restaurant	رستوران
result	نتیجه (نتایج)
retired	بازنشسته
return flight	پرواز دوسره / دوطرفه
revolution	انقلاب
revolutionary	انقلابی (انقلابیون)
rewriting	بازنویسی
rice (cooked)	پلو
rice (uncooked)	برنج
rich	غنی؛ پولدار
right; correct	درست
rioter	شورشی (شورشیان)
room	اتاق
root	ریشه

rough; violent	خشن
royal	سلطنتی
running race	مسابقه دو
Russia	روسیه
Russian	روسی
sad (people)	غمگین
sad (things)	غم انگیز
salad	سالاد
salary; law (the subject); (pl.) rights	حق (حقوق)
salt	نمک
salty	شور
same	یکسان
satire	طنز
satirical	طنزگونه
Saturday	شنبه
savings account	حساب پس انداز
scary; frightening	ترسناک
scholar	محقق (محققین)
school	مدرسه (مدارس)
screening (of a film)	سانس
screw; bend (in the road)	پیچ
sea	دریا
seagull	پرنده دریایی
season; chapter	فصل (فصول)
seat belt	کمربند ایمنی
second (of time)	ثانیه
secretary	منشی
section; part	بخش
security	امنیت
self; own	خود

English–Persian Glossary 256

seller	فروشنده
sender	فرستنده
sentence	جمله (جملات)
service	خدمت (خدمات)
several	چندین
sewing	خیاطی
shah	شاه
shape; look; appearance; form	شکل
shell	صدف
sherbet	شربت
shield	سپر
ship	کشتی
shoe	کفش
shop	فروشگاه؛ مغازه؛ دکان
shop window	ویترین
shopping	خرید
short; low	کوتاه
shroud	کفن
side	طرف (اطراف)
sights	دیدنی ها
similar to	شبیه
simple	ساده
since; because	چون؛ چونکه
singer; reader	خواننده (خوانندگان)
single (i.e. unmarried)	مجرد
sister	خواهر
size	اندازه ؛ سایز
skiing	اسکی
sleep; dream	خواب
snake	مار

so far	تا بحال
so much/many. . .that	آنقدر .... که ....
so much; so	چندان
sociology	جامعه شناسی
sofa	مبل
soft drink	نوشابه
soldier	سرباز
some	بعضی؛ برخی
some of	بعضی از
sometimes	بعضی وقت ها؛ گاهی
song	آواز
south	جنوب
Spain	اسپانیا
sparrow	گنجشک
special	ویژه
special delivery	پست سفارشی
speech	سخنرانی
spicy	تند
spoiled (person) (adj.)	لوس
spoon	قاشق
sport	ورزش
spring	بهار
stamp	تمبر
stand; stall	غرفه؛ باجه
star	ستاره (ستارگان)
state (of being)	حال (احوال)
state; government (adj.)	دولتی
state	ایالت (ایالات)
statistics	آمار
statue	تندیس؛ مجسمه

English–Persian Glossary   258

stew	خورش
still; yet	هنوز
stingy	خسیس
stomach ache	معده درد
stork	لک لک
storm	طوفان
story	داستان
stove	اجاق
straight; straight on	مستقیم
strange	عجیب
street; avenue	خیابان
strong	قوی
student	محصل (محصلین)
studies	مطالعات
style	سبک
suddenly	ناگهان
sugar	شکر
suitcase	چمدان
summary	خلاصه
summer	تابستان
Sunday	یکشنبه
sunset	غروب
supermarket	سوپر مارکت
surface mail	پست زمینی
suspicious	مشکوک
swear word	حرف زشت
sweet	شیرین
sweet pastries	شیرینی
sweetcorn	ذرت
table	میز

table cloth	سفره
tape recorder	ضبط صوت
taste (aesthetic)	سلیقه
taxi	تاکسی
teacher	معلم (معلمین)
teaching; tenet	تعلیم (تعالیم)
teahouse	چایخانه
team	تیم
telephone	تلفن
term; semester	ترم
terminal	ترمینال
text	متن (متون)
textbook	کتاب درسی (کتب درسی)
Thai	تایلندی
Thank you	متشکرم
thanks	مرسی
thanks; grateful	ممنون
that	آن
that is why	ازینرو؛ به این دلیل؛ لذا
the day after tomorrow	پس فردا
the day before yesterday	پریروز
the present	حال
the year before last	پیرارسال
theatre	تئاتر
theft	سرقت
then; afterwards	سپس
there	آنجا
thesis	تز
thief	دزد
thin	لاغر

thing	چیز
a third	ثلث
this	این
this year	امسال
those; they	آنها
thought	فکر (افکار)
throat	گلو
through; via	از طریق
Thursday	پنج شنبه
ticket	بلیت
time	وقت (اوقات)
time; moment	موقع (مواقع)
tiny; fine	ریز
to abide by	رعایت کردن (کن)
to achieve; to arrive at	رسیدن (رس) به
to act; to operate	عمل کردن (کن)
to add	اضافه کردن (کن)
to adore; to worship	پرستیدن (پرست)
to agree	موافقت کردن (کن)
to agree (to be in agreement)	موافق بودن
to allow	اجازه دادن (ده)
to announce	اعلان کردن (کن)
to answer	پاسخ دادن (ده)
to apologize to	معذرت خواستن (خواه) از
to arrive	فرا رسیدن (رس)
to ask	سؤال کردن (کن)
to ask for help	کمک خواستن (خواه)
to attract; to absorb	جذب کردن (کن)
to bargain	چانه زدن (زن)
to be accepted; to pass (an exam)	قبول شدن (شو)

to be added	اضافه شدن (شو)
to be admitted	پذیرفته شدن (شو)
to be born	به دنیا آمدن (آ)
to be careful	مواظب بودن
to be displayed	عرضه شدن (شو)
to be engaged in	سر و کار داشتن (دار) با
to be forced to; to have to	مجبور بودن
to be held	برگزار شدن (شو)
to be hidden	پنهان شدن (شو)
to be interested in	علاقه داشتن (دار) به
to be located	قرار داشتن (دار)
to be mentioned	ذکر شدن (شو)
to be nominated	نامزد شدن (شو)
to be painful	درد کردن (کن)
to be persistent	میدان را خالی نکردن (کن)
to be proud of	افتخار کردن (کن)
to be published	چاپ شدن (شو)
to be scared	ترسیدن (ترس)
to be sure	مطمئن بودن
to be surprised	تعجب کردن (کن)
to be upset	ناراحت شدن (شو)
to become acquainted with	آشنا شدن (شو)
to become separated from	جدا شدن (شو)
to begin (transitive)	شروع کردن (کن)
to begin (intransitive)	شروع شدن (شو)
to believe	باور کردن (کن)
to believe in	اعتقاد داشتن (دار) به
to boil (intransitive)	جوشیدن (جوش)
to bother someone	مزاحم شدن (شو)
to break into small pieces	خرد کردن (کن)

English–Persian Glossary   **262**

to bring	آوردن (آور)
to brush one's teeth	مسواک زدن (زن)
to build	ساختن (ساز)
to burn something	به آتش کشیدن (کش)
to burst into laughter	خنده . . . گرفتن (گیر)
to burst into tears	گریه . . . گرفتن (گیر)
to buy	خریدن (خر)
to carry out; to perform	انجام دادن (ده)
to celebrate	جشن گرفتن (گیر)
to change	عوض کردن (کن)
to change (intransitive)	فرق کردن (کن)
to change something	تغییر دادن (ده)
to cheat	تقلب کرد ن (کن)
to choose	انتخاب کردن (کن)
to close; to tie	بستن (بند)
to come to an end	به سر رسیدن (رس)
to compare	مقایسه کردن (کن)
to confirm	تأیید کردن (کن)
to consider at fault	مقصر دانستن (دان)
to continue	ادامه دادن (ده)
to cook	پختن (پز)
to cry	گریه کردن (کن)
to cut	بریدن (بر)
to decorate	تزئین کردن (کن)
to deposit	واریز کردن (کن)
to destroy	از بین بردن (بر)
to die	جان خود را از دست دادن (ده)
to die	فوت کردن (کن)
to discuss something	در میان گذاشتن (گذار)
to dislike	بد . . . آمدن (آ) از

to divide	تقسیم کردن (کن)
to doubt	شک داشتن (دار)
to drink	نوشیدن (نوش)
to drive	رانندگی کردن (کن)
to dry something	خشک کردن (کن)
to dust	گردگیری کردن (کن)
to eat	خوردن (خور)
to emigrate	مهاجرت کردن (کن)
to empty	خالی کردن (کن)
to encourage	تشویق کردن (کن)
to enjoy	لذت بردن از (بر)
to enter	وارد شدن (شو)
to establish	تأسیس کردن (کن)
to exchange; to transform	تبدیل کردن (کن)
to exist	وجود داشتن (دار)
to explain	توضیح دادن (ده)
to explain	شرح دادن (ده)
to fail	در . . . رد شدن (شو)
to fall	افتادن (افت)
to fall asleep	خواب . . . بردن (بر)
to fall over	زمین خوردن (خور)
to feel cold	سرد . . . بودن
to feel hot	گرم . . . بودن
to fill	پر کردن (کن)
to find	پیدا کردن (کن)
to finish	تمام کردن (کن)
to finish something	به پایان بردن (بر)
to flee; to escape	فرار کردن (کن)
to fly	پرواز کردن (کن)
to follow someone	به دنبال کسی آمدن (آ)

English–Persian Glossary

to follow; to abide by	پیروی کردن (کن)
to forget	فراموش کردن (کن)
to forgive; to bestow	بخشیدن (بخش)
to frighten someone	ترساندن (ترسان)
to gather	جمع شدن (شو)
to get a discount	تخفیف گرفتن (گیر)
to get a visa	ویزا گرفتن (گیر)
to get; to take; to hold	گرفتن (گیر)
to give a speech	سخنرانی کردن (کن)
to give somebody a ride	رساندن (رسان)
to go on foot	پیاده رفتن (رو)
to go to work	سرکار رفتن (رو)
to grow	رشد کردن (کن)
to have	داشتن (دار)
to have a bad time	بد گذشتن (گذر) به
to have a good time	خوش گذشتن (گذر) به
to have confidence in	اعتماد داشتن (دار) به
to have permission to	اجازه داشتن (دار)
to have something on someone	چیزی همراه کسی بودن
to hear	شنیدن (شنو)
to help	کمک کردن (کن)
to hit	زدن (زن)
to hope	امیدوار بودن
to imagine	تصور کردن (کن)
to imitate	تقلید کردن (کن)
to increase	افزایش یافتن (یاب)
to inform	اطلاع دادن (ده)
to intend to	قصد داشتن (دار)
to introduce	معرفی کردن (کن)
to invite	دعوت کردن (کن)

to iron	اتو کردن (کن)
to jump	پریدن (پر)
to keep	نگه داشتن (دار)
to keep an eye on	مراقبت کردن (کن)
to kill	کشتن (کش)
to know	شناختن (شناس)
to know how to	بلد بودن
to know something	دانستن (دان)
to last	طول کشیدن (کش)
to learn	یاد گرفتن (گیر)
to leave, to abandon	ترک کردن (کن)
to let, to put	گذاشتن (گذار)
to lie	دروغ گفتن (گو)
to like	خوش . . . آمدن (آ) از
to like	دوست داشتن (دار)
to like to; to want to	مایل بودن
to live	زندگی کردن (کن)
to live	زیستن (زی)
to look at	نگاه کردن (کن)
to lose	گم کردن (کن)
to make	درست کردن (کن)
to make an appointment	وقت گرفتن (گیر)
to make someone cry	گریاندن (گریان)
to make someone laugh	خنداندن (خندان)
to make someone sit	نشاندن (نشان)
to make tired	خسته کردن (کن)
to marry	عقد کردن (کن)
to memorize	حفظ کردن (کن)
to mention	نام بردن (بر)
to miss someone	دل تنگ شدن (شو)

English–Persian Glossary   266

to need	نیاز داشتن (دار)
to open	باز کردن (کن)
to participate in	شرکت کردن (کن) در
to pass	در . . . قبول شدن (شو)
to pass	گذشتن (گذر)
to pay attention	حواس کسی بودن
to pay particular attention	دقت کردن (کن)
to pertain to	مربوط بودن به
to phone	تلفن کردن (کن)
to phone	زنگ زدن (زن)
to pick up	برداشتن (دار)
to play	بازی کردن (کن)
to play the tar	تارزدن (زن)
to practise	تمرین کردن (کن)
to pray (the obligatory prayer)	نمازخواندن (خوان)
to prefer	ترجیح دادن (ده)
to prepare	آماده کردن (کن)
to prepare	تهیه کردن (کن)
to promise	قول دادن (ده)
to publish	منتشر کردن (کن)
to punish	تنبیه کردن (کن)
to put on display	به نمایش گذاشتن (گذار)
to realise	متوجه شدن (شو)
to receive	دریافت کردن (کن) ؛ کسب کردن (کن)
to recommend; to suggest	پیشنهاد کردن (کن)
to record	ضبط کردن (کن)
to recount; to speak highly of	تعریف کردن (کن) از
to reduce (intransitive)	کاهش پیدا کردن (کن)
to register	ثبت نام کردن (کن)
to rely upon	اعتماد کردن (کن) به

to remember	به یاد داشتن (دار)
to respect	احترام گذاشتن (گذار) به
to return	برگشتن (گرد)
to say; to tell	گفتن (گو)
to search	جستجو کردن (کن)
to search for; to become	گشتن (گرد)
to see	دیدن (بین)
to sell	فروختن (فروش)
to send	فرستادن (فرست)
to set (a table); to pluck (a flower)	چیدن (چین)
to set off	راه افتادن (افت)
to set up	بر قرار کردن (کن)
to shop	خرید کردن (کن)
to show	نشان دادن (ده)
to sign	امضاء کردن (کن)
to sit	نشستن (نشین)
to sleep	خوابیدن (خواب)
to smoke	سیگار کشیدن (کش)
to snow	برف آمدن (آ)
to snow	برف باریدن (بار)
to speak	حرف زدن (زن)؛ صحبت کردن (کن)
to spill; to pour	ریختن (ریز)
to stay	ماندن (مان)
to steal	سرقت کردن (کن)؛ دزدیدن (دزد)
to stick something	چسباندن (چسبان)
to stop; to stand	ایستادن (ایست)
to strive	تلاش کردن (کن)
to study	تحصیل کردن (کن)
to study	درس خواندن (خوان)
to study; to read; to recite; to sing	خواندن (خوان)

English–Persian Glossary   **268**

to submit; to hand in	تحویل دادن (ده)
to succeed	موفق شدن (شو)
to suit someone	به کسی آمدن (آ)
to survive	زنده ماندن (مان)
to take an exam	امتحان دادن (ده)
to take into account	در نظر گرفتن (گیر)
to take place	صورت گرفتن (گیر)
to teach	درس دادن (ده)، تدریس کردن (کن)، یاد دادن (ده)
to tell the truth; to be right	راست گفتن (گو)
to test; to try	امتحان کردن (کن)
to be able	توانستن (توان)
to tolerate; to put up with	تحمل کردن (کن)
to travel	سفر کردن (کن) ؛ مسافرت رفتن (رو)
to trust	اطمینان کردن (کن) به
to try; to attempt	سعی کردن (کن)
to turn on	روشن کردن (کن)
to twist; to turn (in a car)	پیچیدن (پیچ)
to use	استفاده کردن (کن)
to vacuum; to sweep the floor	جارو کردن (کن)
to visit	دیدن کردن (کن)
to wake up	بیدار شدن (شو)
to want	خواستن (خواه)
to want to	میل داشتن (دار)
to wash	شستن (شوی)
to watch	تماشا کردن (کن)
to wear	پوشیدن (پوش)
to wear on one's hand	به دست کردن (کن)
to wish	آرزو داشتن (دار)
to work	کار کردن (کن)
to write	نوشتن (نویس)

today	امروز
together	با هم
together with	به همراه
tomb	آرامگاه؛ مقبره (مقابر)
tomorrow	فردا
tonight	امشب
toothache	دندان درد
topic	مطلب (مطالب) ؛ موضوع (موضوعات)
tourist	جهانگرد
towel	حوله
town square; roundabout	میدان (میادین)
traditional	سنتی
traffic light	چراغ راهنمایی
train	قطار
transit hall	سالن ترانزیت
travellers' cheque	چک پول
treasure	گنج
tree	درخت (درختان)
triangle	مثلث
trousers	شلوار
Tuesday	سه شنبه
tuition fee	شهریه
tulip	لاله
Turkey	ترکیه
Turkish	ترکی
TV	تلویزیون
ugly	زشت
umbrella	چتر
uncle (maternal)	دایی
uncle (paternal)	عمو

English–Persian Glossary · 270

under; below	زیر
unfortunately	متأسفانه
unique	بی نظیر ؛ یگانه
university	دانشگاه
university entrance examination	کنکور
university student	دانشجو (دانشجویان)
unlucky	بد یمن
until; so that	تا
usual; customary	معمول
usually	معمولاً
varied; diverse	متنوع
vegetable	سبزی (سبزیجات)
very	بسیار
very; many	خیلی
victorious	پیروز
victory	ظفر
village	ده (دهات) ؛ روستا
vinegar	سرکه
visible	نمایان
visit	دیدار
visitor	بازدید کننده
voice; sound	صدا
volume (of a series of books)	جلد
walnut	گردو
war	جنگ
water	آب
water shortage	کم آبی
wave	موج
wax	موم
way; route	مسیر

we	ما
weather	هوا
wedding	عروسی
wedding ring	حلقه
Wednesday	چهارشنبه
weekend	آخر هفته
well; good	خوب
west	غرب
western; westerner	غربی
wet	تر
whale	نهنگ
what?	چه؛ چه چیزی؟
what day of the week	چند شنبه؟
when	وقتی که
when (at what time)?	ساعت چند؟
when?	کی؟
where?	کجا؟
whereas	درصورتیه
which?	کدام؟
white	سفید
who	کی؛ چه کسی
whole, all	تمام
why?	چرا؟
widespread; common	رایج
window	پنجره
winter coat	پالتو
wise	دانا
withered	پژمرده
without	بدون
woman; wife	زن

English–Persian Glossary 272

wonder	عجب
word	کلمه (کلمات) لغت (لغات)؛ واژه (واژگان)
work	کار
world	جهان
worry	نگرانی
worse	بدتر
worst	بدترین
wrestler	کشتی گیر
wrestling	کشتی
writer	نویسنده (نویسندگان)
written	کتبی
written exam	امتحان کتبی
yard	حیاط
year	سال
yellow	زرد
yesterday	دیروز
yoghurt	ماست
you (informal sing.)	تو
you (plural; formal sing.)	شما
young; young person	جوان
Zoroastrian	زرتشتی (زرتشتیان)

Index

adjectives 23, 32–33, 108–110, 160
adverbs 9, 45–46, 62, 96, 139–140, 160, 162
adverbial clauses 139–140
adjectives: comparative; superlative; demonstrative 32–33, 108–109
alphabet 2–12

causative verbs 169
compounding 160
conditionals: possible; impossible 140
conjunctions 162

definite and indefinite markers 109
demonstrative adjectives 108
demonstrative pronouns 109
derivatives 161
determiners 108
direct object marker (*ra*) 42, 55

emphatic pronouns 122
exclamatory sentences 55, 57
ezafe 23, 32, 62, 107

future tense 71, 172

imperative verbs 84
impersonal constructions 141

months and seasons 86

narrative sentences 55
negation 31
nouns; definite; indefinite 106–110
numbers 59, 61
numericals 107

orthography 5–8, 107

passive constructions 150–151
past progressive tense 94, 140, 170–171

past perfect tense 96, 140, 171
past subjunctive 84, 140, 173
past tense 43, 69–70, 94–96
plurals 106–108
possession, possessives 41, 43
prepositions 120–122
present progressive 71, 171
present perfect tense 95, 171
present subjunctive 82–84, 96, 140, 172–173
present tense 31, 70–72
pronouns; demonstrative; reflexive 109, 122
pronunciation 7, 107

questions 55–57

ra, direct object marker 42, 55
reflexive pronouns 122
relative clauses 131

sentences 55–57
subjunctives: past; present 82–84, 96, 140, 172–173

time expressions 61–62
to be 21
to have 22

verbs: future; imperatives; past; past perfect; past subjunctive;
    present; present continuous; present perfect; present
    subjunctive 31, 43, 69–72, 94–96, 140, 170–171

word order 45, 55